Our National Parks

SEQUOIAS, MARIPOSA GROVE (Page 134)

Our National Parks

John Muir

With a foreword by Richard F. Fleck

The University of Wisconsin Press

Published by
The University of Wisconsin Press
114 North Murray Street
Madison, Wisconsin 53715

The University of Wisconsin Press, Ltd.
1 Gower Street
London WC1E 6HA, England

First Wisconsin printing 1981

Printed in the United States of America

ISBN 0–299–08590–2 cloth; 0–299–08594–5 paper
LC 80–53957

Our National Parks was published in 1901 by Houghton, Mifflin and Company.

TO

CHARLES SPRAGUE SARGENT

STEADFAST LOVER AND DEFENDER

OF OUR COUNTRY'S FORESTS

THIS LITTLE BOOK

Is Affectionately Dedicated

FOREWORD

Richard F. Fleck

John Muir, born in Dunbar, Scotland, in 1838, moved
with his family eleven years later to central Wisconsin,
where his father cleared land for a farm on the edge of
Fountain Lake. Muir's interest in nature, clearly discernible in Scotland, grew considerably in the wilderness
of Wisconsin, where he managed to take occasional
rambles in the woodlands despite the inordinate amount
of labor his stern Calvinistic father, Daniel, demanded of
him. Although most of his boyhood hours were spent in
such hard work on the farm as cutting and splitting rails,
ploughing, planting and harvesting crops, and digging
wells, young John took great delight in observing, at
every chance he had, bird and animal life in the oak and
hickory forests around him. As his biographer, Linnie
Marsh Wolfe, notes, "Had the future naturalist had all
the world from which to choose his training-ground, he
could hardly have found a richer treasure house than
Fountain Lake, the boggy meadow, and the woods that
embosomed them."

While he was growing up on the farm, Muir began to
show an unusual mechanical ability and a talent for
invention. He built such labor-saving devices as a small

self-setting sawmill and an "early-rising machine" which lit fires and lamps automatically. In 1860 he exhibited some of his mechanical inventions at the Wisconsin State Fair at Madison, particularly the remarkable clocks he had made out of wood, where they attracted a good deal of attention. It was after his trip to the State Fair that Muir determined to become a student at the University of Wisconsin. Finding that he could earn his own way and receiving encouragement from the dean, he enrolled, and new horizons were opened up for the young Scotsman. Through Professor Ezra Slocum Carr, he became acquainted with the theories of Louis Agassiz, who maintained that a blanket of continental ice had carved out the main topographical features of Europe. Muir's professor of Latin and Greek, James Davie Butler, urged him to keep a commonplace notebook in the manner of Ralph Waldo Emerson. And at the home of Professor and Mrs. Carr, Muir gained access to the works of Emerson and Henry David Thoreau, two writers who would profoundly influence his later thought and writing. Though he attended the university for only two and a half years, it was one of the factors, along with the woodlands of Wisconsin, that significantly shaped his life's objectives.

In 1866 Muir took a job with an Indianapolis carriage factory, intending to stay only long enough to earn a few hundred dollars which would enable him to continue his studies in the "university of the wilderness," as Thoreau had done before him. He became very much involved with the firm, Osgood, Smith, & Company, however, functioning as a kind of efficiency expert suggesting ways of improving production. But after suffering a terrible accident which nearly cost him the sight of his right eye, he resolved to spend the rest of his life, after his recovery, out in the wilds, joyfully studying God's creation. Prophetically, during his convalescence, someone had given him an illustrated folder of Yosemite.

September 1, 1867, marked the beginning of Muir's self-dedication to nature. He set out on a long walk from Indiana to Florida, which he later recorded in *A Thousand-Mile Walk to the Gulf* (1916)—a book which staunchly defends the rights of wildlife against the callous advances of man. "Now, it never seems to occur to these far-seeing teachers," Muir jotted down in his notebook, "that Nature's object in making animals and plants might possibly be first of all the happiness of each one of them, not the creation of all for the happiness of one. Why should man value himself as more than a small part of the one great unit of creation?" Such a philosophy developed further in his final destination high in the California Sierra, where he first laid eyes on the "range of light" in 1868, six months after he had started out from Jeffersonville, Indiana.

Late in the fall of that year, Muir found employment herding sheep in the region of Yosemite. Remembering the advice of Professor Butler, he kept a journal during that time, and that journal subsequently became the basis of his first book on the West, *My First Summer in the Sierra* (published in 1911). During his days off he hiked the far valleys and peaks to study God's design in nature. With Agassiz's glacial theories in mind, Muir soon came to the conclusion that the U-shaped valleys of the Sierra, including Yosemite, had been carved by giant icefields or glaciers thousands of years earlier. His findings were in direct opposition to those of the State Geologist, Josiah

Dwight Whitney, who believed that Yosemite had been formed by a vast cataclysmic event. With the encouragement of his former professors and a California professor, John Le Conte, Muir undertook to write articles on his theory of the ancient glaciation of the Sierra. He was thus launched into a debate with Whitney which would bring him notoriety both in California and on the East Coast. At the same time, Muir was beginning his career of writing about the West, with numerous articles on the mountains of California, published in such journals as *Overland Monthly*, *San Francisco Bulletin*, *Century*, and eventually *Atlantic Monthly*, *Scribner's*, and *Harper's*. The articles, ultimately collected for the book *The Mountains of California* (1894), emphasized an overriding and harmonious unity in nature. Muir saw a unity in nature even in such devastating or cataclysmic events as earthquakes. Through destruction came re-creation; thus for Muir earthquakes and volcanoes were "joyous" events. In describing talus slopes formed by earthquakes, he writes, "If for a moment you are inclined to regard these taluses as mere draggled, chaotic dumps, climb to the top of one of them, tie your mountain shoes firmly over the instep, and with braced nerves run down without any haggling, puttering hesitation, boldly jumping from boulder to boulder with even speed. You will then find your feet playing a tune, and quickly discover the music and poetry of rock-piles—a fine lesson; and all Nature's wildness tells the same story. Storms of every sort, torrents, earthquakes, cataclysms, 'convulsions of nature,' etc., however mysterious and lawless at first sight they may seem, are only harmonious notes in the song of creation, varied expressions of God's love." Muir's favorite animals, the water ouzel and the Douglas squirrel, also have a prominent place in *The Mountains of California*. From Muir's point of view, these two creatures, and others as well, are as deserving of their habitat as humans are of towns and cities. Animals need to be protected from the devastation of self-centered man.

In 1874 John Muir met Louie Wanda Strentzel, daughter of a Polish-born horticulturalist and fruitgrower of Contra Costa County, California. Six years later they were married. It would have been difficult to find any woman more ideally suited to the wandering Muir. She encouraged him to continue his travels and writing, rather than spending his time in working with fruit production on the Strentzel ranch. One year before their marriage, in fact, Muir left for Alaska on the first of several Arctic trips. Here, he was able to observe "unfinished Yosemites" with miles of ice curving down Alaskan fiords. Two Alaskan books resulted from his journeys: *Travels in Alaska* (1915) and *The Cruise of the Corwin* (1917), both published posthumously. Both concern glaciers and glaciated landscapes, which Muir saw as living manifestations of God's design. Describing the Stickeen Glaciers, he writes, "I greatly enjoyed my walk up the majestic ice-river, charmed by the pale-blue, ineffably fine light in the crevasses, molins, and wells, and the innumerable azure pools in basins of azure ice, and the network of surface streams, large and small, gliding, swirling with wonderful grace of motion in their frictionless channels, calling forth devout admiration at almost every step and filling the mind with a sense of Nature's endless beauty and power."

During the same period of his life Muir met in person

two eminent nineteenth-century philosophers, Ralph Waldo Emerson and Henry George, in 1871 and 1875 respectively. These two men and their writings helped to shape his ideas for preserving wilderness by means of a national park system. Although Emerson spent only a brief time with him in Yosemite, Muir was deeply impressed by Emerson's profound serenity of character, as he had previously been impressed by his book *Nature* (1836), which he read and re-read. Muir believed, with Emerson, that nature is a symbol of spiritual fact. For Muir, nature was God's temple, complete with living pillars. Since destruction of this sacred temple was clearly a sacrilege, it was therefore essential to preserve God's temples wherever they might be.

Muir met and talked with the philosopher-economist Henry George in his San Francisco home, and, according to Linnie Marsh Wolfe, he must have also read George's momentous pamphlet, *Our Land and Land Policy*. Wolfe sums up George's pamphlet: "The earth as our common mother should belong to all the people of the planet. Land with the inherent raw resources is the source of all wealth. Poverty, ignorance, sickness, and crime stem from Land Monopoly. 'Man is a land animal,' and dispossessed of land, is reduced to serfdom. 'Each for all and all for each,' is the Law of the Universe. But man has revised that to read: 'All for a few.'" Reinforcing his own thought with that of George, Muir began a campaign to establish Yosemite as a national park, part of a larger system of parks throughout North America. Muir's compelling articles, his founding of the Sierra Club in 1892, and his strong influence on politicians, including President Theodore Roosevelt, helped the national park cause. Like Henry David Thoreau in his book *The Maine Woods* (1864), Muir spoke out against lumber company interests by advocating firm governmental policies. At times, his critique of commercial interests and the politicians who supported them could be scathing. Muir knew of the destruction of Maine's white pines and black spruce, and was determined not to let the Sierra's sequoias suffer the same fate. Although Muir did lose some significant battles, chief among them the attempt to keep the gorgeous Hetch Hetchy Valley from becoming a reservoir for San Francisco, he also won many. Two years after his death, in 1916, the National Park Service was founded. It offered federal protection, at its inception, to sixteen national parks and twenty-one national monuments.

Our National Parks was first published in 1901 by Houghton, Mifflin and Company and issued again in 1916 as Volume VI of a ten-volume set. At the same time, a "manuscript edition" of 750 copies, each containing one handwritten manuscript page, and a more accessible Sierra edition were published. The book consists of ten essays originally published in the *Atlantic Monthly* between August, 1897, and September, 1901 (see the list following this foreword). With one exception, the titles of the original essays are the present chapter headings— "The Sequoia and General Grant National Parks" was originally "Hunting Big Redwoods." The *Atlantic Monthly*, although it had a modest circulation of twelve to twenty thousand, was one of the four most prominent journals in America at the turn of the century. According to Frank Mott, in *A History of American Magazines*, the *Atlantic Monthly* was turning to political controversy, social reform, and exposure of corruption in government at the very time that John Muir's articles were appearing. Certainly, it was attracting the attention of government officials of the day. And as a result of these articles, when *Our National Parks* first appeared as a book in 1901, it became a minor bestseller, helping further to arouse interest in the cause of conservation and supplementing Muir's own political efforts before legislative bodies. Less than four years after the publication of the book, the California State Legislature passed a bill releasing Yosemite from state control, thus paving the way for it to become the nation's second national park, Yellowstone being the first.

In 1901, in the original preface to *Our National Parks*, Muir wrote, "I have done the best I could to show forth the beauty, grandeur, and all-embracing usefulness of our wild mountain forest reservations and parks, with a view to inciting the people to come and enjoy them, and get them into their hearts, that so at length their preservation and right use might be made sure." That this book played its part in gaining public support for that "right use" there can be little doubt.

Muir holds the modern reader's attention with his rich and sometimes radiant descriptions of colorful landscapes, informative catalogs of plants, trees, and rocks, geological narratives which intuitively re-create events from the dawn of time to present, and numerous allusions to the Bible and to his favorite writers, Emerson and Thoreau. But above all else, he constantly reminds us of our need for the wilderness and our responsibility to it. As Muir concludes, "God has cared for these trees, saved them from drought, disease, avalanches, and a thousand straining, leveling tempests and floods; but he cannot save them from fools,—only Uncle Sam can do that."

University of Wyoming
Laramie, Wyoming
July, 1980

Chronological List of the *Atlantic Monthly* Essays
Constituting *Our National Parks*

"The American Forests," *Atlantic Monthly* 80 (August,
1897), 145–157.

"Wild Parks and Forest Reservations of the West," *Atlantic
Monthly* 81 (January, 1898), 15–28.

"The Yellowstone National Park," *Atlantic Monthly* 81
(April, 1898), 509–522.

"Among the Animals of the Yosemite," *Atlantic Monthly* 82
(November, 1898), 617–631.

"Among the Birds of the Yosemite," *Atlantic Monthly* 82
(December, 1898), 751–760.

"Yosemite National Park," *Atlantic Monthly* 84 (August,
1899), 145–152.

"Forests of the Yosemite," *Atlantic Monthly* 85 (April,
1900), 493–507.

"The Wild Gardens of the Yosemite," *Atlantic Monthly* 86
(August, 1900), 167–179.

"Fountains and Streams of Yosemite," *Atlantic Monthly* 87
(April, 1901), 556–565.

"Hunting Big Redwoods," *Atlantic Monthly* 88 (September,
1901), 304–320.

A Note on the Text

When these articles were incorporated into a book, Muir added a few notes. The notes (Chapters I and X) are now, of course, sadly outdated, but they are being retained because they were in the original text. Similarly, in fidelity to the original text, the scientific names of plants and animals have been kept as Muir gave them.

PREFACE

In this book, made up of sketches first published in the Atlantic Monthly, I have done the
best I could to show forth the beauty, grandeur, and all-embracing usefulness of our wild
mountain forest reservations and parks, with a
view to inciting the people to come and enjoy
them, and get them into their hearts, that so at
length their preservation and right use might be
made sure

Martinez, California
September, 1901

CONTENTS

LIST OF ILLUSTRATIONS

OUR NATIONAL PARKS

CHAPTER I

THE WILD PARKS AND FOREST RESERVATIONS
OF THE WEST

"Keep not standing fix'd and rooted,
    Briskly venture, briskly roam;
Head and hand, where'er thou foot it,
    And stout heart are still at home.
In each land the sun does visit
    We are gay, whate'er betide:
To give room for wandering is it
    That the world was made so wide."

THE tendency nowadays to wander in wildernesses is delightful to see. Thousands of tired, nerve-shaken, over-civilized people are beginning to find out that going to the mountains is going home; that wildness is a necessity; and that mountain parks and reservations are useful not only as fountains of timber and irrigating rivers, but as fountains of life. Awakening from the stupefying effects of the vice of over-industry and the deadly apathy of luxury, they are trying as best they can to mix and enrich their own little ongoings with those of Nature, and to get rid of rust and disease. Briskly venturing and

roaming, some are washing off sins and cobweb
cares of the devil's spinning in all-day storms on
mountains ; sauntering in rosiny pinewoods or
in gentian meadows, brushing through chaparral,
bending down and parting sweet, flowery sprays ;
tracing rivers to their sources, getting in touch
with the nerves of Mother Earth ; jumping from
rock to rock, feeling the life of them, learning
the songs of them, panting in whole-souled exercise, and rejoicing in deep, long-drawn breaths
of pure wildness.   This is fine and natural and
full of promise.   So also is the growing interest in the care and preservation of forests
and wild places in general, and in the half wild
parks and gardens of towns.   Even the scenery
habit in its most artificial forms, mixed with
spectacles, silliness, and kodaks ; its devotees
arrayed more gorgeously than scarlet tanagers,
frightening the wild game with red umbrellas,
— even this is encouraging, and may well be
regarded as a hopeful sign of the times.

All the Western mountains are still rich in
wildness, and by means of good roads are being
brought nearer civilization every year.   To the
sane and free it will hardly seem necessary to
cross the continent in search of wild beauty,
however easy the way, for they find it in abundance wherever they chance to be.   Like Thoreau they see forests in orchards and patches of
huckleberry brush, and oceans in ponds and

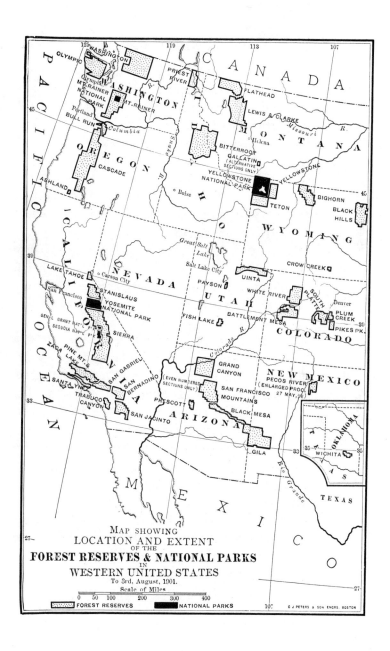

MAP SHOWING
LOCATION AND EXTENT
OF THE
FOREST RESERVES & NATIONAL PARKS
IN
WESTERN UNITED STATES
To 3rd, August, 1901.
Scale of Miles

drops of dew. Few in these hot, dim, strenuous times are quite sane or free; choked with care like clocks full of dust, laboriously doing so much good and making so much money, — or so little, — they are no longer good for themselves.

When, like a merchant taking a list of his goods, we take stock of our wildness, we are glad to see how much of even the most destructible kind is still unspoiled. Looking at our continent as scenery when it was all wild, lying between beautiful seas, the starry sky above it, the starry rocks beneath it, to compare its sides, the East and the West, would be like comparing the sides of a rainbow. But it is no longer equally beautiful. The rainbows of to-day are, I suppose, as bright as those that first spanned the sky; and some of our landscapes are growing more beautiful from year to year, notwithstanding the clearing, trampling work of civilization. New plants and animals are enriching woods and gardens, and many landscapes wholly new, with divine sculpture and architecture, are just now coming to the light of day as the mantling folds of creative glaciers are being withdrawn, and life in a thousand cheerful, beautiful forms is pushing into them, and new-born rivers are beginning to sing and shine in them. The old rivers, too, are growing longer, like healthy trees, gaining new branches and lakes as the residual glaciers at their highest sources on the mountains recede, while the rootlike branches in their flat deltas are at the same time spreading farther and wider into the seas and making new lands.

Under the control of the vast mysterious forces of the interior of the earth all the continents and islands are slowly rising or sinking. Most of the mountains are diminishing in size under the wearing action of the weather, though a few are increasing in height and girth, especially the volcanic ones, as fresh floods of molten rocks are piled on their summits and spread in successive layers, like the wood-rings of trees, on their sides. New mountains, also, are being created from time to time as islands in lakes and seas, or as subordinate cones on the slopes of old ones, thus in some measure balancing the waste of old beauty with new. Man, too, is making many far-reaching changes. This most influential half animal, half angel is rapidly multiplying and spreading, covering the seas and lakes with ships, the land with huts, hotels, cathedrals, and clustered city shops and homes, so that soon, it would seem, we may have to go farther than Nansen to find a good sound solitude. None of Nature's landscapes are ugly so long as they are wild; and much, we can say comfortingly, must always be in great part wild, particularly the sea and the sky, the floods of light from the stars, and the warm, unspoilable heart of the earth, infinitely beautiful, though only dimly visible to the eye of imagination. The geysers, too, spouting from the hot underworld ; the steady, long-lasting glaciers on the mountains, obedient only to the sun ; Yosemite domes and the tremendous grandeur of rocky cañons and mountains in general, — these must always be wild, for man can change them and mar them hardly more than can the butterflies that hover above them. But the continent's outer beauty is fast passing away, especially the plant part of it, the most destructible and most universally charming of all.

Only thirty years ago, the great Central Valley of California, five hundred miles long and fifty miles wide, was one bed of golden and purple flowers. Now it is ploughed and pastured out of existence, gone forever, — scarce a memory of it left in fence corners and along the bluffs of the streams. The gardens of the Sierra, also, and the noble forests in both the reserved and unreserved portions are sadly hacked and trampled, notwithstanding the ruggedness of the topography, — all excepting those of the parks guarded by a few soldiers. In the noblest forests of the world, the ground, once divinely beautiful, is desolate and repulsive, like a face ravaged by disease. This is true also of many other Pacific Coast and Rocky Mountain valleys and forests. The same fate, sooner or later, is awaiting them all, unless awakening public opinion comes forward to stop it. Even the great deserts in Arizona, Nevada, Utah, and New Mexico, which offer so little to attract settlers, and which a few years ago pioneers were afraid of, as places of desolation and death, are now taken as pastures at the rate of one or two square miles per cow, and of course their plant treasures are passing away, — the delicate abronias, phloxes, gilias, etc. Only a few of the bitter, thorny, unbitable shrubs are left, and the sturdy cactuses that defend themselves with bayonets and spears.

Most of the wild plant wealth of the East also has vanished, — gone into dusty history. Only vestiges of its glorious prairie and woodland wealth remain to bless humanity in boggy, rocky, unploughable places. Fortunately, some of these are purely wild, and go far to keep Nature's love visible. White water-lilies, with rootstocks deep and safe in mud, still send up every summer a Milky Way of starry, fragrant flowers around a thousand lakes, and many a tuft of wild grass waves its panicles on mossy rocks, beyond reach of trampling feet, in company with saxifrages, bluebells, and ferns. Even in the midst of farmers' fields, precious sphagnum bogs, too soft for the feet of cattle, are preserved with their charming plants unchanged, — chiogenes, Andromeda, Kalmia, Linnæa, Arethusa, etc. Ca-

lypso borealis still hides in the arbor vitæ swamps
of Canada, and away to the southward there are
a few unspoiled swamps, big ones, where miasma,
snakes, and alligators, like guardian angels, defend their treasures and keep them as pure as
paradise. And beside a' that and a' that, the
East is blessed with good winters and blossoming
clouds that shed white flowers over all the land,
covering every scar and making the saddest landscape divine at least once a year.

The most extensive, least spoiled, and most
unspoilable of the gardens of the continent are
the vast tundras of Alaska. In summer they
extend smooth, even, undulating, continuous beds
of flowers and leaves from about lat. 62° to
the shores of the Arctic Ocean; and in winter
sheets of snowflowers make all the country shine,
one mass of white radiance like a star. Nor are
these Arctic plant people the pitiful frost-pinched
unfortunates they are guessed to be by those who
have never seen them. Though lowly in stature,
keeping near the frozen ground as if loving it,
they are bright and cheery, and speak Nature's
love as plainly as their big relatives of the South.
Tenderly happed and tucked in beneath downy
snow to sleep through the long, white winter,
they make haste to bloom in the spring without
trying to grow tall, though some rise high enough
to ripple and wave in the wind, and display
masses of color, — yellow, purple, and blue, — so

rich that they look like beds of rainbows, and
are visible miles and miles away.

As early as June one may find the showy Geum
glaciale in flower, and the dwarf willows putting
forth myriads of fuzzy catkins, to be followed
quickly, especially on the dryer ground, by mer-
tensia, eritrichium, polemonium, oxytropis, astragalus, lathyrus, lupinus, myosotis, dodecatheon,
arnica, chrysanthemum, nardosmia, saussurea,
senecio, erigeron, matrecaria, caltha, valeriana,
stellaria, Tofieldia, polygonum, papaver, phlox,
lychnis, cheiranthus, Linnæa, and a host of drabas, saxifrages, and heathworts, with bright stars
and bells in glorious profusion, particularly Cassiope, Andromeda, ledum, pyrola, and vaccinium,
— Cassiope the most abundant and beautiful of
them all. Many grasses also grow here, and
wave fine purple spikes and panicles over the
other flowers, — poa, aira, calamagrostis, alope-
curus, trisetum, elymus, festuca, glyceria, etc.
Even ferns are found thus far north, carefully
and comfortably unrolling their precious fronds,
— aspidium, cystopteris, and woodsia, all growing on a sumptuous bed of mosses and lichens;
not the scaly lichens seen on rails and trees and
fallen logs to the southward, but massive, round-
headed, finely colored plants like corals, wonderfully beautiful, worth going round the world to
see. I should like to mention all the plant
friends I found in a summer's wanderings in

this cool reserve, but I fear few would care to read their names, although everybody, I am sure, would love them could they see them blooming and rejoicing at home.

On my last visit to the region about Kotzebue Sound, near the middle of September, 1881, the weather was so fine and mellow that it suggested the Indian summer of the Eastern States. The winds were hushed, the tundra glowed in creamy golden sunshine, and the colors of the ripe foliage of the heathworts, willows, and birch — red, purple, and yellow, in pure bright tones — were enriched with those of berries which were scattered everywhere, as if they had been showered from the clouds like hail. When I was back a mile or two from the shore, reveling in this color-glory, and thinking how fine it would be could I cut a square of the tundra sod of conventional picture size, frame it, and hang it among the paintings on my study walls at home, saying to myself, " Such a Nature painting taken at random from any part of the thousand-mile bog would make the other pictures look dim and coarse," I heard merry shouting, and, looking round, saw a band of Eskimos — men, women, and children, loose and hairy like wild animals — running towards me. I could not guess at first what they were seeking, for they seldom leave the shore ; but soon they told me, as they threw themselves down, sprawling and laughing, on the mellow bog, and began to feast on the berries. A lively picture they made, and a pleasant one, as they frightened the whirring ptarmigans, and surprised their oily stomachs with the beautiful acid berries of many kinds, and filled sealskin bags with them to carry away for festive days in winter.

Nowhere else on my travels have I seen so much warm-blooded, rejoicing life as in this grand Arctic reservation, by so many regarded as desolate. Not only are there whales in abundance along the shores, and innumerable seals, walruses, and white bears, but on the tundras great herds of fat reindeer and wild sheep, foxes, hares, mice, piping marmots, and birds. Perhaps more birds are born here than in any other region of equal extent on the continent. Not only do strong-winged hawks, eagles, and water-fowl, to whom the length of the continent is merely a pleasant excursion, come up here every summer in great numbers, but also many short-winged warblers, thrushes, and finches, repairing hither to rear their young in safety, reinforce the plant bloom with their plumage, and sweeten the wilderness with song; flying all the way, some of them, from Florida, Mexico, and Central America. In coming north they are coming home, for they were born here, and they go south only to spend the winter months, as New Englanders go to Florida. Sweet-voiced troubadours, they sing in orange groves and vine-clad magnolia woods in winter, in thickets of dwarf birch and alder in summer, and sing and chatter more or less all the way back and forth, keeping the whole country glad. Oftentimes, in New England, just as the last snow-patches are melting and the sap in the maples begins to flow, the blessed wanderers may be heard about orchards and the edges of fields where they have stopped to glean a scanty meal, not tarrying long, knowing they have far to go. Tracing the footsteps of spring, they arrive in their tundra homes in June or July, and set out on their return journey in September, or as soon as their families are able to fly well.

This is Nature's own reservation, and every lover of wildness will rejoice with me that by kindly frost it is so well defended. The discovery lately made that it is sprinkled with gold may cause some alarm; for the strangely exciting stuff makes the timid bold enough for anything, and the lazy destructively industrious. Thousands at least half insane are now pushing their way into it, some by the southern passes over the mountains, perchance the first mountains they have ever seen, — sprawling, struggling, gasping for breath, as, laden with awkward, merciless burdens of provisions and tools, they climb over rough-angled boulders and cross thin miry bogs. Some are going by the mountains

and rivers to the eastward through Canada,
tracing the old romantic ways of the Hudson
Bay traders; others by Bering Sea and the Yu-
kon, sailing all the way, getting glimpses perhaps of the famous fur-seals, the ice-floes, and
the innumerable islands and bars of the great
Alaska river. In spite of frowning hardships
and the frozen ground, the Klondike gold will
increase the crusading crowds for years to come,
but comparatively little harm will be done.
Holes will be burned and dug into the hard
ground here and there, and into the quartz-ribbed
mountains and hills; ragged towns like beaver
and muskrat villages will be built, and mills and
locomotives will make rumbling, screeching, dis-
enchanting noises; but the miner's pick will not
be followed far by the plough, at least not until
Nature is ready to unlock the frozen soil-beds
with her slow-turning climate key. On the other
hand, the roads of the pioneer miners will lead
many a lover of wildness into the heart of the
reserve, who without them would never see it.

In the meantime, the wildest health and pleasure grounds accessible and available to tourists
seeking escape from care and dust and early
death are the parks and reservations of the West.
There are four national parks,[1] — the Yellowstone, Yosemite, General Grant, and Sequoia, —
all within easy reach, and thirty forest reserva-

[1] There are now five parks and thirty-eight reservations.

tions, a magnificent realm of woods, most of which, by railroads and trails and open ridges, is also fairly accessible, not only to the determined traveler rejoicing in difficulties, but to those (may their tribe increase) who, not tired, not sick, just naturally take wing every summer in search of wildness. The forty million acres of these reserves are in the main unspoiled as yet, though sadly wasted and threatened on their more open margins by the axe and fire of the lumberman and prospector, and by hoofed locusts, which, like the winged ones, devour every leaf within reach, while the shepherds and owners set fires with the intention of making a blade of grass grow in the place of every tree, but with the result of killing both the grass and the trees.

In the million acre Black Hills Reserve of South Dakota, the easternmost of the great forest reserves, made for the sake of the farmers and miners, there are delightful, reviving saunteringgrounds in open parks of yellow pine, planted well apart, allowing plenty of sunshine to warm the ground. This tree is one of the most variable and most widely distributed of American pines. It grows sturdily on all kinds of soil and rocks, and, protected by a mail of thick bark, defies frost and fire and disease alike, daring every danger in firm, calm beauty and strength. It occurs here mostly on the outer hills and slopes where no other tree can grow. The ground beneath it

is yellow most of the summer with showy Wythia,
arnica, applopappus, solidago, and other sun-lov-
ing plants, which, though they form no heavy
entangling growth, yet give abundance of color
and make all the woods a garden. Beyond the
yellow pine woods there lies a world of rocks
of wildest architecture, broken, splintery, and
spiky, not very high, but the strangest in form
and style of grouping imaginable. Countless
towers and spires, pinnacles and slender domed
columns, are crowded together, and feathered
with sharp-pointed Engelmann spruces, making
curiously mixed forests, — half trees, half rocks.
Level gardens here and there in the midst of
them offer charming surprises, and so do the
many small lakes with lilies on their meadowy
borders, and bluebells, anemones, daises, castilleias, comandras, etc., together forming landscapes delightfully novel, and made still wilder
by many interesting animals, — elk, deer, beavers,
wolves, squirrels, and birds. Not very long ago
this was the richest of all the red man's hunting-
grounds hereabout. After the season's buffalo
hunts were over, — as described by Parkman,
who, with a picturesque cavalcade of Sioux sav-
ages, passed through these famous hills in 1846,
— every winter deficiency was here made good,
and hunger was unknown until, in spite of most
determined, fighting, killing opposition, the
white gold-hunters entered the fat game reserve

and spoiled it. The Indians are dead now, and so are most of the hardly less striking free trappers of the early romantic Rocky Mountain times. Arrows, bullets, scalping-knives, need no longer be feared; and all the wilderness is peacefully open.

The Rocky Mountain reserves are the Teton, Yellowstone, Lewis and Clark, Bitter Root, Priest River and Flathead, comprehending more than twelve million acres of mostly unclaimed, rough, forest-covered mountains in which the great rivers of the country take their rise. The commonest tree in most of them is the brave, indomitable, and altogether admirable Pinus contorta, widely distributed in all kinds of climate and soil, growing cheerily in frosty Alaska, breathing the damp salt air of the sea as well as the dry biting blasts of the Arctic interior, and making itself at home on the most dangerous flame-swept slopes and ridges of the Rocky Mountains in immeasurable abundance and variety of forms. Thousands of acres of this species are destroyed by running fires nearly every summer, but a new growth springs quickly from the ashes. It is generally small, and yields few sawlogs of commercial value, but is of incalculable importance to the farmer and miner; supplying fencing, mine timbers, and firewood, holding the porous soil on steep slopes, preventing landslips and avalanches, and giving kindly, nourishing shelter to animals and the widely outspread sources of the life-giving rivers. The other trees are mostly spruce, mountain pine, cedar, juniper, larch, and balsam fir; some of them, especially on the western slopes of the mountains, attaining grand size and furnishing abundance of fine timber.

Perhaps the least known of all this grand group of reserves is the Bitter Root, of more than four million acres. It is the wildest, shaggiest block of forest wildness in the Rocky Mountains, full of happy, healthy, storm-loving trees, full of streams that dance and sing in glorious array, and full of Nature's animals, — elk, deer, wild sheep, bears, cats, and innumerable smaller people.

In calm Indian summer, when the heavy winds are hushed, the vast forests covering hill and dale, rising and falling over the rough topography and vanishing in the distance, seem lifeless. No moving thing is seen as we climb the peaks, and only the low, mellow murmur of falling water is heard, which seems to thicken the silence. Nevertheless, how many hearts with warm red blood in them are beating under cover of the woods, and how many teeth and eyes are shining! A multitude of animal people, intimately related to us, but of whose lives we know almost nothing, are as busy about their own affairs as we are about ours: beavers are building and mending dams and huts for winter, and

storing them with food; bears are studying
winter quarters as they stand thoughtful in open
spaces, while the gentle breeze ruffles the long
hair on their backs; elk and deer, assembling
on the heights, are considering cold pastures
where they will be farthest away from the
wolves; squirrels and marmots are busily laying
up provisions and lining their nests against coming frost and snow foreseen; and countless
thousands of birds are forming parties and gathering their young about them for flight to the
southlands; while butterflies and bees, apparently with no thought of hard times to come,
are hovering above the late-blooming goldenrods,
and, with countless other insect folk, are dancing and humming right merrily in the sunbeams
and shaking all the air into music.

Wander here a whole summer, if you can.
Thousands of God's wild blessings will search
you and soak you as if you were a sponge, and
the big days will go by uncounted. If you
are business-tangled, and so burdened with duty
that only weeks can be got out of the heavy-
laden year, then go to the Flathead Reserve;
for it is easily and quickly reached by the Great
Northern Railroad. Get off the track at Belton
Station, and in a few minutes you will find yourself in the midst of what you are sure to say is
the best care-killing scenery on the continent, —
beautiful lakes derived straight from glaciers,

lofty mountains steeped in lovely nemophila-blue
skies and clad with forests and glaciers, mossy,
ferny waterfalls in their hollows, nameless and
numberless, and meadowy gardens abounding in
the best of everything. When you are calm
enough for discriminating observation, you will
find the king of the larches, one of the best of
the Western giants, beautiful, picturesque, and
regal in port, easily the grandest of all the
larches in the world. It grows to a height of
one hundred and fifty to two hundred feet, with
a diameter at the ground of five to eight feet,
throwing out its branches into the light as no
other tree does. To those who before have seen
only the European larch or the Lyall species of
the eastern Rocky Mountains, or the little tamarack or hackmatack of the Eastern States and
Canada, this Western king must be a revelation.

Associated with this grand tree in the making
of the Flathead forests is the large and beautiful
mountain pine, or Western white pine (Pinus
monticola), the invincible contorta or lodge-pole
pine, and spruce and cedar. The forest floor is
covered with the richest beds of Linnæa borealis
I ever saw, thick fragrant carpets, enriched with
shining mosses here and there, and with Clintonia, pyrola, moneses, and vaccinium, weaving
hundred-mile beds of bloom that would have
made blessed old Linnæus weep for joy.

Lake McDonald, full of brisk trout, is in the

heart of this forest, and Avalanche Lake is ten miles above McDonald, at the feet of a group of glacier-laden mountains. Give a month at least to this precious reserve. The time will not be taken from the sum of your life. Instead of shortening, it will indefinitely lengthen it and make you truly immortal. Nevermore will time seem short or long, and cares will never again fall heavily on you, but gently and kindly as gifts from heaven.

The vast Pacific Coast reserves in Washington and Oregon — the Cascade, Washington, Mount Rainier, Olympic, Bull Run, and Ashland, named in order of size — include more than 12,500,000 acres of magnificent forests of beautiful and gigantic trees. They extend over the wild, unexplored Olympic Mountains and both flanks of the Cascade Range, the wet and the dry. On the east side of the Cascades the woods are sunny and open, and contain principally yellow pine, of moderate size, but of great value as a cover for the irrigating streams that flow into the dry interior, where agriculture on a grand scale is being carried on. Along the moist, balmy, foggy, west flank of the mountains, facing the sea, the woods reach their highest development, and, excepting the California redwoods, are the heaviest on the continent. They are made up mostly of the Douglas spruce (Pseudotsuga taxifolia), with the giant arbor vitæ, or cedar, and several species of fir and hemlock in varying abundance, forming a forest kingdom unlike any other, in which limb meets limb, touching and overlapping in bright, lively, triumphant exuberance, two hundred and fifty, three hundred, and even four hundred feet above the shady, mossy ground. Over all the other species the Douglas spruce reigns supreme. It is not only a large tree, the tallest in America next to the redwood, but a very beautiful one, with bright green drooping foliage, handsome pendent cones, and a shaft exquisitely straight and round and regular. Forming extensive forests by itself in many places, it lifts its spiry tops into the sky close together with as even a growth as a well-tilled field of grain. No ground has been better tilled for wheat than these Cascade Mountains for trees : they were ploughed by mighty glaciers, and harrowed and mellowed and outspread by the broad streams that flowed from the ice-ploughs as they were withdrawn at the close of the glacial period.

In proportion to its weight when dry, Douglas spruce timber is perhaps stronger than that of any other large conifer in the country, and being tough, durable, and elastic, it is admirably suited for ship-building, piles, and heavy timbers in general; but its hardness and liability to warp when it is cut into boards render it unfit for fine work. In the lumber markets of California it is

called "Oregon pine." When lumbering is
going on in the best Douglas woods, especially
about Puget Sound, many of the long, slender
boles are saved for spars; and so superior is
their quality that they are called for in almost
every shipyard in the world, and it is interesting
to follow their fortunes. Felled and peeled and
dragged to tide-water, they are raised again as
yards and masts for ships, given iron roots and
canvas foliage, decorated with flags, and sent to
sea, where in glad motion they go cheerily over
the ocean prairie in every latitude and longitude,
singing and bowing responsive to the same winds
that waved them when they were in the woods.
After standing in one place for centuries they
thus go round the world like tourists, meeting
many a friend from the old home forest; some
traveling like themselves, some standing head
downward in muddy harbors, holding up the
platforms of wharves, and others doing all kinds
of hard timber work, showy or hidden.

This wonderful tree also grows far northward
in British Columbia, and southward along the
coast and middle regions of Oregon and California; flourishing with the redwood wherever it
can find an opening, and with the sugar pine,
yellow pine, and libocedrus in the Sierra. It extends into the San Gabriel, San Bernardino, and
San Jacinto Mountains of southern California.
It also grows well on the Wasatch Mountains,

where it is called " red pine," and on many parts
of the Rocky Mountains and short interior ranges
of the Great Basin. But though thus widely
distributed, only in Oregon, Washington, and
some parts of British Columbia does it reach perfect development.

To one who looks from some high standpoint
over its vast breadth, the forest on the west side
of the Cascades seems all one dim, dark, monotonous field, broken only by the white volcanic
cones along the summit of the range. Back in
the untrodden wilderness a deep furred carpet of
brown and yellow mosses covers the ground like
a garment, pressing about the feet of the trees,
and rising in rich bosses softly and kindly over
every rock and mouldering trunk, leaving no spot
uncared for ; and dotting small prairies, and
fringing the meadows and the banks of streams
not seen in general views, we find, besides the
great conifers, a considerable number of hard-
wood trees, — oak, ash, maple, alder, wild apple,
cherry, arbutus, Nuttall's flowering dogwood,
and in some places chestnut. In a few favored
spots the broad-leaved maple grows to a height
of a hundred feet in forests by itself, sending out
large limbs in magnificent interlacing arches covered with mosses and ferns, thus forming lofty
sky-gardens, and rendering the underwoods delightfully cool. No finer forest ceiling is to be
found than these maple arches, while the floor,

ornamented with tall ferns and rubus vines, and cast into hillocks by the bulging, moss-covered roots of the trees, matches it well.

Passing from beneath the heavy shadows of the woods, almost anywhere one steps into lovely gardens of lilies, orchids, heathworts, and wild roses. Along the lower slopes, especially in Oregon, where the woods are less dense, there are miles of rhododendron, making glorious masses of purple in the spring, while all about the streams and the lakes and the beaver meadows there is a rich tangle of hazel, plum, cherry, crab-apple, cornel, gaultheria, and rubus, with myriads of flowers and abundance of other more delicate bloomers, such as erythronium, brodiæa, fritillaria, calochortus, Clintonia, and the lovely hider of the north, Calypso. Beside all these bloomers there are wonderful ferneries about the many misty waterfalls, some of the fronds ten feet high, others the most delicate of their tribe, the maidenhair fringing the rocks within reach of the lightest dust of the spray, while the shading trees on the cliffs above them, leaning over, look like eager listeners anxious to catch every tone of the restless waters. In the autumn berries of every color and flavor abound, enough for birds, bears, and everybody, particularly about the stream-sides and meadows where sunshine reaches the ground : huckleberries, red, blue, and black, some growing close to the ground others on

bushes ten feet high; gaultheria berries, called
" sal-al " by the Indians ; salmon berries, an inch
in diameter, growing in dense prickly tangles, the
flowers, like wild roses, still more beautiful than
the fruit; raspberries, gooseberries, currants,
blackberries, and strawberries.   The underbrush
and meadow fringes are in great part made up of
these berry bushes and vines ; but in the depths
of the woods there is not much underbrush of
any kind, — only a thin growth of rubus, huckleberry, and vine-maple.

Notwithstanding the outcry against the reservations last winter in Washington, that uncounted farms, towns, and villages were included
in them, and that all business was threatened or
blocked, nearly all the mountains in which the
reserves lie are still covered with virgin forests.
Though lumbering has long been carried on with
tremendous energy along their boundaries, and
home-seekers have explored the woods for openings available for farms, however small, one may
wander in the heart of the reserves for weeks
without meeting a human being, Indian or white
man, or any conspicuous trace of one.   Indians
used to ascend the main streams on their way to
the mountains for wild goats, whose wool furnished them clothing.   But with food in abundance on the coast there was little to draw them
into the woods, and the monuments they have
left there are scarcely more conspicuous than

those of birds and squirrels; far less so than
those of the beavers, which have dammed streams
and made clearings that will endure for centuries. Nor is there much in these woods to attract cattle-keepers. Some of the first settlers
made farms on the small bits of prairie and in
the comparatively open Cowlitz and Chehalis
valleys of Washington; but before the gold
period most of the immigrants from the Eastern
States settled in the fertile and open Willamette
Valley of Oregon. Even now, when the search
for tillable land is so keen, excepting the bottom-
lands of the rivers around Puget Sound, there
are few cleared spots in all western Washington.
On every meadow or opening of any sort some
one will be found keeping cattle, raising hops,
or cultivating patches of grain, but these spots
are few and far between. All the larger spaces
were taken long ago; therefore most of the
newcomers build their cabins where the beavers
built theirs. They keep a few cows, laboriously
widen their little meadow openings by hacking,
girdling, and burning the rim of the close-press-
ing forest, and scratch and plant among the huge
blackened logs and stumps, girdling and killing
themselves in killing the trees.

Most of the farm lands of Washington and
Oregon, excepting the valleys of the Willamette
and Rogue rivers, lie on the east side of the
mountains. The forests on the eastern slopes

of the Cascades fail altogether ere the foot of the range is reached, stayed by drought as suddenly as on the west side they are stopped by the sea; showing strikingly how dependent are these forest giants on the generous rains and fogs so often complained of in the coast climate. The lower portions of the reserves are solemnly soaked and poulticed in rain and fog during the winter months, and there is a sad dearth of sunshine, but with a little knowledge of woodcraft any one may enjoy an excursion into these woods even in the rainy season. The big, gray days are exhilarating, and the colors of leaf and branch and mossy bole are then at their best. The mighty trees getting their food are seen to be wide-awake, every needle thrilling in the welcome nourishing storms, chanting and bowing low in glorious harmony, while every raindrop and snowflake is seen as a beneficent messenger from the sky. The snow that falls on the lower woods is mostly soft, coming through the trees in downy tufts, loading their branches, and bending them down against the trunks until they look like arrows, while a strange muffled silence prevails, making everything impressively solemn. But these lowland snowstorms and their effects quickly vanish. The snow melts in a day or two, sometimes in a few hours, the bent branches spring up again, and all the forest work is left to the fog and the rain. At the same time, dry

snow is falling on the upper forests and mountain tops. Day after day, often for weeks, the
big clouds give their flowers without ceasing, as
if knowing how important is the work they have
to do. The glinting, swirling swarms thicken
the blast, and the trees and rocks are covered
to a depth of ten to twenty feet. Then the
mountaineer, snug in a grove with bread and
fire, has nothing to do but gaze and listen and
enjoy. Ever and anon the deep, low roar of the
storm is broken by the booming of avalanches,
as the snow slips from the overladen heights and
rushes down the long white slopes to fill the
fountain hollows. All the smaller streams are
hushed and buried, and the young groves of
spruce and fir near the edge of the timber-line
are gently bowed to the ground and put to sleep,
not again to see the light of day or stir branch
or leaf until the spring.

These grand reservations should draw thousands of admiring visitors at least in summer, yet
they are neglected as if of no account, and spoil-
ers are allowed to ruin them as fast as they like.[1]
A few peeled spars cut here were set up in London, Philadelphia, and Chicago, where they

[1] The outlook over forest affairs is now encouraging. Popular interest, more practical than sentimental in whatever touches the welfare
of the country's forests, is growing rapidly, and a hopeful beginning has been made by the Government in real protection for the reservations as well as for the parks. From July 1, 1900, there have
been 9 superintendents, 39 supervisors, and from 330 to 445 rangers of
reservations.

excited wondering attention; but the countless hosts of living trees rejoicing at home on the mountains are scarce considered at all. Most travelers here are content with what they can see from car windows or the verandas of hotels, and in going from place to place cling to their precious trains and stages like wrecked sailors to rafts. When an excursion into the woods is proposed, all sorts of dangers are imagined, — snakes, bears, Indians. Yet it is far safer to wander in God's woods than to travel on black highways or to stay at home. The snake danger is so slight it is hardly worth mentioning. Bears are a peaceable people, and mind their own business, instead of going about like the devil seeking whom they may devour. Poor fellows, they have been poisoned, trapped, and shot at until they have lost confidence in brother man, and it is not now easy to make their acquaintance. As to Indians, most of them are dead or civilized into useless innocence. No American wilderness that I know of is so dangerous as a city home " with all the modern improvements." One should go to the woods for safety, if for nothing else. Lewis and Clark, in their famous trip across the continent in 1804–1805, did not lose a single man by Indians or animals, though all the West was then wild. Captain Clark was bitten on the hand as he lay asleep. That was one bite among more than a hundred men while traveling nine thou-

sand miles. Loggers are far more likely to be
met than Indians or bears in the reserves or about
their boundaries, brown weather-tanned men with
faces furrowed like bark, tired-looking, moving
slowly, swaying like the trees they chop. A
little of everything in the woods is fastened to
their clothing, rosiny and smeared with balsam,
and rubbed into it, so that their scanty outer gar-
ments grow thicker with use and never wear out.
Many a forest giant have these old woodmen
felled, but, round-shouldered and stooping, they
too are leaning over and tottering to their fall.
Others, however, stand ready to take their places,
stout young fellows, erect as saplings; and
always the foes of trees outnumber their friends.
Far up the white peaks one can hardly fail to
meet the wild goat, or American chamois, — an
admirable mountaineer, familiar with woods and
glaciers as well as rocks, — and in leafy thickets
deer will be found ; while gliding about unseen
there are many sleek furred animals enjoying
their beautiful lives, and birds also, notwithstanding few are noticed in hasty walks. The ousel
sweetens the glens and gorges where the streams
flow fastest, and every grove has its singers, however silent it seems, — thrushes, linnets, warblers ;
humming-birds glint about the fringing bloom of
the meadows and peaks, and the lakes are stirred
into lively pictures by water-fowl.

The Mount Rainier Forest Reserve should be

made a national park and guarded while yet its
bloom is on ;[1] for if in the making of the West
Nature had what we call parks in mind, — places
for rest, inspiration, and prayers, — this Rainier
region must surely be one of them.   In the
centre of it there is a lonely mountain capped
with ice ; from the ice-cap glaciers radiate in
every direction, and young rivers from the glaciers ; while its flanks, sweeping down in beautiful curves, are clad with forests and gardens, and
filled with birds and animals.   Specimens of the
best of Nature's treasures have been lovingly
gathered here and arranged in simple symmetrical
beauty within regular bounds.

Of all the fire-mountains which, like beacons,
once blazed along the Pacific Coast, Mount
Rainier is the noblest in form, has the most interesting forest cover, and, with perhaps the exception of Shasta, is the highest and most
flowery.   Its massive white dome rises out of its
forests, like a world by itself, to a height of fourteen thousand to fifteen thousand feet.   The forests reach to a height of a little over six thousand
feet, and above the forests there is a zone of the
loveliest flowers, fifty miles in circuit and nearly

---

[1] This was done shortly after the above was written. "One of the
most important measures taken during the past year in connection
with forest reservations was the action of Congress in withdrawing
from the Mount Rainier Forest Reserve a portion of the region immediately surrounding Mount Rainier and setting it apart as a national
park." (*Report of Commissioner of General Land Office*, for the year
ended June, 1899.)   But the park as it now stands is far too small.

two miles wide, so closely planted and luxuriant
that it seems as if Nature, glad to make an open
space between woods so dense and ice so deep,
were economizing the precious ground, and trying to see how many of her darlings she can get
together in one mountain wreath, — daisies,
anemones, geraniums, columbines, erythroniums,
larkspurs, etc., among which we wade knee-deep
and waist-deep, the bright corollas in myriads
touching petal to petal. Picturesque detached
groups of the spiry Abies lasiocarpa stand like
islands along the lower margin of the garden
zone, while on the upper margin there are extensive beds of bryanthus, Cassiope, Kalmia, and other
heathworts, and higher still saxifrages and drabas,
more and more lowly, reach up to the edge of the
ice. Altogether this is the richest subalpine
garden I ever found, a perfect floral elysium.
The icy dome needs none of man's care, but unless the reserve is guarded the flower bloom will
soon be killed, and nothing of the forests will be
left but black stump monuments.

The Sierra of California is the most openly
beautiful and useful of all the forest reserves,
and the largest excepting the Cascade Reserve of
Oregon and the Bitter Root of Montana and
Idaho. It embraces over four million acres of
the grandest scenery and grandest trees on the
continent, and its forests are planted just where
they do the most good, not only for beauty, but

for farming in the great San Joaquin Valley beneath them. It extends southward from the
Yosemite National Park to the end of the range,
a distance of nearly two hundred miles. No
other coniferous forest in the world contains so
many species or so many large and beautiful
trees, — Sequoia gigantea, king of conifers, " the
noblest of a noble race," as Sir Joseph Hooker
well says; the sugar pine, king of all the
world's pines, living or extinct; the yellow pine,
next in rank, which here reaches most perfect
development, forming noble towers of verdure
two hundred feet high; the mountain pine,
which braves the coldest blasts far up the mountains on grim, rocky slopes; and five others,
flourishing each in its place, making eight species
of pine in one forest, which is still further enriched by the great Douglas spruce, libocedrus,
two species of silver fir, large trees and exquisitely
beautiful, the Paton hemlock, the most graceful
of evergreens, the curious tumion, oaks of many
species, maples, alders, poplars, and flowering
dogwood, all fringed with flowery underbrush,
manzanita, ceanothus, wild rose, cherry, chestnut,
and rhododendron. Wandering at random
through these friendly, approachable woods, one
comes here and there to the loveliest lily gardens,
some of the lilies ten feet high, and the smooth-
est gentian meadows, and Yosemite valleys known
only to mountaineers.   Once I spent a night by

a camp-fire on Mount Shasta with Asa Gray and
Sir Joseph Hooker, and, knowing that they were
acquainted with all the great forests of the
world, I asked whether they knew any coniferous forest that rivaled that of the Sierra. They
unhesitatingly said: " No. In the beauty and
grandeur of individual trees, and in number and
variety of species, the Sierra forests surpass all
others."

This Sierra Reserve, proclaimed by the President of the United States in September, 1893, is
worth the most thoughtful care of the government for its own sake, without considering its
value as the fountain of the rivers on which the
fertility of the great San Joaquin Valley depends. Yet it gets no care at all. In the fog
of tariff, silver, and annexation politics it is left
wholly unguarded, though the management of
the adjacent national parks by a few soldiers
shows how well and how easily it can be preserved. In the meantime, lumbermen are allowed to spoil it at their will, and sheep in
uncountable ravenous hordes to trample it and
devour every green leaf within reach ; while the
shepherds, like destroying angels, set innumerable fires, which burn not only the undergrowth
of seedlings on which the permanence of the
forest depends, but countless thousands of the
venerable giants. If every citizen could take
one walk through this reserve, there would be

no more trouble about its care; for only in darkness does vandalism flourish.[1]

The reserves of southern California, — the San Gabriel, San Bernardino, San Jacinto, and Trabuco, — though not large, only about two million acres together, are perhaps the best appreciated. Their slopes are covered with a close, almost impenetrable growth of flowery bushes, beginning on the sides of the fertile coast valleys and the dry interior plains. Their higher ridges, however, and mountains are open, and fairly well forested with sugar pine, yellow pine, Douglas spruce, libocedrus, and white fir. As timber fountains they amount to little, but as bird and bee pastures, cover for the precious streams that irrigate the lowlands, and quickly available retreats from dust and heat and care, their value is incalculable. Good roads have been graded into them, by which in a few hours lowlanders can get well up into the sky and find refuge in hospitable camps and club-houses, where, while breathing reviving ozone, they may absorb the beauty about them, and look comfortably down on the busy towns and the most beautiful orange groves ever planted since gardening began.

The Grand Cañon Reserve of Arizona, of nearly two million acres, or the most interesting part of it, as well as the Rainier region, should

[1] See note, p. 27.

be made into a national park, on account of their
supreme grandeur and beauty. Setting out
from Flagstaff, a station on the Atchison, To-
peka, and Santa Fé Railroad, on the way to the
cañon you pass through beautiful forests of
yellow pine, — like those of the Black Hills, but
more extensive, — and curious dwarf forests of
nut pine and juniper, the spaces between the
miniature trees planted with many interesting
species of eriogonum, yucca, and cactus. After
riding or walking seventy-five miles through
these pleasure-grounds, the San Francisco and
other mountains, abounding in flowery parklike
openings and smooth shallow valleys with long
vistas which in fineness of finish and arrangement suggest the work of a consummate landscape artist, watching you all the way, you come
to the most tremendous cañon in the world. It
is abruptly countersunk in the forest plateau, so
that you see nothing of it until you are suddenly
stopped on its brink, with its immeasurable
wealth of divinely colored and sculptured buildings before you and beneath you. No matter
how far you have wandered hitherto, or how
many famous gorges and valleys you have seen,
this one, the Grand Cañon of the Colorado, will
seem as novel to you, as unearthly in the color
and grandeur and quantity of its architecture, as
if you had found it after death, on some other
star ; so incomparably lovely and grand and

supreme is it above all the other cañons in our
fire-moulded, earthquake-shaken, rain-washed,
wave-washed, river and glacier sculptured world.
It is about six thousand feet deep where you
first see it, and from rim to rim ten to fifteen
miles wide. Instead of being dependent for
interest upon waterfalls, depth, wall sculpture,
and beauty of parklike floor, like most other
great cañons, it has no waterfalls in sight, and
no appreciable floor spaces. The big river has
just room enough to flow and roar obscurely,
here and there groping its way as best it can,
like a weary, murmuring, overladen traveler trying to escape from the tremendous, bewildering
labyrinthic abyss, while its roar serves only to
deepen the silence. Instead of being filled with
air, the vast space between the walls is crowded
with Nature's grandest buildings, — a sublime
city of them, painted in every color, and adorned
with richly fretted cornice and battlement spire
and tower in endless variety of style and architecture. Every architectural invention of man
has been anticipated, and far more, in this
grandest of God's terrestrial cities.

CHAPTER II

OF the four national parks of the West, the Yellowstone is far the largest. It is a big, wholesome wilderness on the broad summit of the Rocky Mountains, favored with abundance of rain and snow, — a place of fountains where the greatest of the American rivers take their rise. The central portion is a densely forested and comparatively level volcanic plateau with an average elevation of about eight thousand feet above the sea, surrounded by an imposing host of mountains belonging to the subordinate Gallatin, Wind River, Teton, Absaroka, and snowy ranges. Unnumbered lakes shine in it, united by a famous band of streams that rush up out of hot lava beds, or fall from the frosty peaks in channels rocky and bare, mossy and bosky, to the main rivers, singing cheerily on through every difficulty, cunningly dividing and finding their way east and west to the two far-off seas.

Glacier meadows and beaver meadows are outspread with charming effect along the banks of the streams, parklike expanses in the woods, and innumerable small gardens in rocky recesses of the mountains, some of them containing more petals than leaves, while the whole wilderness is enlivened with happy animals.

Beside the treasures common to most mountain regions that are wild and blessed with a kind climate, the park is full of exciting wonders. The wildest geysers in the world, in bright, triumphant bands, are dancing and singing in it amid thousands of boiling springs, beautiful and awful, their basins arrayed in gorgeous colors like gigantic flowers ; and hot paint-pots, mud springs, mud volcanoes, mush and broth caldrons whose contents are of every color and consistency, plash and heave and roar in bewildering abundance. In the adjacent mountains, beneath the living trees the edges of petrified forests are exposed to view, like specimens on the shelves of a museum, standing on ledges tier above tier where they grew, solemnly silent in rigid crystalline beauty after swaying in the winds thousands of centuries ago, opening marvelous views back into the years and climates and life of the past. Here, too, are hills of sparkling crystals, hills of sulphur, hills of glass, hills of cinders and ashes, mountains of every style of architecture, icy or forested, mountains covered with honey-bloom sweet as Hymettus, mountains boiled soft like potatoes and colored like a sunset sky. A' that and a' that, and twice as muckle 's a' that,

Nature has on show in the Yellowstone Park. Therefore it is called Wonderland, and thousands of tourists and travelers stream into it every summer, and wander about in it enchanted.

Fortunately, almost as soon as it was discovered it was dedicated and set apart for the benefit of the people, a piece of legislation that shines benignly amid the common dust-and-ashes history of the public domain, for which the world must thank Professor Hayden above all others; for he led the first scientific exploring party into it, described it, and with admirable enthusiasm urged Congress to preserve it. As delineated in the year 1872, the park contained about 3344 square miles. On March 30, 1891 it was to all intents and purposes enlarged by the Yellowstone National Park Timber Reserve, and in December, 1897, by the Teton Forest Reserve; thus nearly doubling its original area, and extending the southern boundary far enough to take in the sublime Teton range and the famous pasture-lands of the big Rocky Mountain game animals. The withdrawal of this large tract from the public domain did no harm to any one; for its height, 6000 to over 13,000 feet above the sea, and its thick mantle of volcanic rocks, prevent its ever being available for agriculture or mining, while on the other hand its geographical position, reviving climate, and wonderful scenery combine to make it a grand health, pleasure, and study resort, — a gathering-place for travelers from all the world.

The national parks are not only withdrawn from sale and entry like the forest reservations, but are efficiently managed and guarded by small troops of United States cavalry, directed by the Secretary of the Interior. Under this care the forests are flourishing, protected from both axe and fire ; and so, of course, are the shaggy beds of underbrush and the herbaceous vegetation. The so-called curiosities, also, are preserved, and the furred and feathered tribes, many of which, in danger of extinction a short time ago, are now increasing in numbers, — a refreshing thing to see amid the blind, ruthless destruction that is going on in the adjacent regions. In pleasing contrast to the noisy, ever changing management, or mismanagement, of blundering, plundering, money-making vote-sellers who receive their places from boss politicians as purchased goods, the soldiers do their duty so quietly that the traveler is scarce aware of their presence.

This is the coolest and highest of the parks. Frosts occur every month of the year. Nevertheless, the tenderest tourist finds it warm enough in summer. The air is electric and full of ozone, healing, reviving, exhilarating, kept pure by frost and fire, while the scenery is wild enough to awaken the dead. It is a glorious place to grow in and rest in ; camping on the shores of the

lakes, in the warm openings of the woods golden
with sunflowers, on the banks of the streams, by
the snowy waterfalls, beside the exciting wonders
or away from them in the scallops of the mountain walls sheltered from every wind, on smooth
silky lawns enameled with gentians, up in the
fountain hollows of the ancient glaciers between
the peaks, where cool pools and brooks and gardens of precious plants charmingly embowered
are never wanting, and good rough rocks with
every variety of cliff and scaur are invitingly
near for outlooks and exercise.

From these lovely dens you may make excursions whenever you like into the middle of the
park, where the geysers and hot springs are reeking and spouting in their beautiful basins, displaying an exuberance of color and strange motion and energy admirably calculated to surprise
and frighten, charm and shake up the least sensitive out of apathy into newness of life.

However orderly your excursions or aimless,
again and again amid the calmest, stillest scenery
you will be brought to a standstill hushed and
awe-stricken before phenomena wholly new to
you. Boiling springs and huge deep pools of
purest green and azure water, thousands of them,
are plashing and heaving in these high, cool
mountains as if a fierce furnace fire were burning
beneath each one of them; and a hundred geysers, white torrents of boiling water and steam,

like inverted waterfalls, are ever and anon rushing up out of the hot, black underworld. Some
of these ponderous geyser columns are as large as
sequoias, — five to sixty feet in diameter, one
hundred and fifty to three hundred feet high,
— and are sustained at this great height with
tremendous energy for a few minutes, or perhaps nearly an hour, standing rigid and erect,
hissing, throbbing, booming, as if thunderstorms
were raging beneath their roots, their sides
roughened or fluted like the furrowed boles of
trees, their tops dissolving in feathery branches,
while the irised spray, like misty bloom is at times
blown aside, revealing the massive shafts shining
against a background of pine-covered hills.
Some of them lean more or less, as if storm-bent,
and instead of being round are flat or fan-shaped,
issuing from irregular slits in silex pavements
with radiate structure, the sunbeams sifting
through them in ravishing splendor. Some are
broad and round-headed like oaks; others are
low and bunchy, branching near the ground like
bushes; and a few are hollow in the centre like
big daisies or water-lilies. No frost cools them,
snow never covers them nor lodges in their
branches; winter and summer they welcome alike;
all of them, of whatever form or size, faithfully
rising and sinking in fairy rhythmic dance night
and day, in all sorts of weather, at varying periods
of minutes, hours, or weeks, growing up rapidly,

uncontrollable as fate, tossing their pearly
branches in the wind, bursting into bloom and
vanishing like the frailest flowers, — plants of
which Nature raises hundreds or thousands of
crops a year with no apparent exhaustion of the
fiery soil.

The so-called geyser basins, in which this rare
sort of vegetation is growing, are mostly open
valleys on the central plateau that were eroded
by glaciers after the greater volcanic fires had
ceased to burn. Looking down over the forests
as you approach them from the surrounding
heights, you see a multitude of white columns,
broad, reeking masses, and irregular jets and
puffs of misty vapor ascending from the bottom
of the valley, or entangled like smoke among the
neighboring trees, suggesting the factories of
some busy town or the camp-fires of an army.
These mark the position of each mush-pot, paint-
pot, hot spring, and geyser, or gusher, as the
Icelandic words mean. And when you saunter
into the midst of them over the bright sinter
pavements, and see how pure and white and
pearly gray they are in the shade of the mountains, and how radiant in the sunshine, you are
fairly enchanted. So numerous they are and
varied, Nature seems to have gathered them
from all the world as specimens of her rarest
fountains, to show in one place what she can do.
Over four thousand hot springs have been counted

in the park, and a hundred geysers; how many more there are nobody knows.

These valleys at the heads of the great rivers may be regarded as laboratories and kitchens, in which, amid a thousand retorts and pots, we may see Nature at work as chemist or cook, cunningly compounding an infinite variety of mineral messes; cooking whole mountains; boiling and steaming flinty rocks to smooth paste and mush, — yellow, brown, red, pink, lavender, gray, and creamy white, — making the most beautiful mud in the world; and distilling the most ethereal essences. Many of these pots and caldrons have been boiling thousands of years. Pots of sulphurous mush, stringy and lumpy, and pots of broth as black as ink, are tossed and stirred with constant care, and thin transparent essences, too pure and fine to be called water, are kept simmering gently in beautiful sinter cups and bowls that grow ever more beautiful the longer they are used. In some of the spring basins, the waters, though still warm, are perfectly calm, and shine blandly in a sod of overleaning grass and flowers, as if they were thoroughly cooked at last, and set aside to settle and cool. Others are wildly boiling over as if running to waste, thousands of tons of the precious liquids being thrown into the air to fall in scalding floods on the clean coral floor of the establishment, keeping onlookers at a distance. Instead of holding limpid pale

green or azure water, other pots and craters are
filled with scalding mud, which is tossed up from
three or four feet to thirty feet, in sticky, rank-
smelling masses, with gasping, belching, thudding sounds, plastering the branches of neighboring trees; every flask, retort, hot spring, and
geyser has something special in it, no two being
the same in temperature, color, or composition.

In these natural laboratories one needs stout
faith to feel at ease. The ground sounds hollow
underfoot, and the awful subterranean thunder
shakes one's mind as the ground is shaken, especially at night in the pale moonlight, or when
the sky is overcast with storm-clouds. In the
solemn gloom, the geysers, dimly visible, look
like monstrous dancing ghosts, and their wild
songs and the earthquake thunder replying to
the storms overhead seem doubly terrible, as if
divine government were at an end. But the
trembling hills keep their places. The sky clears,
the rosy dawn is reassuring, and up comes the
sun like a god, pouring his faithful beams across
the mountains and forest, lighting each peak
and tree and ghastly geyser alike, and shining
into the eyes of the reeking springs, clothing
them with rainbow light, and dissolving the
seeming chaos of darkness into varied forms of
harmony. The ordinary work of the world goes
on. Gladly we see the flies dancing in the sunbeams, birds feeding their young, squirrels gath-

ering nuts, and hear the blessed ouzel singing
confidingly in the shallows of the river, — most
faithful evangel, calming every fear, reducing
everything to love.

The variously tinted sinter and travertine
formations, outspread like pavements over large
areas of the geyser valleys, lining the spring
basins and throats of the craters, and forming
beautiful coral-like rims and curbs about them,
always excite admiring attention; so also does
the play of the waters from which they are deposited. The various minerals in them are rich
in colors, and these are greatly heightened by a
smooth, silky growth of brilliantly colored confervæ which lines many of the pools and channels and terraces. No bed of flower-bloom is
more exquisite than these myriads of minute
plants, visible only in mass, growing in the hot
waters. Most of the spring borders are low and
daintily scalloped, crenelated, and beaded with
sinter pearls. Some of the geyser craters are
massive and picturesque, like ruined castles or
old burned-out sequoia stumps, and are adorned
on a grand scale with outbulging, cauliflower-
like formations. From these as centres the silex
pavements slope gently away in thin, crusty,
overlapping layers, slightly interrupted in some
places by low terraces. Or, as in the case of the
Mammoth Hot Springs, at the north end of the
park, where the building waters issue from the

side of a steep hill, the deposits form a succession of higher and broader terraces of white travertine tinged with purple, like the famous Pink Terrace at Rotomahana, New Zealand, draped in front with clustering stalactites, each terrace having a pool of indescribably beautiful water upon it in a basin with a raised rim that glistens with confervæ, — the whole, when viewed at a distance of a mile or two, looking like a broad, massive cascade pouring over shelving rocks in snowy purpled foam.

The stones of this divine masonry, invisible particles of lime or silex, mined in quarries no eye has seen, go to their appointed places in gentle, tinkling, transparent currents or through the dashing turmoil of floods, as surely guided as the sap of plants streaming into bole and branch, leaf and flower. And thus from century to century this beauty-work has gone on and is going on.

Passing though many a mile of pine and spruce woods, toward the centre of the park you come to the famous Yellowstone Lake. It is about twenty miles long and fifteen wide, and lies at a height of nearly 8000 feet above the level of the sea, amid dense black forests and snowy mountains. Around its winding, wavering shores, closely forested and picturesquely varied with promontories and bays, the distance is more than 100 miles. It is not very deep,

only from 200 to 300 feet, and contains less
water than the celebrated Lake Tahoe of the
California Sierra, which is nearly the same size,
lies at a height of 6400 feet, and is over 1600
feet deep. But no other lake in North America
of equal area lies so high as the Yellowstone, or
gives birth to so noble a river. The terraces
around its shores show that at the close of the
glacial period its surface was about 160 feet
higher than it is now, and its area nearly twice as
great.

It is full of trout, and a vast multitude of
birds — swans, pelicans, geese, ducks, cranes,
herons, curlews, plovers, snipe — feed in it and
upon its shores; and many forest animals come
out of the woods, and wade a little way in shallow, sandy places to drink and look about them,
and cool themselves in the free flowing breezes.

In calm weather it is a magnificent mirror for
the woods and mountains and sky, now pattered
with hail and rain, now roughened with sudden
storms that send waves to fringe the shores and
wash its border of gravel and sand. The Absaroka Mountains and the Wind River Plateau on
the east and south pour their gathered waters
into it, and the river issues from the north side
in a broad, smooth, stately current, silently gliding with such serene majesty that one fancies it
knows the vast journey of four thousand miles
that lies before it, and the work it has to do.

For the first twenty miles its course is in a level, sunny valley lightly fringed with trees, through which it flows in silvery reaches stirred into spangles here and there by ducks and leaping trout, making no sound save a low whispering among the pebbles and the dipping willows and sedges of its banks. Then suddenly, as if preparing for hard work, it rushes eagerly, impetuously forward rejoicing in its strength, breaks into foam-bloom, and goes thundering down into the Grand Cañon in two magnificent falls, one hundred and three hundred feet high.

The cañon is so tremendously wild and impressive that even these great falls cannot hold your attention. It is about twenty miles long and a thousand feet deep, — a weird, unearthly-looking gorge of jagged, fantastic architecture, and most brilliantly colored. Here the Washburn range, forming the northern rim of the Yellowstone basin, made up mostly of beds of rhyolite decomposed by the action of thermal waters, has been cut through and laid open to view by the river; and a famous section it has made. It is not the depth or the shape of the cañon, nor the waterfall, nor the green and gray river chanting its brave song as it goes foaming on its way, that most impresses the observer, but the colors of the decomposed volcanic rocks. With few exceptions, the traveler in strange lands finds that, however much the scenery and vegetation in different countries may change, Mother Earth is ever familiar and the same. But here the very ground is changed, as if belonging to some other world. The walls of the cañon from top to bottom burn in a perfect glory of color, confounding and dazzling when the sun is shining, — white, yellow, green, blue, vermilion, and various other shades of red indefinitely blending. All the earth hereabouts seems to be paint. Millions of tons of it lie in sight, exposed to wind and weather as if of no account, yet marvelously fresh and bright, fast colors not to be washed out or bleached out by either sunshine or storms. The effect is so novel and awful, we imagine that even a river might be afraid to enter such a place. But the rich and gentle beauty of the vegetation is reassuring. The lovely Linnæa borealis hangs her twin bells over the brink of the cliffs, forests and gardens extend their treasures in smiling confidence on either side, nuts and berries ripen well whatever may be going on below; blind fears vanish, and the grand gorge seems a kindly, beautiful part of the general harmony, full of peace and joy and good will.

The park is easy of access. Locomotives drag you to its northern boundary at Cinnabar, and horses and guides do the rest. From Cinnabar you will be whirled in coaches along the foaming Gardiner River to Mammoth Hot Springs;

thence through woods and meadows, gulches and ravines along branches of the Upper Gallatin, Madison, and Firehole rivers to the main geyser basins; thence over the Continental Divide and back again, up and down through dense pine, spruce, and fir woods to the magnificent Yellowstone Lake, along its northern shore to the outlet, down the river to the falls and Grand Cañon, and thence back through the woods to Mammoth Hot Springs and Cinnabar; stopping here and there at the so-called points of interest among the geysers, springs, paint-pots, mud volcanoes, etc., where you will be allowed a few minutes or hours to saunter over the sinter pavements, watch the play of a few of the geysers, and peer into some of the most beautiful and terrible of the craters and pools. These wonders you will enjoy, and also the views of the mountains, especially the Gallatin and Absaroka ranges, the long, willowy glacier and beaver meadows, the beds of violets, gentians, phloxes, asters, phacelias, goldenrods, eriogonums, and many other flowers, some species giving color to whole meadows and hillsides. And you will enjoy your short views of the great lake and river and cañon. No scalping Indians will you see. The Blackfeet and Bannocks that once roamed here are gone; so are the old beaver-catchers, the Coulters and Bridgers, with all their attractive buckskin and romance. There are several bands

of buffaloes in the park, but you will not thus
cheaply in tourist fashion see them nor many of
the other large animals hidden in the wilderness.
The song-birds, too, keep mostly out of sight of
the rushing tourist, though off the roads thrushes,
warblers, orioles, grosbeaks, etc., keep the air
sweet and merry. Perhaps in passing rapids and
falls you may catch glimpses of the water-ouzel,
but in the whirling noise you will not hear his
song. Fortunately, no road noise frightens the
Douglas squirrel, and his merry play and gossip
will amuse you all through the woods. Here
and there a deer may be seen crossing the road,
or a bear. Most likely, however, the only bears
you will see are the half tame ones that go to the
hotels every night for dinner-table scraps, —
yeast-powder biscuit, Chicago canned stuff, mixed
pickles, and beefsteaks that have proved too
tough for the tourists.

Among the gains of a coach trip are the ac-
quaintances made and the fresh views into human nature ; for the wilderness is a shrewd
touchstone, even thus lightly approached, and
brings many a curious trait to view. Setting
out, the driver cracks his whip, and the four
horses go off at half gallop, half trot, in trained,
showy style, until out of sight of the hotel. The
coach is crowded, old and young side by side,
blooming and fading, full of hope and fun and
care. Some look at the scenery or the horses,

and all ask questions, an odd mixed lot of them :
" Where is the umbrella ? What is the name of
that blue flower over there ? Are you sure the
little bag is aboard ? Is that hollow yonder a
crater ? How is your throat this morning ?
How high did you say the geysers spout ? How
does the elevation affect your head ? Is that a
geyser reeking over there in the rocks, or only a
hot spring ? " A long ascent is made, the solemn
mountains come to view, small cares are quenched,
and all become natural and silent, save perhaps
some unfortunate expounder who has been reading guidebook geology, and rumbles forth foggy
subsidences and upheavals until he is in danger
of being heaved overboard. The driver will
give you the names of the peaks and meadows
and streams as you come to them, call attention
to the glass road, tell how hard it was to build,
— how the obsidian cliffs naturally pushed the
surveyor's lines to the right, and the industrious
beavers, by flooding the valley in front of the
cliff, pushed them to the left.

Geysers, however, are the main objects, and as
soon as they come in sight other wonders are forgotten. All gather around the crater of the one
that is expected to play first. During the erup-
tions of the smaller geysers, such as the Beehive
and Old Faithful, though a little frightened at
first, all welcome the glorious show with enthusiasm, and shout, " Oh, how wonderful, beautiful,

splendid, majestic ! " Some venture near enough
to stroke the column with a stick, as if it were
a stone pillar or a tree, so firm and substantial
and permanent it seems. While tourists wait
around a large geyser, such as the Castle or the
Giant, there is a chatter of small talk in anything
but solemn mood; and during the intervals
between the preliminary splashes and upheavals
some adventurer occasionally looks down the
throat of the crater, admiring the silex formations and wondering whether Hades is as beautiful. But when, with awful uproar as if avalanches were falling and storms thundering in
the depths, the tremendous outburst begins,
all run away to a safe distance, and look on,
awe-stricken and silent, in devout, worshiping
wonder.

The largest and one of the most wonderfully
beautiful of the springs is the Prismatic, which
the guide will be sure to show you. With a circumference of 300 yards, it is more like a lake
than a spring. The water is pure deep blue in
the centre, fading to green on the edges, and its
basin and the slightly terraced pavement about
it are astonishingly bright and varied in color.
This one of the multitude of Yellowstone fountains is of itself object enough for a trip across
the continent. No wonder that so many fine
myths have originated in springs; that so many
fountains were held sacred in the youth of the

world, and had miraculous virtues ascribed to
them.   Even in these cold, doubting, question-
ing, scientific times many of the Yellowstone
fountains seem able to work miracles.   Near the
Prismatic Spring is the great Excelsior Geyser,
which is said to throw a column of boiling water
60 to 70 feet in diameter to a height of from 50
to 300 feet, at irregular periods.   This is the
greatest of all the geysers yet discovered anywhere.
The Firehole River, which sweeps past it, is, at
ordinary stages, a stream about 100 yards wide
and 3 feet deep; but when the geyser is in
eruption, so great is the quantity of water dis-
charged that the volume of the river is doubled,
and it is rendered too hot and rapid to be forded.

Geysers are found in many other volcanic regions, — in Iceland, New Zealand, Japan, the
Himalayas, the Eastern Archipelago, South
America, the Azores, and elsewhere; but only in
Iceland, New Zealand, and this Rocky Mountain
park do they display their grandest forms, and of
these three famous regions the Yellowstone is
easily first, both in the number and in the size of
its geysers.   The greatest height of the column
of the Great Geyser of Iceland actually measured
was 212 feet, and of the Strokhr 162 feet.

In New Zealand, the Te Pueia at Lake Taupo,
the Waikite at Rotorna, and two others are said
to lift their waters occasionally to a height of 100
feet, while the celebrated Te Tarata at Rotomahana

sometimes lifts a boiling column 20 feet in diameter to a height of 60 feet. But all these are far surpassed by the Excelsior. Few tourists, however, will see the Excelsior in action, or a thousand other interesting features of the park that lie beyond the wagon-roads and the hotels. The regular trips — from three to five days — are too short. Nothing can be done well at a speed of forty miles a day. The multitude of mixed, novel impressions rapidly piled on one another make only a dreamy, bewildering, swirling blur, most of which is unrememberable. Far more time should be taken. Walk away quietly in any direction and taste the freedom of the mountaineer. Camp out among the grass and gentians of glacier meadows, in craggy garden nooks full of Nature's darlings. Climb the mountains and get their good tidings. Nature's peace will flow into you as sunshine flows into trees. The winds will blow their own freshness into you, and the storms their energy, while cares will drop off like autumn leaves. As age comes on, one source of enjoyment after another is closed, but Nature's sources never fail. Like a generous host, she offers here brimming cups in endless variety, served in a grand hall, the sky its ceiling, the mountains its walls, decorated with glorious paintings and enlivened with bands of music ever playing. The petty discomforts that beset the awkward guest, the unskilled camper, are quickly forgotten, while all that is precious remains. Fears vanish as soon as one is fairly free in the wilderness.

Most of the dangers that haunt the unseasoned citizen are imaginary; the real ones are perhaps too few rather than too many for his good. The bears that always seem to spring up thick as trees, in fighting, devouring attitudes before the frightened tourist whenever a camping trip is proposed, are gentle now, finding they are no longer likely to be shot; and rattlesnakes, the other big irrational dread of over-civilized people, are scarce here, for most of the park lies above the snake-line. Poor creatures, loved only by their Maker, they are timid and bashful, as mountaineers know; and though perhaps not possessed of much of that charity that suffers long and is kind, seldom, either by mistake or by mishap, do harm to any one. Certainly they cause not the hundredth part of the pain and death that follow the footsteps of the admired Rocky Mountain trapper. Nevertheless, again and again, in season and out of season, the question comes up, "What are rattlesnakes good for?" As if nothing that does not obviously make for the benefit of man had any right to exist; as if our ways were God's ways. Long ago, an Indian to whom a French traveler put this old question replied that their tails were good for toothache, and their heads for fever.

Anyhow, they are all, head and tail, good for
themselves, and we need not begrudge them their
share of life.

Fear nothing. No town park you have been
accustomed to saunter in is so free from danger
as the Yellowstone. It is a hard place to leave.
Even its names in your guidebook are attractive,
and should draw you far from wagon-roads, — all
save the early ones, derived from the infernal regions: Hell Roaring River, Hell Broth Springs,
The Devil's Caldron, etc. Indeed, the whole region was at first called Coulter's Hell, from the
fiery brimstone stories told by trapper Coulter,
who left the Lewis and Clark expedition and
wandered through the park, in the year 1807,
with a band of Bannock Indians. The later
names, many of which we owe to Mr. Arnold
Hague of the U. S. Geological Survey, are so
telling and exhilarating that they set our pulses
dancing and make us begin to enjoy the pleas-
ures of excursions ere they are commenced.
Three River Peak, Two Ocean Pass, Continental
Divide, are capital geographical descriptions, suggesting thousands of miles of rejoicing streams
and all that belongs to them. Big Horn Pass,
Bison Peak, Big Game Ridge, bring brave mountain animals to mind. Birch Hills, Garnet Hills,
Amethyst Mountain, Storm Peak, Electric Peak,
Roaring Mountain, are bright, bracing names.
Wapiti, Beaver, Tern, and Swan lakes, conjure

up fine pictures, and so also do Osprey and Ouzel falls. Antelope Creek, Otter, Mink, and Grayling creeks, Geode, Jasper, Opal, Carnelian, and Chalcedony creeks, are lively and sparkling names that help the streams to shine; and Azalea, Stellaria, Arnica, Aster, and Phlox creeks, what pictures these bring up! Violet, Morning Mist, Hygeia, Beryl, Vermilion, and Indigo springs, and many beside, give us visions of fountains more beautifully arrayed than Solomon in all his purple and golden glory. All these and a host of others call you to camp. You may be a little cold some nights, on mountain tops above the timber-line, but you will see the stars, and by and by you can sleep enough in your town bed, or at least in your grave. Keep awake while you may in mountain mansions so rare.

If you are not very strong, try to climb Electric Peak when a big bossy, well-charged thunder-cloud is on it, to breathe the ozone set free, and get yourself kindly shaken and shocked. You are sure to be lost in wonder and praise, and every hair of your head will stand up and hum and sing like an enthusiastic congregation.

After this reviving experience, you should take a look into a few of the tertiary volumes of the grand geological library of the park, and see how God writes history. No technical knowledge is required; only a calm day and a calm mind. Perhaps nowhere else in the Rocky Mountains have

the volcanic forces been so busy. More than
ten thousand square miles hereabouts have been
covered to a depth of at least five thousand feet
with material spouted from chasms and craters
during the tertiary period, forming broad sheets
of basalt, andesite, rhyolite, etc., and marvelous
masses of ashes, sand, cinders, and stones now
consolidated into conglomerates, charged with the
remains of plants and animals that lived in the
calm, genial periods that separated the volcanic
outbursts.

Perhaps the most interesting and telling of
these rocks, to the hasty tourist, are those that
make up the mass of Amethyst Mountain. On its
north side it presents a section two thousand feet
high of roughly stratified beds of sand, ashes, and
conglomerates coarse and fine, forming the un-
trimmed edges of a wonderful set of volumes lying on their sides, — books a million years old,
well bound, miles in size, with full-page illustra-
tions. On the ledges of this one section we see
trunks and stumps of fifteen or twenty ancient
forests ranged one above another, standing where
they grew, or prostrate and broken like the pillars of ruined temples in desert sands, — a forest
fifteen or twenty stories high, the roots of each
spread above the tops of the next beneath it, telling wonderful tales of the bygone centuries, with
their winters and summers, growth and death,
fire, ice, and flood.

There were giants in those days. The largest of the standing opal and agate stumps and prostrate sections of the trunks are from two or three to fifty feet in height or length, and from five to ten feet in diameter ; and so perfect is the petrifaction that the annual rings and ducts are clearer and more easily counted than those of living trees, centuries of burial having brightened the records instead of blurring them. They show that the winters of the tertiary period gave as decided a check to vegetable growth as do those of the present time. Some trees favorably located grew rapidly, increasing twenty inches in diameter in as many years, while others of the same species, on poorer soil or overshadowed, increased only two or three inches in the same time.

Among the roots and stumps on the old forest floors we find the remains of ferns and bushes, and the seeds and leaves of trees like those now growing on the southern Alleghanies, — such as magnolia, sassafras, laurel, linden, persimmon, ash, alder, dogwood. Studying the lowest of these forests, the soil it grew on and the deposits it is buried in, we see that it was rich in species, and flourished in a genial, sunny climate. When its stately trees were in their glory, volcanic fires broke forth from chasms and craters, like larger geysers, spouting ashes, cinders, stones, and mud, which fell on the doomed forest like hail and snow; sifting, hurtling through the leaves and branches, choking the streams, covering the ground, crushing bushes and ferns, rapidly deepening, packing around the trees and breaking them, rising higher until the topmost boughs of the giants were buried, leaving not a leaf or twig in sight, so complete was the desolation. At last the volcanic storm began to abate, the fiery soil settled; mud floods and boulder floods passed over it, enriching it, cooling it; rains fell and mellow sunshine, and it became fertile and ready for another crop. Birds, and the winds, and roaming animals brought seeds from more fortunate woods, and a new forest grew up on the top of the buried one. Centuries of genial growing seasons passed. The seedling trees became giants, and with strong outreaching branches spread a leafy canopy over the gray land.

The sleeping subterranean fires again awake and shake the mountains, and every leaf trembles. The old craters, with perhaps new ones, are opened, and immense quantities of ashes, pumice, and cinders are again thrown into the sky. The sun, shorn of his beams, glows like a dull red ball, until hidden in sulphurous clouds. Volcanic snow, hail, and floods fall on the new forest, burying it alive, like the one beneath its roots. Then come another noisy band of mud floods and boulder floods, mixing, settling, enriching the new ground, more seeds, quickening sunshine and showers; and a third noble magnolia forest is carefully raised on the top of the second. And so on. Forest was planted above forest and destroyed, as if Nature were ever repenting, undoing the work she had so industriously done, and burying it.

Of course this destruction was creation, progress in the march of beauty through death. How quickly these old monuments excite and hold the imagination ! We see the old stone stumps budding and blossoming and waving in the wind as magnificent trees, standing shoulder to shoulder, branches interlacing in grand varied round-headed forests ; see the sunshine of morning and evening gilding their mossy trunks, and at high noon spangling on the thick glossy leaves of the magnolia, filtering through translucent canopies of linden and ash, and falling in mellow patches on the ferny floor ; see the shining after rain, breathe the exhaling fragrance, and hear the winds and birds and the murmur of brooks and insects. We watch them from season to season ; see the swelling buds when the sap begins to flow in the spring, the opening leaves and blossoms, the ripening of summer fruits, the colors of autumn, and the maze of leafless branches and sprays in winter ; and we see the sudden oncome of the storms that overwhelmed them.

One calm morning at sunrise I saw the oaks

and pines in Yosemite Valley shaken by an earthquake, their tops swishing back and forth, and
every branch and needle shuddering as if in distress like the frightened screaming birds. One
may imagine the trembling, rocking, tumultuous
waving of those ancient Yellowstone woods, and
the terror of their inhabitants when the first
foreboding shocks were felt, the sky grew dark,
and rock-laden floods began to roar. But though
they were close pressed and buried, cut off from
sun and wind, all their happy leaf-fluttering and
waving done, other currents coursed through
them, fondling and thrilling every fibre, and
beautiful wood was replaced by beautiful stone.
Now their rocky sepulchres are partly open, and
show forth the natural beauty of death.

After the forest times and fire times had
passed away, and the volcanic furnaces were
banked and held in abeyance, another great
change occurred. The glacial winter came on.
The sky was again darkened, not with dust and
ashes, but with snow which fell in glorious abundance, piling deeper, deeper, slipping from the
overladen heights in booming avalanches, compacting into glaciers, that flowed over all the
landscape, wiping off forests, grinding, sculpturing, fashioning the comparatively featureless
lava beds into the beautiful rhythm of hill and
dale and ranges of mountains we behold to-day;
forming basins for lakes, channels for streams,

new soils for forests, gardens, and meadows. While this ice-work was going on, the slumbering volcanic fires were boiling the subterranean waters, and with curious chemistry decomposing the rocks, making beauty in the darkness; these forces, seemingly antagonistic, working harmoniously together. How wild their meetings on the surface were we may imagine. When the glacier period began, geysers and hot springs were playing in grander volume, it may be, than those of to-day. The glaciers flowed over them while they spouted and thundered, carrying away their fine sinter and travertine structures, and shortening their mysterious channels.

The soils made in the down-grinding required to bring the present features of the landscape into relief are possibly no better than were some of the old volcanic soils that were carried away, and which, as we have seen, nourished magnificent forests, but the glacial landscapes are incomparably more beautiful than the old volcanic ones were. The glacial winter has passed away, like the ancient summers and fire periods, though in the chronolgy of the geologist all these times are recent. Only small residual glaciers on the cool northern slopes of the highest mountains are left of the vast all-embracing ice-mantle, as solfataras and geysers are all that are left of the ancient volcanoes.

Now the post-glacial agents are at work on the

grand old palimpsest of the park region, inscrib-
ing new characters; but still in its main telling
features it remains distinctly glacial. The
moraine soils are being leveled, sorted, refined,
re-formed, and covered with vegetation; the polished pavements and scoring and other superficial
glacial inscriptions on the crumbling lavas are
being rapidly obliterated; gorges are being cut in
the decomposed rhyolites and loose conglomerates, and turrets and pinnacles seem to be
springing up like growing trees; while the geysers are depositing miles of sinter and travertine.
Nevertheless, the ice-work is scarce blurred as
yet. These later effects are only spots and
wrinkles on the grand glacial countenance of the
park.

Perhaps you have already said that you have
seen enough for a lifetime. But before you go
away you should spend at least one day and a
night on a mountain top, for a last general,
calming, settling view. Mount Washburn is a
good one for the purpose, because it stands in
the middle of the park, is unencumbered with
other peaks, and is so easy of access that the
climb to its summit is only a saunter. First your
eye goes roving around the mountain rim amid
the hundreds of peaks: some with plain flowing
skirts, others abruptly precipitous and defended
by sheer battlemented escarpments; flat-topped
or round; heaving like sea-waves or spired and

turreted like Gothic cathedrals; streaked with
snow in the ravines, and darkened with files of
adventurous trees climbing the ridges.   The
nearer peaks are perchance clad in sapphire
blue, others far off in creamy white.   In the
broad glare of noon they seem to shrink and
crouch to less than half their real stature, and
grow dull and uncommunicative, — mere dead,
draggled heaps of waste ashes and stone, giving
no hint of the multitude of animals enjoying life
in their fastnesses, or of the bright bloom-
bordered streams and lakes.   But when storms
blow they awake and arise, wearing robes of
cloud and mist in majestic speaking attitudes like
gods.   In the color glory of morning and evening
they become still more impressive ; steeped in
the divine light of the alpenglow their earthi-
ness disappears, and, blending with the heavens,
they seem neither high nor low.

Over all the central plateau, which from here
seems level, and over the foothills and lower
slopes of the mountains, the forest extends like a
black uniform bed of weeds, interrupted only
by lakes and meadows and small burned spots
called parks, — all of them, except the Yellowstone Lake, being mere dots and spangles in general views, made conspicuous by their color and
brightness.   About eighty-five per cent of the
entire area of the park is covered with trees,
mostly the indomitable lodge-pole pine (*Pinus*

contorta, var. *Murrayana*), with a few patches
and sprinklings of Douglas spruce, Engelmann
spruce, silver fir (*Abies lasiocarpa*), Pinus flexilis, and a few alders, aspens, and birches.   The
Douglas spruce is found only on the lowest portions, the silver fir on the highest, and the Engelmann spruce on the dampest places, best defended
from fire.   Some fine specimens of the flexilis
pine are growing on the margins of openings, —
wide-branching, sturdy trees, as broad as high,
with trunks five feet in diameter, leafy and
shady, laden with purple cones and rose-colored
flowers.   The Engelmann spruce and sub-alpine
silver fir are beautiful and notable trees, —
tall, spiry, hardy, frost and snow defying, and
widely distributed over the West, wherever there
is a mountain to climb or a cold moraine slope
to cover.   But neither of these is a good fire-
fighter.   With rather thin bark, and scattering
their seeds every year as soon as they are ripe,
they are quickly driven out of fire-swept regions.   When the glaciers were melting, these
hardy mountaineering trees were probably among
the first to arrive on the new moraine soil beds;
but as the plateau became drier and fires began
to run, they were driven up the mountains, and
into the wet spots and islands where we now find
them, leaving nearly all the park to the lodge-
pole pine, which, though as thin-skinned as they
and as easily killed by fire, takes pains to store

up its seeds in firmly closed cones, and holds
them from three to nine years, so that, let the
fire come when it may, it is ready to die and
ready to live again in a new generation. For
when the killing fires have devoured the leaves
and thin resinous bark, many of the cones, only
scorched, open as soon as the smoke clears away;
the hoarded store of seeds is sown broadcast on
the cleared ground, and a new growth immediately springs up triumphant out of the ashes.
Therefore, this tree not only holds its ground,
but extends its conquests farther after every fire.
Thus the evenness and closeness of its growth are
accounted for. In one part of the forest that I
examined, the growth was about as close as a cane-
brake. The trees were from four to eight inches
in diameter, one hundred feet high, and one hundred and seventy-five years old. The lower limbs
die young and drop off for want of light. Life
with these close-planted trees is a race for light,
more light, and so they push straight for the sky.
Mowing off ten feet from the top of the forest
would make it look like a crowded mass of tele-
graph-poles; for only the sunny tops are leafy. A
sapling ten years old, growing in the sunshine,
has as many leaves as a crowded tree one or two
hundred years old. As fires are multiplied and the
mountains become drier, this wonderful lodge-
pole pine bids fair to obtain possession of nearly
all the forest ground in the West.

How still the woods seem from here, yet how lively a stir the hidden animals are making; digging, gnawing, biting, eyes shining, at work and play, getting food, rearing young, roving through the underbrush, climbing the rocks, wading solitary marshes, tracing the banks of the lakes and streams! Insect swarms are dancing in the sunbeams, burrowing in the ground, diving, swimming, — a cloud of witnesses telling Nature's joy. The plants are as busy as the animals, every cell in a swirl of enjoyment, humming like a hive, singing the old new song of creation. A few columns and puffs of steam are seen rising above the treetops, some near, but most of them far off, indicating geysers and hot springs, gentle-looking and noiseless as downy clouds, softly hinting the reaction going on between the surface and the hot interior. From here you see them better than when you are standing beside them, frightened and confused, regarding them as lawless cataclysms. The shocks and outbursts of earthquakes, volcanoes, geysers, storms, the pounding of waves, the uprush of sap in plants, each and all tell the orderly love-beats of Nature's heart.

Turning to the eastward, you have the Grand Cañon and reaches of the river in full view; and yonder to the southward lies the great lake, the largest and most important of all the high fountains of the Missouri-Mississippi, and the last to be discovered.

In the year 1541, when De Soto, with a romantic band of adventurers, was seeking gold
and glory and the fountain of youth, he found
the Mississippi a few hundred miles above its
mouth, and made his grave beneath its floods.
La Salle, in 1682, after discovering the Ohio,
one of the largest and most beautiful branches of
the Mississippi, traced the latter to the sea from
the mouth of the Illinois, through adventures and
privations not easily realized now. About the
same time Joliet and Father Marquette reached
the " Father of Waters " by way of the Wisconsin, but more than a century passed ere its highest sources in these mountains were seen. The
advancing stream of civilization has ever followed
its guidance toward the west, but none of the
thousand tribes of Indians living on its banks
could tell the explorer whence it came. From
those romantic De Soto and La Salle days to
these times of locomotives and tourists, how much
has the great river seen and done! Great as it
now is, and still growing longer through the
ground of its delta and the basins of receding glaciers at its head, it was immensely broader toward
the close of the glacial period, when the ice-mantle of the mountains was melting : then with its
three hundred thousand miles of branches outspread over the plains and valleys of the continent, laden with fertile mud, it made the biggest
and most generous bed of soil in the world.

Think of this mighty stream springing in the first place in vapor from the sea, flying on the wind, alighting on the mountains in hail and snow and rain, lingering in many a fountain feeding the trees and grass; then gathering its scattered waters, gliding from its noble lake, and going back home to the sea, singing all the way! On it sweeps, through the gates of the mountains, across the vast prairies and plains, through many a wild, gloomy forest, cane-brake, and sunny savanna; from glaciers and snowbanks and pine woods to warm groves of magnolia and palm; geysers dancing at its head keeping time with the sea-waves at its mouth; roaring and gray in rapids, booming in broad, bossy falls, murmuring, gleaming in long, silvery reaches, swaying now hither, now thither, whirling, bending in huge doubling, eddying folds, serene, majestic, ungovernable, overflowing all its metes and bounds, frightening the dwellers upon its banks; building, wasting, uprooting, planting; engulfing old islands and making new ones, taking away fields and towns as if in sport, carrying canoes and ships of commerce in the midst of its spoils and drift, fertilizing the continent as one vast farm. Then, its work done, it gladly vanishes in its ocean home, welcomed by the waiting waves.

Thus naturally, standing here in the midst of its fountains, we trace the fortunes of the great river. And how much more comes to mind as

we overlook this wonderful wilderness! Fountains of the Columbia and Colorado lie before
us, interlaced with those of the Yellowstone and
Missouri, and fine it would be to go with them to
the Pacific; but the sun is already in the west,
and soon our day will be done.

Yonder is Amethyst Mountain, and other
mountains hardly less rich in old forests, which
now seem to spring up again in their glory ; and
you see the storms that buried them, — the ashes
and torrents laden with boulders and mud, the
centuries of sunshine, and the dark, lurid nights.
You see again the vast floods of lava, red-hot and
white-hot, pouring out from gigantic geysers,
usurping the basins of lakes and streams, absorb-
ing or driving away their hissing, screaming
waters, flowing around hills and ridges, submerg-
ing every subordinate feature. Then you see
the snow and glaciers taking possession of the
land, making new landscapes. How admirable
it is that, after passing through so many vicissi-
tudes of frost and fire and flood, the physiognomy and even the complexion of the landscape
should still be so divinely fine !

Thus reviewing the eventful past, we see Nature working with enthusiasm like a man, blowing
her volcanic forges like a blacksmith blowing
his smithy fires, shoving glaciers over the landscapes like a carpenter shoving his planes, clearing, ploughing, harrowing, irrigating, planting,

and sowing broadcast like a farmer and gardener, doing rough work and fine work, planting sequoias and pines, rosebushes and daisies; working in gems, filling every crack and hollow with them; distilling fine essences; painting plants and shells, clouds, mountains, all the earth and heavens, like an artist, — ever working toward beauty higher and higher. Where may the mind find more stimulating, quickening pasturage? A thousand Yellowstone wonders are calling, " Look up and down and round about you !" And a multitude of still, small voices may be heard directing you to look through all this transient, shifting show of things called " substantial " into the truly substantial, spiritual world whose forms flesh and wood, rock and water, air and sunshine, only veil and conceal, and to learn that here is heaven and the dwelling-place of the angels.

The sun is setting; long, violet shadows are growing out over the woods from the mountains along the western rim of the park; the Absaroka range is baptized in the divine light of the alpenglow, and its rocks and trees are transfigured. Next to the light of the dawn on high mountain tops, the alpenglow is the most impressive of all the terrestrial manifestations of God.

Now comes the gloaming. The alpenglow is fading into earthy, murky gloom, but do not let your town habits draw you away to the hotel.

Stay on this good fire-mountain and spend the night among the stars. Watch their glorious bloom until the dawn, and get one more baptism of light. Then, with fresh heart, go down to your work, and whatever your fate, under whatever ignorance or knowledge you may afterward chance to suffer, you will remember these fine, wild views, and look back with joy to your wanderings in the blessed old Yellowstone Wonderland.

CHAPTER III

Of all the mountain ranges I have climbed, I like the Sierra Nevada the best. Though extremely rugged, with its main features on the grandest scale in height and depth, it is nevertheless easy of access and hospitable; and its marvelous beauty, displayed in striking and alluring forms, wooes the admiring wanderer on and on, higher and higher, charmed and enchanted. Benevolent, solemn, fateful, pervaded with divine light, every landscape glows like a countenance hallowed in eternal repose; and every one of its living creatures, clad in flesh and leaves, and every crystal of its rocks, whether on the surface shining in the sun or buried miles deep in what we call darkness, is throbbing and pulsing with the heartbeats of God. All the world lies warm in one heart, yet the Sierra seems to get more light than other mountains. The weather is mostly sunshine embellished with magnificent storms, and nearly everything shines from base to summit, — the rocks, streams, lakes, glaciers, irised falls, and the forests of silver fir

and silver pine.   And how bright is the shining
after summer showers and dewy nights, and after
frosty nights in spring and autumn, when the
morning sunbeams are pouring through the
crystals on the bushes and grass, and in winter
through the snow-laden trees !

The average cloudiness for the whole year is
perhaps less than ten hundredths.   Scarcely a
day of all the summer is dark, though there is
no lack of magnificent thundering cumuli.   They
rise in the warm midday hours, mostly over the
middle region, in June and July, like new mountain ranges, higher Sierras, mightily augmenting
the grandeur of the scenery while giving rain to
the forests and gardens and bringing forth their
fragrance.   The wonderful weather and beauty
inspire everybody to be up and doing.   Every
summer day is a workday to be confidently
counted on, the short dashes of rain forming,
not interruptions, but rests.   The big blessed
storm days of winter, when the whole range
stands white, are not a whit less inspiring and
kind.   Well may the Sierra be called the Range
of Light, not the Snowy Range; for only in
winter is it white, while all the year it is bright.

Of this glorious range the Yosemite National
Park is a central section, thirty-six miles in
length and forty-eight miles in breadth.   The
famous Yosemite Valley lies in the heart of it,
and it includes the head waters of the Tuolumne

and Merced rivers, two of the most songful
streams in the world; innumerable lakes and
waterfalls and smooth silky lawns; the noblest
forests, the loftiest granite domes, the deepest
ice-sculptured cañons, the brightest crystalline
pavements, and snowy mountains soaring into
the sky twelve and thirteen thousand feet, arrayed in open ranks and spiry pinnacled groups
partially separated by tremendous cañons and
amphitheatres; gardens on their sunny brows,
avalanches thundering down their long white
slopes, cataracts roaring gray and foaming in
the crooked rugged gorges, and glaciers in their
shadowy recesses working in silence, slowly com-
pleting their sculpture; new-born lakes at their
feet, blue and green, free or encumbered with
drifting icebergs like miniature Arctic Oceans,
shining, sparkling, calm as stars.

Nowhere will you see the majestic operations
of nature more clearly revealed beside the frailest, most gentle and peaceful things. Nearly
all the park is a profound solitude. Yet it is
full of charming company, full of God's thoughts,
a place of peace and safety amid the most exalted
grandeur and eager enthusiastic action, a new
song, a place of beginnings abounding in first
lessons on life, mountain-building, eternal, invincible, unbreakable order; with sermons in stones,
storms, trees, flowers, and animals brimful of
humanity. During the last glacial period, just

past, the former features of the range were rubbed off as a chalk sketch from a blackboard, and a new beginning was made.   Hence the wonderful clearness and freshness of the rocky pages.

But to get all this into words is a hopeless task.   The leanest sketch of each feature would need a whole chapter.   Nor would any amount of space, however industriously scribbled, be of much avail.   To defrauded town toilers, parks in magazine articles are like pictures of bread to the hungry.   I can write only hints to incite good wanderers to come to the feast.

While this glorious park embraces big, generous samples of the very best of the Sierra treasures, it is, fortunately, at the same time, the most accessible portion.   It lies opposite San Francisco, at a distance of about one hundred and forty miles.   Railroads connected with all the continent reach into the foothills, and three good carriage roads, from Big Oak Flat, Coulterville, and Raymond, run into Yosemite Valley.   Another, called the Tioga road, runs from Crocker's Station on the Yosemite Big Oak Flat road near the Tuolumne Big Tree Grove, right across the park to the summit of the range by way of Lake Tenaya, the Big Tuolumne Meadows, and Mount Dana.   These roads, with many trails that radiate from Yosemite Valley, bring most of the park within reach of everybody, well or half well.

The three main natural divisions of the park, the lower, middle, and alpine regions, are fairly well defined in altitude, topographical features, and vegetation. The lower, with an average elevation of about five thousand feet, is the region of the great forests, made up of sugar pine, the largest and most beautiful of all the pines in the world; the silvery yellow pine, the next in rank; Douglas spruce, libocedrus, the white and red silver firs, and the Sequoia gigantea, or "big tree," the king of conifers, the noblest of a noble race. On warm slopes next the foothills there are a few Sabine nut pines; oaks make beautiful groves in the cañon valleys; and poplar, alder, maple, laurel, and Nuttall's flowering dogwood shade the banks of the streams. Many of the pines are more than two hundred feet high, but they are not crowded together. The sunbeams streaming through their feathery arches brighten the ground, and you walk beneath the radiant ceiling in devout subdued mood, as if you were in a grand cathedral with mellow light sifting through colored windows, while the flowery pillared aisles open enchanting vistas in every direction. Scarcely a peak or ridge in the whole region rises bare above the forests, though they are thinly planted in some places where the soil is shallow. From the cool breezy heights you look abroad over a boundless waving sea of evergreens, covering hill and ridge and smooth-flowing slope as far as the eye can reach, and filling every hollow and down-plunging ravine in glorious triumphant exuberance.

Perhaps the best general view of the pine forests of the park, and one of the best in the range, is obtained from the top of the Merced and Tuolumne divide near Hazel Green. On the long, smooth, finely folded slopes of the main ridge, at a height of five to six thousand feet above the sea, they reach most perfect development and are marshaled to view in magnificent towering ranks, their colossal spires and domes and broad palmlike crowns, deep in the kind sky, rising above one another, — a multitude of giants in perfect health and beauty, — sun-fed mountaineers rejoicing in their strength, chanting with the winds, in accord with the falling waters. The ground is mostly open and inviting to walkers. The fragrant chamæbatia is outspread in rich carpets miles in extent; the manzanita, in orchard-like groves, covered with pink bell-shaped flowers in the spring, grows in openings facing the sun, hazel and buckthorn in the dells; warm brows are purple with mint, yellow with sunflowers and violets; and tall lilies ring their bells around the borders of meadows and along the ferny, mossy banks of the streams. Never was mountain forest more lavishly furnished.

Hazel Green is a good place quietly to camp and study, to get acquainted with the trees and birds, to drink the reviving water and weather, and to watch the changing lights of the big charmed days. The rose light of the dawn, creeping higher among the stars, changes to daffodil yellow; then come the level enthusiastic sunbeams pouring across the feathery ridges, touching pine after pine, spruce and fir, libocedrus and lordly sequoia, searching every recess, until all are awakened and warmed. In the white noon they shine in silvery splendor, every needle and cell in bole and branch thrilling and tingling with ardent life; and the whole landscape glows with consciousness, like the face of a god. The hours go by uncounted. The evening flames with purple and gold. The breeze that has been blowing from the lowlands dies away, and far and near the mighty host of trees baptized in the purple flood stand hushed and thoughtful, awaiting the sun's blessing and farewell, — as impressive a ceremony as if it were never to rise again. When the daylight fades, the night breeze from the snowy summits begins to blow, and the trees, waving and rustling beneath the stars, breathe free again.

It is hard to leave such camps and woods; nevertheless, to the large majority of travelers the middle region of the park is still more interesting, for it has the most striking features of all the Sierra scenery, — the deepest sections of the famous cañons, of which the Yosemite Valley, Hetch-Hetchy Valley, and many smaller ones are wider portions, with level parklike floors and walls of immense height and grandeur of sculpture. This middle region holds also the greater number of the beautiful glacier lakes and glacier meadows, the great granite domes, and the most brilliant and most extensive of the glacier pavements. And though in large part it is severely rocky and bare, it is still rich in trees. The magnificent silver fir (*Abies magnifica*), which ranks with the giants, forms a continuous belt across the park above the pines at an elevation of from seven to nine thousand feet, and north and south of the park boundaries to the extremities of the range, only slightly interrupted by the main cañons. The two-leaved or tamarack pine makes another less regular belt along the upper margin of the region, while between these two belts, and mingling with them, in groves or scattered, are the mountain hemlock, the most graceful of evergreens; the noble mountain pine; the Jeffrey form of the yellow pine, with big cones and long needles; and the brown, burly, sturdy Western juniper. All these, except the juniper, which grows on bald rocks, have plenty of flowery brush about them, and gardens in open spaces.

Here, too, lies the broad, shining, heavily

sculptured region of primeval granite, which
best tells the story of the glacial period on the
Pacific side of the continent. No other mountain chain on the globe, as far as I know, is so
rich as the Sierra in bold, striking, well-preserved
glacial monuments, easily understood by anybody capable of patient observation. Every feature is more or less glacial, and this park portion
of the range is the brightest and clearest of all.
Not a peak, ridge, dome, cañon, lake basin, garden, forest, or stream but in some way explains
the past existence and modes of action of flowing, grinding, sculpturing, soil-making, scenery-
making ice. For, notwithstanding the post-
glacial agents — air, rain, frost, rivers, earthquakes, avalanches — have been at work upon
the greater part of the range for tens of thousands of stormy years, engraving their own
characters over those of the ice, the latter are so
heavily emphasized and enduring they still rise
in sublime relief, clear and legible through every
after inscription. The streams have traced only
shallow wrinkles as yet, and avalanche, wind,
rain, and melting snow have made blurs and
scars, but the change effected on the face of the
landscape is not greater than is made on the face
of a mountaineer by a single year of weathering.

Of all the glacial phenomena presented here,
the most striking and attractive to travelers are
the polished pavements, because they are so

beautiful, and their beauty is of so rare a kind, — unlike any part of the loose earthy lowlands where people dwell and earn their bread. They are simply flat or gently undulating areas of solid resisting granite, the unchanged surface over which the ancient glaciers flowed. They are found in the most perfect condition at an elevation of from eight to nine thousand feet above sea level. Some are miles in extent, only slightly blurred or scarred by spots that have at last yielded to the weather; while the best preserved portions are brilliantly polished, and reflect the sunbeams as calm water or glass, shining as if rubbed and burnished every day, notwithstanding they have been exposed to plashing, corroding rains, dew, frost, and melting sloppy snows for thousands of years.

The attention of hunters and prospectors, who see so much in their wild journeys, is seldom attracted by moraines, however regular and artificial-looking; or rocks, however boldly sculptured; or cañons, however deep and sheer-walled. But when they come to these pavements, they go down on their knees and rub their hands admiringly on the glistening surface, and try hard to account for its mysterious smoothness and brightness. They may have seen the winter avalanches come down the mountains, through the woods, sweeping away the trees and scouring the ground; but they conclude that this cannot be the work of avalanches, because the striæ show that the agent, whatever it was, flowed along and around and over the top of high ridges and domes, and also filled the deep cañons. Neither can they see how water could be the agent, for the strange polish is found thousands of feet above the reach of any conceivable flood. Only the winds seem capable of moving over the face of the country in the directions indicated by the lines and grooves.

The pavements are particularly fine around Lake Tenaya, and have suggested the Indian name Py-we-ack, the Lake of the Shining Rocks. Indians seldom trouble themselves with geological questions, but a Mono Indian once came to me and asked if I could tell him what made the rocks so smooth at Tenaya. Even dogs and horses, on their first journeys into this region, study geology to the extent of gazing wonderingly at the strange brightness of the ground, and pawing it and smelling it, as if afraid of falling or sinking.

In the production of this admirable hard finish, the glaciers in many places exerted a pressure of more than a hundred tons to the square foot, planing down granite, slate, and quartz alike, showing their structure, and making beautiful mosaics where large feldspar crystals form the greater part of the rock. On such pavements the sunshine is at times dazzling, as if the surface were of burnished silver.

PAVEMENT OF BASALTIC COLUMNS WORN BY GLACIAL ACTION, YOSEMITE

Here, also, are the brightest of the Sierra landscapes in general. The regions lying at the same elevation to the north and south were perhaps subjected to as long and intense a glaciation; but because the rocks are less resisting, their polished surfaces have mostly given way to the weather, leaving here and there only small imperfect patches on the most enduring portions of cañon walls protected from the action of rain and snow, and on hard bosses kept comparatively dry by boulders. The short, steeply inclined cañons of the east flank of the range are in some places brightly polished, but they are far less magnificent than those of the broad west flank.

One of the best general views of the middle region of the park is to be had from the top of a majestic dome which long ago I named the Glacier Monument. It is situated a few miles to the north of Cathedral Peak, and rises to a height of about fifteen hundred feet above its base and ten thousand above the sea. At first sight it seems sternly inaccessible, but a good climber will find that it may be scaled on the south side. Approaching it from this side you pass through a dense bryanthus-fringed grove of mountain hemlock, catching glimpses now and then of the colossal dome towering to an immense height above the dark evergreens; and when at last you have made your way across woods, wading through azalea and ledum thickets, you step abruptly out of the tree shadows and mossy leafy softness upon a bare porphyry pavement, and behold the dome unveiled in all its grandeur. Fancy a nicely proportioned monument, eight or ten feet high, hewn from one stone, standing in a pleasure ground; magnify it to a height of fifteen hundred feet, retaining its simplicity of form and fineness, and cover its surface with crystals; then you may gain an idea of the sublimity and beauty of this ice-burnished dome, one of many adorning this wonderful park.

In making the ascent, one finds that the curve of the base rapidly steepens, until one is in danger of slipping; but feldspar crystals, two or three inches long, that have been weathered into relief, afford slight footholds. The summit is in part burnished, like the sides and base, the striæ and scratches indicating that the mighty Tuolumne Glacier, two or three thousand feet deep, overwhelmed it while it stood firm like a boulder at the bottom of a river. The pressure it withstood must have been enormous. Had it been less solidly built, it would have been ground and crushed into moraine fragments, like the general mass of the mountain flank in which at first it lay imbedded; for it is only a hard residual knob or knot with a concentric structure of superior strength, brought into relief by the removal of the less resisting rock about it, — an illustration in stone of the survival of the strongest and most favorably situated.

Hardly less wonderful, when we contemplate the storms it has encountered since first it saw the light, is its present unwasted condition. The whole quantity of postglacial wear and tear it has suffered has not diminished its stature a single inch, as may be readily shown by measuring from the level of the unchanged polished portions of the surface. Indeed, the average postglacial denudation of the entire region, measured in the same way, is found to be less than two inches, — a mighty contrast to that of the ice; for the glacial denudation here has been not less than a mile; that is, in developing the present landscapes, an amount of rock a mile in average thickness has been silently carried away by flowing ice during the last glacial period.

A few erratic boulders nicely poised on the rounded summit of the monument tell an interesting story. They came from a mountain on the crest of the range, about twelve miles to the eastward, floating like chips on the frozen sea, and were stranded here when the top of the monument emerged to the light of day, while the companions of these boulders, whose positions chanced to be over the slopes where they could not find rest, were carried farther on by the shallowing current.

The general view from the summit consists of a sublime assemblage of iceborn mountains and rocks and long wavering ridges, lakes and

streams and meadows, moraines in wide-sweeping
belts, and beds covered and dotted with forests
and groves, — hundreds of square miles of them
composed in wild harmony. The snowy mountains on the axis of the range, mostly sharp-
peaked and crested, rise in noble array along the
sky to the eastward and northward; the gray-
pillared Hoffman spur and the Yosemite domes
and a countless number of others to the westward; Cathedral Peak with its many spires and
companion peaks and domes to the southward;
and a smooth billowy multitude of rocks, from
fifty feet or less to a thousand feet high, which
from their peculiar form seem to be rolling on
westward, fill most of the middle ground. Immediately beneath you are the Big Tuolumne
Meadows, with an ample swath of dark pine
woods on either side, enlivened by the young
river, that is seen sparkling and shimmering as
it sways from side to side, tracing as best it can
its broad glacial channel.

The ancient Tuolumne Glacier, lavishly flooded
by many a noble affluent from the snow-laden
flanks of Mounts Dana, Gibbs, Lyell, Maclure,
and others nameless as yet, poured its majestic overflowing current, four or five miles wide,
directly against the high outstanding mass of
Mount Hoffman, which divided and deflected it
right and left, just as a river is divided against
an island that stands in the middle of its chan-

nel. Two distinct glaciers were thus formed, one of which flowed through the Big Tuolumne Cañon and Hetch-Hetchy Valley, while the other swept upward five hundred feet in a broad current across the divide between the basins of the Tuolumne and Merced into the Tenaya basin, and thence down through the Tenaya Cañon and Yosemite Valley.

The maplike distinctness and freshness of this glacial landscape cannot fail to excite the attention of every observer, no matter how little of its scientific significance he may at first recognize. These bald, glossy, westward-leaning rocks in the open middle ground, with their rounded backs and shoulders toward the glacier fountains of the summit mountains and their split angular fronts looking in the opposite direction, every one of them displaying the form of greatest strength with reference to physical structure and glacial action, show the tremendous force with which through unnumbered centuries the ice flood swept over them, and also the direction of the flow; while the mountains, with their sharp summits and abraded sides, indicate the height to which the glacier rose; and the moraines, curving and swaying in beautiful lines, mark the boundaries of the main trunk and its tributaries as they existed toward the close of the glacial winter. None of the commercial highways of the sea or land, marked with buoys and lamps, fences and guideboards, is so unmistakably indicated as are these channels of the vanished Tuolumne glaciers.

The action of flowing ice, whether in the form of river-like glaciers or broad mantling folds, is but little understood as compared with that of other sculpturing agents. Rivers work openly where people dwell, and so do the rain, and the sea thundering on all the shores of the world; and the universal ocean of air, though unseen, speaks aloud in a thousand voices and explains its modes of working and its power. But glaciers, back in their cold solitudes, work apart from men, exerting their tremendous energies in silence and darkness. Coming in vapor from the sea, flying invisible on the wind, descending in snow, changing to ice, white, spiritlike, they brood outspread over the predestined landscapes, working on unwearied through unmeasured ages, until in the fullness of time the mountains and valleys are brought forth, channels furrowed for the rivers, basins made for meadows and lakes, and soil beds spread for the forests and fields that man and beast may be fed. Then vanishing like clouds, they melt into streams and go singing back home to the sea.

To an observer upon this adamantine old monument in the midst of such scenery, getting glimpses of the thoughts of God, the day seems endless, the sun stands still. Much faithless fuss

is made over the passage in the Bible telling of the
standing still of the sun for Joshua. Here you
may learn that the miracle occurs for every devout mountaineer, for everybody doing anything
worth doing, seeing anything worth seeing. One
day is as a thousand years, a thousand years as
one day, and while yet in the flesh you enjoy
immortality.

From the monument you will find an easy way
down through the woods and along the Big
Tuolumne Meadows to Mount Dana, the summit
of which commands a grand telling view of the
alpine region. The scenery all the way is inspiring, and you saunter on without knowing
that you are climbing. The spacious sunny
meadows, through the midst of which the bright
river glides, extend with but little interruption
ten miles to the eastward, dark woods rising
on either side to the limit of tree growth, and
above the woods a picturesque line of gray peaks
and spires dotted with snow banks ; while, on the
axis of the Sierra, Mount Dana and his noble
compeers repose in massive sublimity, their vast
size and simple flowing contours contrasting in
the most striking manner with the clustering
spires and thin-pinnacled crests crisply outlined
on the horizon to the north and south of them.

Tracing the silky lawns, gradually ascending,
gazing at the sublime scenery more and more
openly unfolded, noting the avalanche gaps in

the upper forests, lingering over beds of blue
gentians and purple-flowered bryanthus and cassiope, and dwarf willows an inch high in close-
felted gray carpets, brightened here and there
with kalmia and soft creeping mats of vaccinium
sprinkled with pink bells that seem to have been
showered down from the sky like hail, — thus
beguiled and enchanted, you reach the base of
the mountain wholly unconscious of the miles
you have walked. And so on to the summit.
For all the way up the long red slate slopes, that
in the distance seemed barren, you find little garden beds and tufts of dwarf phlox, ivesia, and
blue arctic daisies that go straight to your heart,
blessed fellow mountaineers kept safe and warm
by a thousand miracles. You are now more than
thirteen thousand feet above the sea, and to the
north and south you behold a sublime wilderness
of mountains in glorious array, their snowy summits towering together in crowded, bewildering
abundance, shoulder to shoulder, peak beyond
peak. To the east lies the Great Basin, barren-
looking and silent, apparently a land of pure
desolation, rich only in beautiful light. Mono
Lake, fourteen miles long, is outspread below
you at a depth of nearly seven thousand feet, its
shores of volcanic ashes and sand, treeless and
sunburned; a group of volcanic cones, with
well-formed, unwasted craters rises to the south
of the lake ; while up from its eastern shore in-

numerable mountains with soft flowing outlines
extend range beyond range, gray, and pale purple,
and blue, — the farthest gradually fading on the
glowing horizon. Westward you look down and
over the countless moraines, glacier meadows,
and grand sea of domes and rock waves of the
upper Tuolumne basin, the Cathedral and Hoffman mountains with their wavering lines and
zones of forest, the wonderful region to the north
of the Tuolumne Cañon, and across the dark belt
of silver firs to the pale mountains of the coast.

In the icy fountains of the Mount Lyell and
Ritter groups of peaks, to the south of Dana,
three of the most important of the Sierra rivers
— the Tuolumne, Merced, and San Joaquin —
take their rise, their highest tributaries being
within a few miles of one another as they rush
forth on their adventurous courses from beneath
snow banks and glaciers.

Of the small shrinking glaciers of the Sierra,
remnants of the majestic system that sculptured
the range, I have seen sixty-five. About twenty-
five of them are in the park, and eight are in
sight from Mount Dana.

The glacier lakes are sprinkled over all the
alpine and subalpine regions, gleaming like eyes
beneath heavy rock brows, tree-fringed or bare,
embosomed in the woods, or lying in open basins
with green and purple meadows around them;
but the greater number are in the cool shadowy

hollows of the summit mountains not far from
the glaciers, the highest lying at an elevation of
from eleven to nearly twelve thousand feet above
the sea. The whole number in the Sierra, not
counting the smallest, can hardly be less than
fifteen hundred, of which about two hundred
and fifty are in the park. From one standpoint,
on Red Mountain, I counted forty-two, most of
them within a radius of ten miles. The glacier
meadows, which are spread over the filled-up
basins of vanished lakes and form one of the
most charming features of the scenery, are still
more numerous than the lakes.

An observer stationed here, in the glacial
period, would have overlooked a wrinkled mantle
of ice as continuous as that which now covers the
continent of Greenland; and of all the vast
landscape now shining in the sun, he would
have seen only the tops of the summit peaks,
rising darkly like storm-beaten islands, lifeless
and hopeless, above rock-encumbered ice waves.
If among the agents that nature has employed
in making these mountains there be one that
above all others deserves the name of Destroyer,
it is the glacier. But we quickly learn that destruction is creation. During the dreary centuries through which the Sierra lay in darkness,
crushed beneath the ice folds of the glacial winter, there was a steady invincible advance toward
the warm life and beauty of to-day; and it is

just where the glaciers crushed most destructively
that the greatest amount of beauty is made man-
ifest. But as these landscapes have succeeded
the preglacial landscapes, so they in turn are
giving place to others already planned and foreseen. The granite domes and pavements, apparently imperishable, we take as symbols of
permanence, while these crumbling peaks, down
whose frosty gullies avalanches are ever falling,
are symbols of change and decay. Yet all alike,
fast or slow, are surely vanishing away.

Nature is ever at work building and pulling
down, creating and destroying, keeping everything whirling and flowing, allowing no rest but
in rhythmical motion, chasing everything in endless song out of one beautiful form into another.

CHAPTER IV

THE FORESTS OF THE YOSEMITE PARK

THE coniferous forests of the Yosemite Park, and of the Sierra in general, surpass all others of their kind in America or indeed in the world, not only in the size and beauty of the trees, but in the number of species assembled together, and the grandeur of the mountains they are growing on. Leaving the workaday lowlands, and wandering into the heart of the mountains, we find a new world, and stand beside the majestic pines and firs and sequoias silent and awestricken, as if in the presence of superior beings new arrived from some other star, so calm and bright and godlike they are.

Going to the woods is going home; for I suppose we came from the woods originally. But in some of nature's forests the adventurous traveler seems a feeble, unwelcome creature; wild beasts and the weather trying to kill him, the rank, tangled vegetation, armed with spears and stinging needles, barring his way and making life a hard struggle. Here everything is hospitable and kind, as if planned for your pleasure,

ministering to every want of body and soul.
Even the storms are friendly and seem to regard
you as a brother, their beauty and tremendous
fateful earnestness charming alike. But the
weather is mostly sunshine, both winter and
summer, and the clear sunny brightness of the
park is one of its most striking characteristics.
Even the heaviest portions of the main forest
belt, where the trees are tallest and stand closest,
are not in the least gloomy. The sunshine falls
in glory through the colossal spires and crowns,
each a symbol of health and strength, the noble
shafts faithfully upright like the pillars of
temples, upholding a roof of infinite leafy interlacing arches and fretted skylights. The more
open portions are like spacious parks, carpeted
with small shrubs, or only with the fallen needles
sprinkled here and there with flowers. In some
places, where the ground is level or slopes gently,
the trees are assembled in groves, and the flowers and underbrush in trim beds and thickets as
in landscape gardens or the lovingly planted
grounds of homes ; or they are drawn up in orderly rows around meadows and lakes and along
the brows of cañons. But in general the forests
are distributed in wide belts in accordance with
climate and the comparative strength of each
kind in gaining and holding possession of the
ground, while anything like monotonous uniformity is prevented by the grandly varied topo-

graphy, and by the arrangement of the best soil-
beds in intricate patterns like embroidery ; for
these soilbeds are the moraines of ancient glaciers
more or less modified by weathering and stream
action, and the trees trace them over the hills
and ridges, and far up the sides of the mountains, rising with even growth on levels, and
towering above one another on the long rich
slopes prepared for them by the vanished glaciers.

Had the Sierra forests been cheaply accessible,
the most valuable of them commercially would
ere this have fallen a prey to the lumberman.
Thus far the redwood of the Coast Mountains
and the Douglas spruce of Oregon and Washington have been more available for lumber
than the pine of the Sierra. It cost less to go a
thousand miles up the coast for timber, where
the trees came down to the shores of navigable
rivers and bays, than fifty miles up the mountains. Nevertheless, the superior value of the
sugar pine for many purposes has tempted capitalists to expend large sums on flumes and railroads to reach the best forests, though perhaps
none of these enterprises has paid. Fortunately,
the lately established system of parks and reservations has put a stop to any great extension of
the business hereabouts in its most destructive
forms. And as the Yosemite Park region has
escaped the millmen, and the all-devouring

TIMBER LINE AT THOUSAND ISLET LAKE, NEAR MT. RITTER, YOSEMITE

hordes of hoofed locusts have been banished, it is still in the main a pure wilderness, unbroken by axe clearings except on the lower margin, where a few settlers have opened spots beside hay meadows for their cabins and gardens. But these are mere dots of cultivation, in no appreciable degree disturbing the grand solitude. Twenty or thirty years ago a good many trees were felled for their seeds; traces of this destructive method of seed-collecting are still visible along the trails; but these as well as the shingle-makers' ruins are being rapidly overgrown, the gardens and beds of underbrush once devastated by sheep are blooming again in all their wild glory, and the park is a paradise that makes even the loss of Eden seem insignificant.

On the way to Yosemite Valley, you get some grand views over the forests of the Merced and Tuolumne basins and glimpses of some of the finest trees by the roadside without leaving your seat in the stage. But to learn how they live and behave in pure wildness, to see them in their varying aspects through the seasons and weather, rejoicing in the great storms, in the spiritual mountain light, putting forth their new leaves and flowers when all the streams are in flood and the birds are singing, and sending away their seeds in the thoughtful Indian summer when all the landscape is glowing in deep calm enthusiasm, — for this you must love them and live with them, as free from schemes and cares and time as the trees themselves.

And surely nobody will find anything hard in this. Even the blind must enjoy these woods, drinking their fragrance, listening to the music of the winds in their groves, and fingering their flowers and plumes and cones and richly furrowed boles. The kind of study required is as easy and natural as breathing. Without any great knowledge of botany or wood-craft, in a single season you may learn the name and something more of nearly every kind of tree in the park.

With few exceptions all the Sierra trees are growing in the park, — nine species of pine, two of silver fir, one each of Douglas spruce, libocedrus, hemlock, juniper, and sequoia, — sixteen conifers in all, and about the same number of round-headed trees, oaks, maples, poplars, laurel, alder, dogwood, tumion, etc.

The first of the conifers you meet in going up the range from the west is the digger nut-pine (*Pinus Sabiniana*), a remarkably open, airy, wide-branched tree, forty to sixty feet high, with long, sparse, grayish green foliage and large cones. At a height of fifteen to thirty feet from the ground the trunk usually divides into several main branches, which, after bearing away from one another, shoot straight up and form separate heads as if the axis of the tree had been broken,

while the secondary branches divide again and
again into rather slender sprays loosely tasseled,
with leaves eight to twelve inches long.   The
yellow and purple flowers are about an inch long,
the staminate in showy clusters.   The big, rough,
burly cones, five to eight or ten inches in length
and five or six in diameter, are rich brown in
color when ripe, and full of hard-shelled nuts
that are greatly prized by Indians and squirrels.
This strange-looking pine, enjoying hot sunshine
like a palm, is sparsely distributed along the
driest part of the Sierra among small oaks and
chaparral, and with its gray mist of foliage, strong
trunk and branches, and big cones seen in relief
on the glowing sky, forms the most striking
feature of the foothill vegetation.

Pinus attenuata is a small, slender, arrowy
tree, with pale green leaves in threes, clustered
flowers half an inch long, brownish yellow and
crimson, and cones whorled in conspicuous clusters around the branches and also around the
trunk.   The cones never fall off or open until
the tree dies.   They are about four inches long,
exceedingly strong and solid, and varnished with
hard resin forming a waterproof and almost
worm and squirrel proof package, in which the
seeds are kept fresh and safe during the lifetime
of the tree.   Sometimes one of the trunk cones
is overgrown and imbedded in the heart wood
like a knot, but nearly all are pushed out and

kept on the surface by the pressure of the successive layers of wood against the base.

This admirable little tree grows on brushy, sun-beaten slopes, which from their position and the inflammable character of the vegetation are most frequently fire-swept. These grounds it is able to hold against all comers, however big and strong, by saving its seeds until death, when all it has produced are scattered over the bare cleared ground, and a new generation quickly springs out of the ashes. Thus the curious fact that all the trees of extensive groves and belts are of the same age is accounted for, and their slender habit; for the lavish abundance of seed sown at the same time makes a crowded growth, and the seedlings with an even start rush up in a hurried race for light and life.

Only a few of the attenuata and Sabiniana pines are within the boundaries of the park, the former on the side of the Merced Cañon, the latter on the walls of Hetch-Hetchy Valley and in the cañon below it.

The nut-pine (*Pinus monophylla*) is a small, hardy, contented-looking tree, about fifteen or twenty feet high and a foot in diameter. In its youth the close radiating and aspiring branches form a handsome broad-based pyramid, but when fully grown it becomes round-topped, knotty, and irregular, throwing out crooked divergent limbs like an apple tree. The leaves are pale grayish green, about an inch and a half long, and instead of being divided into clusters they are single, round, sharp-pointed, and rigid like spikes, amid which in the spring the red flowers glow brightly. The cones are only about two inches in length and breadth, but nearly half of their bulk is made up of sweet nuts.

This fruitful little pine grows on the dry east side of the park, along the margin of the Mono sage plain, and is the commonest tree of the short mountain ranges of the Great Basin. Tens of thousands of acres are covered with it, forming bountiful orchards for the Red-man. Being so low and accessible, the cones are easily beaten off with poles, and the nuts procured by roasting until the scales open. To the tribes of the desert and sage plains these seeds are the staff of life. They are eaten either raw or parched, or in the form of mush or cakes after being pounded into meal. The time of nut harvest in the autumn is the Indian's merriest time of all the year. An industrious squirrelish family can gather fifty or sixty bushels in a single month before the snow comes, and then their bread for the winter is sure.

The white pine (*Pinus flexilis*) is widely distributed through the Rocky Mountains and the ranges of the Great Basin, where in many places it grows to a good size, and is an important timber tree where none better is to be found. In the park it is sparsely scattered along the eastern flank of the range from Mono Pass southward, above the nut-pine, at an elevation of from eight to ten thousand feet, dwarfing to a tangled bush near the timber-line, but under favorable conditions attaining a height of forty or fifty feet, with a diameter of three to five. The long branches show a tendency to sweep out in bold curves, like those of the mountain and sugar pines to which it is closely related. The needles are in clusters of five, closely packed on the ends of the branchlets. The cones are about five inches long, — the smaller ones nearly oval, the larger cylindrical. But the most interesting feature of the tree is its bloom, the vivid red pistillate flowers glowing among the leaves like coals of fire.

The dwarfed pine or white-barked pine (*Pinus albicaulis*) is sure to interest every observer on account of its curious low matted habit, and the great height on the snowy mountains at which it bravely grows. It forms the extreme edge of the timber-line on both flanks of the summit mountains — if so lowly a tree can be called timber — at an elevation of ten to twelve thousand feet above the level of the sea. Where it is first met on the lower limit of its range it may be thirty or forty feet high, but farther up the rocky wind-swept slopes, where the snow lies deep and heavy for six months of the year, it makes shaggy clumps and beds, crinkled and pressed flat, over which you can easily walk. Nevertheless in this crushed, down-pressed, felted condition it clings hardily to life, puts forth fresh leaves every spring on the ends of its tasseled branchlets, blooms bravely in the lashing blasts with abundance of gay red and purple flowers, matures its seeds in the short summers, and often outlives the favored giants of the sun lands far below. One of the trees that I examined was only about three feet high, with a stem six inches in diameter at the ground, and branches that spread out horizontally as if they had grown up against a ceiling; yet it was four hundred and twenty-six years old, and one of its supple branchlets, about an eighth of an inch in diameter inside the bark, was seventy-five years old, and so tough that I tied it into knots. At the age of this dwarf many of the sugar and yellow pines and sequoias are seven feet in diameter and over two hundred feet high.

In detached clumps never touched by fire the fallen needles of centuries of growth make fine elastic mattresses for the weary mountaineer, while the tasseled branchlets spread a roof over him, and the dead roots, half resin, usually found in abundance, make capital camp-fires, unquenchable in thickest storms of rain or snow. Seen from a distance the belts and patches darkening the mountain sides look like mosses on a roof, and bring to mind Dr. Johnson's remarks on the trees of Scotland. His guide, anxious for the honor of Mull, was still talking of its woods and pointing them out. "Sir," said Johnson, "I saw at Tobermory what they called a wood, which I unluckily took for heath. If you show me what I shall take for furze, it will be something."

The mountain pine (*Pinus monticola*) is far the largest of the Sierra tree mountaineers. Climbing nearly as high as the dwarf albicaulis, it is still a giant in size, bold and strong, standing erect on the storm-beaten peaks and ridges, tossing its cone-laden branches in the rough winds, living a thousand years, and reaching its greatest size — ninety to a hundred feet in height, six to eight in diameter — just where other trees, its companions, are dwarfed. But it is not able to endure burial in snow so long as the albicaulis and flexilis. Therefore, on the upper limit of its range it is found on slopes which, from their steepness or exposure, are least snowy. Its soft graceful beauty in youth, and its leaves, cones, and outsweeping feathery branches constantly remind you of the sugar pine, to which it is closely allied. An admirable tree, growing nobler in form and size the colder and balder the mountains about it.

The giants of the main forest in the favored middle region are the sequoia, sugar pine, yellow pine, libocedrus, Douglas spruce, and the two silver firs. The park sequoias are restricted to two small groves, a few miles apart, on the Tuolumne and Merced divide, about seventeen miles from Yosemite Valley. The Big Oak Flat road to the valley runs through the Tuolumne Grove, the Coulterville through the Merced. The more famous and better known Mariposa Grove, belonging to the state, lies near the southwest corner of the park, a few miles above Wawona.

The sugar pine (*Pinus Lambertiana*) is first met in the park in open, sunny, flowery woods, at an elevation of about thirty-five hundred feet above the sea, attains full development at a height between five and six thousand feet, and vanishes at the level of eight thousand feet. In many places, especially on the northern slopes of the main ridges between the rivers, it forms the bulk of the forest, but mostly it is intimately associated with its noble companions, above which it towers in glorious majesty on every hill, ridge, and plateau from one extremity of the range to the other, a distance of five hundred miles, — the largest, noblest, and most beautiful of all the seventy or eighty species of pine trees in the world, and of all the conifers second only to King Sequoia.

A good many are from two hundred to two hundred and twenty feet in height, with a diameter at four feet from the ground of six to eight feet, and occasionally a grand patriarch, seven or

eight hundred years old, is found that is ten or
even twelve feet in diameter and two hundred
and forty feet high, with a magnificent crown
seventy feet wide.   David Douglas, who discovered " this most beautiful and immensely grand
tree " in the fall of 1826 in southern Oregon,
says that the largest of several that had been
blown down, " at three feet from the ground
was fifty-seven feet nine inches in circumference"
(or fully eighteen feet in diameter); "at one
hundred and thirty-four feet, seventeen feet five
inches; extreme length, two hundred and forty-
five feet."   Probably for *fifty-seven* we should
read *thirty-seven* for the base measurement,
which would make it correspond with the other
dimensions; for none of this species with anything like so great a girth has since been seen.
A girth of even thirty feet is uncommon.   A
fallen specimen that I measured was nine feet
three inches in diameter inside the bark at four
feet from the ground, and six feet in diameter
at a hundred feet from the ground.   A comparatively young tree, three hundred and thirty
years old, that had been cut down, measured
seven feet across the stump, was three feet three
inches in diameter at a height of one hundred
and fifty feet, and two hundred and ten feet in
length.

The trunk is a round, delicately tapered shaft
with finely furrowed purplish-brown bark, usually

free of limbs for a hundred feet or more.   The
top is furnished with long and comparatively
slender branches, which sweep gracefully downward and outward, feathered with short tasseled
branchlets, and divided only at the ends, forming
a palmlike crown fifty to seventy-five feet wide,
but without the monotonous uniformity of palm
crowns or of the spires of most conifers.   The
old trees are as tellingly varied and picturesque
as oaks.   No two are alike, and we are tempted
to stop and admire every one we come to, whether
as it stands silent in the calm balsam-scented sunshine or waving in accord with enthusiastic
storms.   The leaves are about three or four
inches long, in clusters of five, finely tempered,
bright lively green, and radiant.   The flowers
are but little larger than those of the dwarf pine,
and far less showy.   The immense cylindrical
cones, fifteen to twenty or even twenty-four inches
long and three in diameter, hang singly or in
clusters, like ornamental tassels, at the ends of
the long branches, green, flushed with purple on
the sunward side.   Like those of almost all the
pines they ripen in the autumn of the second
season from the flower, and the seeds of all that
have escaped the Indians, bears, and squirrels
take wing and fly to their places.   Then the
cones become still more effective as ornaments,
for by the spreading of the scales the diameter is
nearly doubled, and the color changes to a rich

brown. They remain on the tree the following winter and summer; therefore few fertile trees are ever found without them. Nor even after they fall is the beauty work of these grand cones done, for they make a fine show on the flowery, needle-strewn ground. The wood is pale yellow, fine in texture, and deliciously fragrant. The sugar, which gives name to the tree, exudes from the heart wood on wounds made by fire or the axe, and forms irregular crisp white candy-like masses. To the taste of most people it is as good as maple sugar, though it cannot be eaten in large quantities.

No traveler, whether a tree lover or not, will ever forget his first walk in a sugar-pine forest. The majestic crowns approaching one another make a glorious canopy, through the feathery arches of which the sunbeams pour, silvering the needles and gilding the stately columns and the ground into a scene of enchantment.

The yellow pine (*Pinus ponderosa*) is surpassed in size and nobleness of port only by its kingly companion. Full-grown trees in the main forest where it is associated with the sugar pine, are about one hundred and seventy-five feet high, with a diameter of five to six feet, though much larger specimens may easily be found. The largest I ever measured was a little over eight feet in diameter four feet above the ground, and two hundred and twenty feet high. Where there is plenty of sunshine and other conditions are favorable, it is a massive symmetrical spire, formed of a strong straight shaft clad with innumerable branches, which are divided again and again into stout branchlets laden with bright shining needles and green or purple cones. Where the growth is at all close half or more of the trunk is branchless. The species attains its greatest size and most majestic form in open groves on the deep, well-drained soil of lake basins at an elevation of about four thousand feet. There nearly all the old trees are over two hundred feet high, and the heavy, leafy, much-divided branches sumptuously clothe the trunk almost to the ground. Such trees are easily climbed, and in going up the winding stairs of knotty limbs to the top you will gain a most telling and memorable idea of the height, the richness and intricacy of the branches, and the marvelous abundance and beauty of the long shining elastic foliage. In tranquil weather, you will see the firm outstanding needles in calm content, shimmering and throwing off keen minute rays of light like lances of ice ; but when heavy winds are blowing, the strong towers bend and wave in the blast with eager wide-awake enthusiasm, and every tree in the grove glows and flashes in one mass of white sunfire.

Both the yellow and sugar pines grow rapidly on good soil where they are not crowded. At

the age of a hundred years they are about two
feet in diameter and a hundred or more high.
They are then very handsome, though very unlike : the sugar pine, lithe, feathery, closely clad
with ascending branches ; the yellow, open,
showing its axis from the ground to the top, its
whorled branches but little divided as yet,
spreading and turning up at the ends with magnificent tassels of long stout bright needles, the
terminal shoot with its leaves being often three
or four feet long and a foot and a half wide, the
most hopeful looking and the handsomest tree-
top in the woods. But instead of increasing,
like its companion, in wildness and individual-
ity of form with age, it becomes more evenly
and compactly spiry. The bark is usually very
thick, four to six inches at the ground, and arranged in large plates, some of them on the
*l*ower part of the trunk four or five feet long
and twelve to eighteen inches wide, forming a
strong defense against fire. The leaves are in
threes, and from three inches to a foot long.
The flowers appear in May : the staminate pink
or brown, in conspicuous clusters two or three
inches wide ; the pistillate crimson, a fourth of
an inch wide, and mostly hidden among the
leaves on the tips of the branchlets. The cones
vary from about three to ten inches in length,
two to five in width, and grow in sessile outstanding clusters near the ends of the upturned
branchlets.

Being able to endure fire and hunger and many climates this grand tree is widely distributed: eastward from the coast across the broad Rocky Mountain ranges to the Black Hills of Dakota, a distance of more than a thousand miles, and southward from British Columbia, near latitude 51°, to Mexico, about fifteen hundred miles. South of the Columbia River it meets the sugar pine, and accompanies it all the way down along the Coast and Cascade mountains and the Sierra and southern ranges to the mountains of the peninsula of Lower California, where they find their southmost homes together. Pinus ponderosa is extremely variable, and much bother it gives botanists who try to catch and confine the unmanageable proteus in two or a dozen species, — Jeffreyi, deflexa, Apacheca latifolia, etc. But in all its wanderings, in every form, it manifests noble strength. Clad in thick bark like a warrior in mail, it extends its bright ranks over all the high ranges of the wild side of the continent: flourishes in the drenching fog and rain of the northern coast at the level of the sea, in the snow-laden blasts of the mountains, and the white glaring sunshine of the interior plateaus and plains, on the borders of mirage-haunted deserts, volcanoes, and lava beds, waving its bright plumes in the hot winds undaunted, blooming every year for centuries, and tossing big ripe cones among the cinders and ashes of nature's hearths.

The Douglas spruce grows with the great pines, especially on the cool north sides of ridges and cañons, and is here nearly as large as the yellow pine, but less abundant. The wood is strong and tough, the bark thick and deeply furrowed, and on vigorous, quick-growing trees the stout, spreading branches are covered with innumerable slender, swaying sprays, handsomely clothed with short leaves. The flowers are about three fourths of an inch in length, red or greenish, not so showy as the pendulous bracted cones. But in June and July, when the young bright yellow leaves appear, the entire tree seems to be covered with bloom.

It is this grand tree that forms the famous forests of western Oregon, Washington, and the adjacent coast regions of British Columbia, where it attains its greatest size and is most abundant, making almost pure forests over thousands of square miles, dark and close and almost inaccessible, many of the trees towering with straight, imperceptibly tapered shafts to a height of three hundred feet, their heads together shutting out the light, — one of the largest, most widely distributed, and most important of all the Western giants.

The incense cedar (*Libocedrus decurrens*), when full grown, is a magnificent tree, one hundred and twenty to nearly two hundred feet high, five to eight and occasionally twelve feet in diameter, with cinnamon-colored bark and warm yellow-green foliage, and in general appearance like an arbor vitæ. It is distributed through the main forest from an elevation of three to six thousand feet, and in sheltered portions of cañons on the warm sides to seven thousand five hundred. In midwinter, when most trees are asleep, it puts forth its flowers. The pistillate are pale green and inconspicuous; but the staminate are yellow, about one fourth of an inch long, and are produced in myriads, tingeing all the branches with gold, and making the tree as it stands in the snow look like a gigantic goldenrod. Though scattered rather sparsely amongst its companions in the open woods, it is seldom out of sight, and its bright brown shafts and warm masses of plumy foliage make a striking feature of the landscape. While young and growing fast in an open situation no other tree of its size in the park forms so exactly tapered a pyramid. The branches, outspread in flat plumes and beautifully fronded, sweep gracefully downward and outward, except those near the top, which aspire; the lowest droop to the ground, overlapping one another, shedding off rain and snow, and making fine tents for stormbound mountaineers and birds. In old age it becomes irregular and picturesque, mostly from accidents: running fires, heavy wet snow breaking the branches, lightning shattering the top, compelling it to try to make new summits out of side branches, etc. Still it frequently lives more than a thousand years, invincibly beautiful, and worthy its place beside the Douglas spruce and the great pines.

This unrivaled forest is still further enriched by two majestic silver firs, Abies magnifica and Abies concolor, bands of which come down from the main fir belt by cool shady ridges and glens. Abies magnifica is the noblest of its race, growing on moraines, at an elevation of seven thousand to eight thousand five hundred feet above the sea, to a height of two hundred or two hundred and fifty feet, and five to seven in diameter; and with these noble dimensions there is a richness and symmetry and perfection of finish not to be found in any other tree in the Sierra. The branches are whorled, in fives mostly, and stand out from the straight red purple bole in level or, on old trees, in drooping collars, every branch regularly pinnated like fern fronds, and clad with silvery needles, making broad plumes singularly rich and sumptuous.

The flowers are in their prime about the middle of June : the staminate red, growing on the underside of the branchlets in crowded profusion, giving a rich color to nearly all the tree; the pistillate greenish yellow tinged with pink, standing erect on the upper side of the topmost branches ; while the tufts of young leaves, about as brightly colored as those of the Douglas spruce, push out their fragrant brown buds a few weeks later, making another grand show.

The cones mature in a single season from the flowers. When full grown they are about six to eight inches long, three or four in diameter, blunt, massive, cylindrical, greenish gray in color, covered with a fine silvery down, and beaded with transparent balsam, very rich and precious-looking, standing erect like casks on the topmost branches. If possible, the inside of the cone is still more beautiful. The scales and bracts are tinged with red, and the seed wings are purple with bright iridescence.

Abies concolor, the white silver fir, grows best about two thousand feet lower than the magnifica. It is nearly as large, but the branches are less regularly pinnated and whorled, the leaves are longer, and instead of standing out around the branchlets or turning up and clasping them they are mostly arranged in two horizontal or ascending rows, and the cones are less than half as large. The bark of the magnifica is reddish purple and closely furrowed, that of the concolor is gray and widely furrowed, — a noble pair, rivaled only by the Abies grandis, amabilis, and nobilis of the forests of Oregon, Washington, and the Northern California Coast Range. But none of these northern species form pure forests that in extent and beauty approach those of the Sierra.

The seeds of the conifers are curiously formed and colored, white, brown, purple, plain or spotted like birds' eggs, and excepting the juniper they are all handsomely and ingeniously winged with reference to their distribution. They are a sort of cunningly devised flying machines, — one-winged birds, birds with but one feather, — and they take but one flight, all save those which, after flying from the cone-nest in calm weather, chance to alight on branches where they have to wait for a wind. And though these seed wings are intended for only a moment's use, they are as thoughtfully colored and fashioned as the wings of birds, and require from one to two seasons to grow. Those of the pine, fir, hemlock, and spruce are curved in such manner that, in being dragged through the air by the seeds, they are made to revolve, whirling the seeds in a close spiral, and sustaining them long enough to allow the winds to carry them to considerable distances, — a style of flying full of quick merry motion, strikingly contrasted to the sober dignified sailing of seeds on tufts of feathery pappus. Surely no merrier adventurers ever set out to seek their fortunes. Only in the fir woods are large flocks seen; for, unlike the cones of the pine, spruce, hemlock, etc., which let the seeds escape slowly, one or two at a time, by spreading the scales, the fir cones when ripe fall to pieces, and let nearly all go at once in

favorable weather. All along the Sierra for hundreds of miles, on dry breezy autumn days, the
sunny spaces in the woods among the colossal
spires are in a whirl with these shining purple-
winged wanderers, notwithstanding the harvesting squirrels have been working at the top of their
speed for weeks trying to cut off every cone before
the seeds were ready to swarm and fly. Sequoia
seeds have flat wings, and glint and glance in
their flight like a boy's kite. The dispersal of
juniper seeds is effected by the plum and cherry
plan of hiring birds at the cost of their board,
and thus obtaining the use of a pair of extra
good wings.

Above the great fir belt, and below the ragged
beds and fringes of the dwarf pine, stretch the
broad dark forests of Pinus contorta, var. Murrayana, usually called tamarack pine. On broad
fields of moraine material it forms nearly pure
forests at an elevation of about eight or nine
thousand feet above the sea, where it is a small,
well proportioned tree, fifty or sixty feet high
and one or two in diameter, with thin gray
bark, crooked much-divided straggling branches,
short needles in clusters of two, bright yellow
and crimson flowers, and small prickly cones.
The very largest I ever measured was ninety
feet in height, and a little over six feet in diameter four feet above the ground. On moist
well-drained soil in sheltered hollows along

streamsides it grows tall and slender with ascending branches, making graceful arrowy spires fifty to seventy-five feet high, with stems only five or six inches thick.

The most extensive forest of this pine in the park lies to the north of the Big Tuolumne Meadows, — a famous deer pasture and hunting ground of the Mono Indians. For miles over wide moraine beds there is an even, nearly pure growth, broken only by glacier meadows, around which the trees stand in trim array, their sharp spires showing to fine advantage both in green flowery summer and white winter. On account of the closeness of its growth in many places, and the thinness and gumminess of its bark, it is easily killed by running fires, which work widespread destruction in its ranks ; but a new generation rises quickly from the ashes, for all or a part of its seeds are held in reserve for a year or two or many years, and when the tree is killed the cones open and the seeds are scattered over the burned ground like those of the attenuata.

Next to the mountain hemlock and the dwarf pine this species best endures burial in heavy snow, while in braving hunger and cold on rocky ridgetops it is not surpassed by any. It is distributed from Alaska to Southern California, and inland across the Rocky Mountains, taking many forms in accordance with demands of climate, soil, rivals, and enemies ; growing patiently in bogs and on sand dunes beside the sea where it is pelted with salt scud, on high snowy mountains and down in the throats of extinct volcanoes; springing up with invincible vigor after every devastating fire and extending its conquests farther.

The sturdy storm-enduring red cedar (*Juniperus occidentalis*) delights to dwell on the tops of granite domes and ridges and glacier pavements of the upper pine belt, at an elevation of seven to ten thousand feet, where it can get plenty of sunshine and snow and elbow-room without encountering quick-growing overshadowing rivals. They never make anything like a forest, seldom come together even in groves, but stand out separate and independent in the wind, clinging by slight joints to the rock, living chiefly on snow and thin air, and maintaining tough health on this diet for two thousand years or more, every feature and gesture expressing steadfast dogged endurance. The largest are usually about six or eight feet in diameter, and fifteen or twenty in height. A very few are ten feet in diameter, and on isolated moraine heaps forty to sixty feet in height. Many are mere stumps, as broad as high, broken by avalanches and lightning, picturesquely tufted with dense gray scalelike foliage, and giving no hint of dying. The staminate flowers are like those of the libocedrus, but smaller; the pistillate are inconspicuous. The wood is red, fine-grained, and fragrant; the bark bright cinnamon and red, and in thrifty trees is strikingly braided and reticulated, flaking off in thin lustrous ribbons, which the Indians used to weave into matting and coarse cloth. These brown unshakable pillars, standing solitary on polished pavements with bossy masses of foliage in their arms, are exceedingly picturesque, and never fail to catch the eye of the artist. They seem sole survivors of some ancient race, wholly unacquainted with their neighbors.

I have spent a good deal of time, trying to determine their age, but on account of dry rot which honeycombs most of the old ones, I never got a complete count of the largest. Some are undoubtedly more than two thousand years old; for though on good moraine soil they grow about as fast as oaks, on bare pavements and smoothly glaciated overswept granite ridges in the dome region they grow extremely slowly. One on the Starr King ridge, only two feet eleven inches in diameter, was eleven hundred and forty years old. Another on the same ridge, only one foot seven and a half inches in diameter, had reached the age of eight hundred and thirty-four years. The first fifteen inches from the bark of a medium-sized tree — six feet in diameter — on the north Tenaya pavement had eight hundred and fifty-nine layers of wood, or fifty-seven to the

inch. Beyond this the count was stopped by
dry rot and scars of old wounds. The largest I
examined was thirty-three feet in girth, or nearly
ten in diameter ; and though I failed to get anything like a complete count, I learned enough
from this and many other specimens to convince
me that most of the trees eight to ten feet thick
standing on pavements are more than twenty centuries of age rather than less. Barring accidents,
for all I can see, they would live forever. When
killed, they waste out of existence about as slowly
as granite. Even when overthrown by avalanches, after standing so long, they refuse to lie
at rest, leaning stubbornly on their big elbows as
if anxious to rise, and while a single root holds
to the rock putting forth fresh leaves with a grim
never-say-die and never-lie-down expression.

As the juniper is the most stubborn and unshakable of trees, the mountain hemlock (*Tsuga
Mertensiana*) is the most graceful and pliant and
sensitive, responding to the slightest touches of
the wind. Until it reaches a height of fifty or
sixty feet it is sumptuously clothed down to the
ground with drooping branches, which are divided into countless delicate waving sprays,
grouped and arranged in most indescribably
beautiful ways, and profusely sprinkled with
handsome brown cones. The flowers also are
peculiarly beautiful and effective : the pistillate
very dark rich purple ; the staminate blue of so

fine and pure a tone that the best azure of the high sky seems to be condensed in them.

Though apparently the most delicate and feminine of all the mountain trees, it grows best where the snow lies deepest, at an elevation of from nine thousand to nine thousand five hundred feet, in hollows on the northern slopes of mountains and ridges. But under all circumstances and conditions of weather and soil, sheltered from the main currents of the winds or in blank exposure to them, well fed or starved, it is always singularly graceful in habit. Even at its highest limit in the park, ten thousand five hundred feet above the sea on exposed ridgetops, where it crouches and huddles close together in low thickets like those of the dwarf pine, it still contrives to put forth its sprays and branches in forms of irrepressible beauty, while on moist well-drained moraines it displays a perfectly tropical luxuriance of foliage, flower, and fruit.

In the first winter storms the snow is oftentimes soft, and lodges in the dense leafy branches, pressing them down against the trunk, and the slender drooping axis bends lower and lower as the load increases, until the top touches the ground and an ornamental arch is made. Then, as storm succeeds storm and snow is heaped on snow, the whole tree is at last buried, not again to see the light or move leaf or limb until set free by the spring thaws in June or July. Not the young saplings only are thus carefully covered and put to sleep in the whitest of white beds for five or six months of the year, but trees thirty and forty feet high. From April to May, when the snow is compacted, you may ride over the prostrate groves without seeing a single branch or leaf of them. In the autumn they are full of merry life, when Clark crows, squirrels, and chipmunks are gathering the abundant crop of seeds while the deer rest beneath the thick concealing branches. The finest grove in the park is near Mount Conness, and the trail from the Tuolumne soda springs to the mountain runs through it. Many of the trees in this grove are three to four or five feet in diameter and about a hundred feet high.

The mountain hemlock is widely distributed from near the south extremity of the high Sierra northward along the Cascade Mountains of Oregon and Washington and the coast ranges of British Columbia to Alaska, where it was first discovered in 1827. Its northmost limit, so far as I have observed, is in the icy fiords of Prince William's Sound in latitude 61°, where it forms pure forests at the level of the sea, growing tall and majestic on the banks of the great glaciers, waving in accord with the mountain winds and the thunder of the falling icebergs. Here as in the Sierra it is ineffably beautiful, the very loveliest evergreen in America.

Of the round-headed dicotyledonous trees in the park the most influential are the black and goldcup oaks. They occur in some parts of the main forest belt, scattered among the big pines like a heavier chaparral, but form extensive groves and reach perfect development only in the Yosemite valleys and flats of the main cañons. The California black oak (*Quercus Californica*) is one of the largest and most beautiful of the Western oaks, attaining under favorable conditions a height of sixty to a hundred feet, with a trunk three to seven feet in diameter, wide-spreading picturesque branches, and smooth lively green foliage handsomely scalloped, purple in the spring, yellow and red in autumn. It grows best in sunny open groves on ground covered with ferns, chokecherry, brier rose, rubus, mints, goldenrods, etc. Few, if any, of the famous oak groves of Europe, however extensive, surpass these in the size and strength and bright, airy beauty of the trees, the color and fragrance of the vegetation beneath them, the quality of the light that fills their leafy arches, and in the grandeur of the surrounding scenery. The finest grove in the park is in one of the little Yosemite valleys of the Tuolumne Cañon, a few miles above Hetch-Hetchy.

The mountain live-oak, or goldcup oak (*Quercus chrysolepis*), forms extensive groves on earthquake and avalanche taluses and terraces

in cañons and Yosemite valleys, from about
three to five thousand feet above the sea. In
tough, sturdy, unwedgeable strength this is the
oak of oaks. In general appearance it resembles
the great live-oak of the Southern states. It
has pale gray bark, a short, uneven, heavily but-
tressed trunk which usually divides a few feet
above the ground into strong wide-reaching
limbs, forming noble arches, and ending in an intricate maze of small branches and sprays, the
outer ones frequently drooping in long tresses to
the ground like those of the weeping willow,
covered with small simple polished leaves, making a canopy broad and bossy, on which the sunshine falls in glorious brightness. The acorn
cups are shallow, thick-walled, and covered with
yellow fuzzy dust. The flowers appear in May
and June with a profusion of pollened tresses,
followed by the bronze-colored young leaves.

No tree in the park is a better measure of altitude. In cañons, at an elevation of four thousand feet, you may easily find a tree six or eight
feet in diameter; and at the head of a side
cañon, three thousand feet higher, up which you
can climb in less than two hours, you find the
knotty giant dwarfed to a slender shrub, with
leaves like those of huckleberry bushes, still
bearing acorns, and seemingly contented, forming dense patches of chaparral, on the top of
which you may make your bed and sleep softly

like a Highlander in heather. About a thousand feet higher it is still smaller, making fringes about a foot high around boulders and along seams in pavements and the brows of cañons, giving hand-holds here and there on cliffs hard to climb. The largest I have measured were from twenty-five to twenty-seven feet in girth, fifty to sixty feet high, and the spread of the limbs was about double the height.

The principal riverside trees are poplar, alder, willow, broad-leaved maple, and Nuttall's flowering dogwood. The poplar (*Populus trichocarpa*), often called balm of Gilead from the gum on its buds, is a tall, stately tree, towering above its companions and gracefully embowering the banks of the main streams at an elevation of about four thousand feet. Its abundant foliage turns bright yellow in the fall, and the Indian-summer sunshine sifts through it in delightful tones over the slow-gliding waters when they are at their lowest ebb.

The flowering dogwood is brighter still in these brooding days, for every branch of its broad head is then a brilliant crimson flame. In the spring, when the streams are in flood, it is the whitest of trees, white as a snow bank with its magnificent flowers four to eight inches in width, making a wonderful show, and drawing swarms of moths and butterflies.

The broad-leaved maple is usually found in the

coolest boulder-choked cañons, where the streams are gray and white with foam, over which it spreads its branches in beautiful arches from bank to bank, forming leafy tunnels full of soft green light and spray, — favorite homes of the water ousel. Around the glacier lakes, two or three thousand feet higher, the common aspen grows in fringing lines and groves which are brilliantly colored in autumn, reminding you of the color glory of the Eastern woods.

Scattered here and there or in groves the botanist will find a few other trees, mostly small, — the mountain mahogany, cherry, chestnut-oak, laurel, and nutmeg. The California nutmeg (*Tumion Californicum*) is a handsome evergreen, belonging to the yew family, with pale bark, prickly leaves, fruit like a green-gage plum, and seed like a nutmeg. One of the best groves of it in the park is at the Cascades below Yosemite.

But the noble oaks and all these rock-shading, stream-embowering trees are as nothing amid the vast abounding billowy forests of conifers. During my first years in the Sierra I was ever calling on everybody within reach to admire them, but I found no one half warm enough until Emerson came. I had read his essays, and felt sure that of all men he would best interpret the sayings of these noble mountains and trees. Nor was my faith weakened when I met him in Yosemite. He seemed as serene as a sequoia, his head in the empyrean ; and forgetting his age, plans, duties, ties of every sort, I proposed an immeasurable camping trip back in the heart of the mountains. He seemed anxious to go, but considerately mentioned his party. I said : " Never mind. The mountains are calling ; run away, and let plans and parties and dragging lowland duties all ' gang tapsal-teerie.' We 'll go up a cañon singing your own song, ' Good-by, proud world ! I 'm going home,' in divine earnest. Up there lies a new heaven and a new earth ; let us go to the show." But alas, it was too late, — too near the sundown of his life. The shadows were growing long, and he leaned on his friends. His party, full of indoor philosophy, failed to see the natural beauty and fullness of promise of my wild plan, and laughed at it in good-natured ignorance, as if it were necessarily amusing to imagine that Boston people might be led to accept Sierra manifestations of God at the price of rough camping. Anyhow, they would have none of it, and held Mr. Emerson to the hotels and trails.

After spending only five tourist days in Yosemite he was led away, but I saw him two days more ; for I was kindly invited to go with the party as far as the Mariposa big trees. I told Mr. Emerson that I would gladly go to the sequoias with him, if he would camp in the grove. He consented heartily, and I felt sure that we would have at least one good wild memorable night around a sequoia camp-fire. Next day we rode through the magnificent forests of the Merced basin, and I kept calling his attention to the sugar pines, quoting his wood-notes, "Come listen what the pine tree saith," etc., pointing out the noblest as kings and high priests, the most eloquent and commanding preachers of all the mountain forests, stretching forth their century-old arms in benediction over the worshiping congregations crowded about them. He gazed in devout admiration, saying but little, while his fine smile faded away.

Early in the afternoon, when we reached Clark's Station, I was surprised to see the party dismount. And when I asked if we were not going up into the grove to camp they said: "No; it would never do to lie out in the night air. Mr. Emerson might take cold; and you know, Mr. Muir, that would be a dreadful thing." In vain I urged, that only in homes and hotels were colds caught, that nobody ever was known to take cold camping in these woods, that there was not a single cough or sneeze in all the Sierra. Then I pictured the big climate-changing, inspiring fire I would make, praised the beauty and fragrance of sequoia flame, told how the great trees would stand about us transfigured in the purple light, while the stars looked down between the great domes ; ending by urging them to come on and make an immortal Emerson night of it. But the house habit was not to be overcome, nor the strange dread of pure night air, though it is only cooled day air with a little dew in it. So the carpet dust and unknowable reeks were preferred. And to think of this being a Boston choice! Sad commentary on culture and the glorious transcendentalism.

Accustomed to reach whatever place I started for, I was going up the mountain alone to camp, and wait the coming of the party next day. But since Emerson was so soon to vanish, I concluded to stop with him. He hardly spoke a word all the evening, yet it was a great pleasure simply to be near him, warming in the light of his face as at a fire. In the morning we rode up the trail through a noble forest of pine and fir into the famous Mariposa Grove, and stayed an hour or two, mostly in ordinary tourist fashion, — looking at the biggest giants, measuring them with a tape line, riding through prostrate fire-bored trunks, etc., though Mr. Emerson was alone occasionally, sauntering about as if under a spell. As we walked through a fine group, he quoted, "There were giants in those days," recognizing the antiquity of the race. To commemorate his visit, Mr. Galen Clark, the guardian of the grove, selected the finest of the unnamed trees and requested him to give it a name. He named it Samoset, after the New England sachem, as the best that occurred to him.

The poor bit of measured time was soon spent, and while the saddles were being adjusted I again urged Emerson to stay. " You are yourself a sequoia," I said. " Stop and get acquainted with your big brethren." But he was past his prime, and was now as a child in the hands of his affectionate but sadly civilized friends, who seemed as full of old-fashioned conformity as of bold intellectual independence. It was the afternoon of the day and the afternoon of his life, and his course was now westward down all the mountains into the sunset. The party mounted and rode away in wondrous contentment, apparently, tracing the trail through ceanothus and dogwood bushes, around the bases of the big trees, up the slope of the sequoia basin, and over the divide. I followed to the edge of the grove. Emerson lingered in the rear of the train, and when he reached the top of the ridge, after all the rest of the party were over and out of sight, he turned his horse, took off his hat and waved me a last good-by. I felt lonely, so sure had I been that Emerson of all men would be the quickest to see the mountains and sing them. Gazing awhile on the spot where he vanished, I sauntered back into the heart of the grove, made a bed of sequoia plumes and ferns by the side of a stream, gathered a store of firewood, and then walked about until sundown. The birds, robins, thrushes, warblers, etc., that had kept out of sight, came

about me, now that all was quiet, and made
cheer. After sundown I built a great fire, and
as usual had it all to myself. And though lone-
some for the first time in these forests, I quickly
took heart again, — the trees had not gone to
Boston, nor the birds; and as I sat by the fire,
Emerson was still with me in spirit, though I
never again saw him in the flesh. He sent books
and wrote, cheering me on; advised me not to
stay too long in solitude. Soon he hoped that
my guardian angel would intimate that my pro-
bation was at a close. Then I was to roll up my
herbariums, sketches, and poems (though I never
knew I had any poems), and come to his house;
and when I tired of him and his humble sur-
roundings, he would show me to better people.

But there remained many a forest to wander
through, many a mountain and glacier to cross,
before I was to see his Wachusett and Monad-
nock, Boston and Concord. It was seventeen
years after our parting on the Wawona ridge
that I stood beside his grave under a pine tree
on the hill above Sleepy Hollow. He had gone
to higher Sierras, and, as I fancied, was again
waving his hand in friendly recognition.

CHAPTER V

THE WILD GARDENS OF THE YOSEMITE PARK

WHEN California was wild, it was the floweri-est part of the continent. And perhaps it is so still, notwithstanding the lowland flora has in great part vanished before the farmers' flocks and ploughs. So exuberant was the bloom of the main valley of the state, it would still have been extravagantly rich had ninety-nine out of every hundred of its crowded flowers been taken away, — far flowerier than the beautiful prairies of Illinois and Wisconsin, or the savan-nas of the Southern states. In the early spring it was a smooth, evenly planted sheet of purple and gold, one mass of bloom more than four hundred miles long, with scarce a green leaf in sight.

Still more interesting is the rich and wonder-fully varied flora of the mountains. Going up the Sierra across the Yosemite Park to the Sum-mit peaks, thirteen thousand feet high, you find as much variety in the vegetation as in the scen-ery. Change succeeds change with bewildering rapidity, for in a few days you pass through as many climates and floras, ranged one above another, as you would in walking along the lowlands to the Arctic Ocean.

And to the variety due to climate there is added that caused by the topographical features of the different regions. Again, the vegetation is profoundly varied by the peculiar distribution of the soil and moisture. Broad and deep moraines, ancient and well weathered, are spread over the lower regions, rough and comparatively recent and unweathered moraines over the middle and upper regions, alternating with bare ridges and domes and glacier-polished pavements, the highest in the icy recesses of the peaks, raw and shifting, some of them being still in process of formation, and of course scarcely planted as yet.

Besides these main soilbeds there are many others comparatively small, reformations of both glacial and weather soils, sifted, sorted out, and deposited by running water and the wind on gentle slopes and in all sorts of hollows, potholes, valleys, lake basins, etc., — some in dry and breezy situations, others sheltered and kept moist by lakes, streams, and waftings of waterfall spray, making comfortable homes for plants widely varied. In general, glaciers give soil to high and low places almost alike, while water currents are dispensers of special blessings, constantly tending to make the ridges poorer and the valleys richer. Glaciers mingle all kinds of material together, mud particles and boulders fifty feet in diameter : water, whether in oozing currents or passionate torrents, discriminates both in the size and shape of the material it carries. Glacier mud is the finest meal ground for any use in the Park, and its transportation into lakes and as foundations for flowery garden meadows was the first work that the young rivers were called on to do. Bogs occur only in shallow alpine basins where the climate is cool enough for sphagnum, and where the surrounding topographical conditions are such that they are safe, even in the most copious rains and thaws, from the action of flood currents capable of carrying rough gravel and sand, but where the water supply is nevertheless constant. The mosses dying from year to year gradually give rise to those rich spongy peat-beds in which so many of our best alpine plants delight to dwell. The strong winds that occasionally sweep the high Sierra play a more important part in the distribution of special soil-beds than is at first sight recognized, carrying forward considerable quantities of sand and gravel, flakes of mica, etc., and depositing them in fields and beds beautifully ruffled and embroidered and adapted to the wants of some of the hardiest and handsomest of the alpine shrubs and flowers. The more resisting of the smooth, solid, glacier-polished domes and ridges can hardly be said to have any soil at all,

while others beginning to give way to the weather are thinly sprinkled with coarse angular
gravel. Some of them are full of crystals, which
as the surface of the rock is decomposed are set
free, covering the summits and rolling down the
sides in minute avalanches, giving rise to zones
and beds of crystalline soil. In some instances
the various crystals occur only here and there,
sprinkled in the gray gravel like daisies in a
sod ; but in others half or more is made up of
crystals, and the glow of the imbedded or loosely
strewn gems and their colored gleams and glint-
ings at different times of the day when the sun
is shining might well exhilarate the flowers that
grow among them, and console them for being
so completely outshone.

These radiant sheets and belts and dome-en-
circling rings of crystals are the most beautiful
of all the Sierra soil-beds, while the huge taluses
ranged along the walls of the great cañons are
the deepest and roughest. Instead of being
slowly weathered and accumulated from the
cliffs overhead like common taluses, they were
all formed suddenly and simultaneously by an
earthquake that occurred at least three centuries
ago. Though thus hurled into existence at a
single effort, they are the least changeable and
destructible of all the soil formations in the
range. Excepting those which were launched
directly into the channels of rivers, scarcely one

of their wedged and interlocked boulders has
been moved since the day of their creation, and
though mostly made up of huge angular blocks
of granite, many of them from ten to fifty feet
cube, trees and shrubs make out to live and
thrive on them, and even delicate herbaceous
plants, — draperia, collomia, zauschneria, etc., —
soothing their rugged features with gardens and
groves. In general views of the Park scarce a
hint is given of its floral wealth. Only by patiently, lovingly sauntering about in it will you
discover that it is all more or less flowery, the
forests as well as the open spaces, and the mountain tops and rugged slopes around the glaciers
as well as the sunny meadows.

Even the majestic cañon cliffs, seemingly absolutely flawless for thousands of feet and necessarily doomed to eternal sterility, are cheered
with happy flowers on invisible niches and ledges
wherever the slightest grip for a root can be
found; as if Nature, like an enthusiastic gardener, could not resist the temptation to plant
flowers everywhere. On high, dry rocky summits and plateaus, most of the plants are so small
they make but little show even when in bloom.
But in the opener parts of the main forests, the
meadows, stream banks, and the level floors of
Yosemite valleys the vegetation is exceedingly
rich in flowers, some of the lilies and larkspurs
being from eight to ten feet high. And on the

upper meadows there are miles of blue gentians
and daisies, white and blue violets; and great
breadths of rosy purple heathworts covering
rocky moraines with a marvelous abundance of
bloom, enlivened by humming-birds, butterflies
and a host of other insects as beautiful as flowers.   In the lower and middle regions, also, many
of the most extensive beds of bloom are in great
part made by shrubs, — adenostoma, manzanita,
ceanothus, chamæbatia, cherry, rose, rubus, spiræa, shad, laurel, azalea, honeysuckle, calycanthus, ribes, philadelphus, and many others, the
sunny spaces about them bright and fragrant
with mints, lupines, geraniums, lilies, daisies,
goldenrods, castilleias, gilias, pentstemons, etc.

Adenostoma fasciculatum is a handsome,
hardy, heathlike shrub belonging to the rose
family, flourishing on dry ground below the pine
belt, and often covering areas of twenty or thirty
square miles of rolling sun-beaten hills and dales
with a dense, dark green, almost impenetrable
chaparral, which in the distance looks like Scotch
heather.   It is about six to eight feet high, has
slender elastic branches, red shreddy bark, needle-
shaped leaves, and small white flowers in panicles
about a foot long, making glorious sheets of fragrant bloom in the spring.   To running fires it
offers no resistance, vanishing with the few
other flowery shrubs and vines and liliaceous
plants that grow with it about as fast as dry

grass, leaving nothing but ashes. But with wonderful vigor it rises again and again in fresh beauty from the root, and calls back to its hospitable mansions the multitude of wild animals that had to flee for their lives.

As soon as you enter the pine woods you meet the charming little Chamæbatia foliolosa, one of the handsomest of the Park shrubs, next in fineness and beauty to the heathworts of the alpine regions. Like adenostoma it belongs to the rose family, is from twelve to eighteen inches high, has brown bark, slender branches, white flowers like those of the strawberry, and thrice-pinnate glandular, yellow-green leaves, finely cut and fernlike, as if unusual pains had been taken in fashioning them. Where there is plenty of sunshine at an elevation of three thousand to six thousand feet, it makes a close, continuous growth, leaf touching leaf over hundreds of acres, spreading a handsome mantle beneath the yellow and sugar pines. Here and there a lily rises above it, an arching bunch of tall bromus, and at wide intervals a rosebush or clump of ceanothus or manzanita, but there are no rough weeds mixed with it, — no roughness of any sort.

Perhaps the most widely distributed of all the Park shrubs and of the Sierra in general, certainly the most strikingly characteristic, are the many species of manzanita (*Arctostaphylos*).

Though one species, the Uva-ursa, or bearberry, — the kinikinic of the Western Indians, — extends around the world, the greater part of them are Californian. They are mostly from four to ten feet high, round-headed, with innumerable branches, brown or red bark, pale green leaves set on edge, and a rich profusion of small, pink, narrow-throated, urn-shaped flowers like those of arbutus. The branches are knotty, zigzaggy, and about as rigid as bones, and the bark is so thin and smooth, both trunk and branches seem to be naked, looking as if they had been peeled, polished, and painted red. The wood also is red, hard, and heavy.

These grand bushes seldom fail to engage the attention of the traveler and hold it, especially if he has to pass through closely planted fields of them such as grow on moraine slopes at an elevation of about seven thousand feet, and in cañons choked with earthquake boulders; for they make the most uncompromisingly stubborn of all chaparral. Even bears take pains to go around the stoutest patches if possible, and when compelled to force a passage leave tufts of hair and broken branches to mark their way, while less skillful mountaineers under like circumstances sometimes lose most of their clothing and all their temper.

The manzanitas like sunny ground. On warm ridges and sandy flats at the foot of sun-beaten cañon cliffs, some of the tallest specimens have well-defined trunks six inches to a foot or more thick, and stand apart in orchard-like growths which in bloomtime are among the finest garden sights in the Park. The largest I ever saw had a round, slightly fluted trunk nearly four feet in diameter, which at a height of only eighteen inches from the ground dissolved into a wilderness of branches, rising and spreading to a height and width of about twelve feet. In spring every bush over all the mountains is covered with rosy flowers, in autumn with fruit. The red pleasantly acid berries, about the size of peas, are like little apples, and the hungry mountaineer is glad to eat them, though half their bulk is made up of hard seeds. Indians, bears, coyotes, foxes, birds, and other mountain people live on them for months.

Associated with manzanita there are six or seven species of ceanothus, flowery, fragrant, and altogether delightful shrubs, growing in glorious abundance in the forests on sunny or half-shaded ground, up to an elevation of about nine thousand feet above the sea. In the sugar-pine woods the most beautiful species is C. integerrimus, often called California lilac, or deer brush. It is five or six feet high, smooth, slender, willowy, with bright foliage and abundance of blue flowers in close, showy panicles. Two species, prostatus and procumbens, spread

handsome blue-flowered mats and rugs on warm
ridges beneath the pines, and offer delightful
beds to the tired mountaineers. The commonest species, C. cordulatus, is mostly restricted to
the silver fir belt. It is white-flowered and
thorny, and makes extensive thickets of tangled
chaparral, far too dense to wade through, and
too deep and loose to walk on, though it is
pressed flat every winter by ten or fifteen feet of
snow.

Above these thorny beds, sometimes mixed
with them, a very wild, red-fruited cherry grows
in magnificent tangles, fragrant and white as
snow when in bloom. The fruit is small and
rather bitter, not so good as the black, puckery
chokecherry that grows in the cañons, but
thrushes, robins, chipmunks like it. Below the
cherry tangles, chinquapin and goldcup oak
spread generous mantles of chaparral, and with
hazel and ribes thickets in adjacent glens help
to clothe and adorn the rocky wilderness, and
produce food for the many mouths Nature has
to fill. Azalea occidentalis is the glory of cool
streams and meadows. It is from two to five feet
high, has bright green leaves and a rich profusion of large, fragrant white and yellow flowers,
which are in prime beauty in June, July, and
August, according to the elevation (from three
thousand to six thousand feet.) Only the purple-flowered rhododendron of the redwood for-

AZALEA THICKET, YOSEMITE

ests rivals or surpasses it in superb abounding bloom.

Back a little way from the azalea-bordered streams, a small wild rose makes thickets, often several acres in extent, deliciously fragrant on dewy mornings and after showers, the fragrance mingled with the music of birds nesting in them. And not far from these rose gardens Rubus Nutkanus covers the ground with broad velvety leaves and pure white flowers as large as those of its neighbor the rose, and finer in texture ; followed at the end of summer by soft red berries good for bird and beast and man also. This is the commonest and the most beautiful of the whole blessed flowery fruity genus.

The glory of the alpine region in bloomtime are the heathworts, cassiope, bryanthus, kalmia, and vaccinium, enriched here and there by the alpine honeysuckle, Lonicera conjugialis, and by the purple-flowered Primula suffruticosa, the only primrose discovered in California, and the only shrubby species in the genus. The lowly, hardy, adventurous cassiope has exceedingly slender creeping branches, scalelike leaves, and pale pink or white waxen bell flowers. Few plants, large or small, so well endure hard weather and rough ground over so great a range. In July it spreads a wavering, interrupted belt of the loveliest bloom around glacier lakes and meadows and across wild moory expanses, between roaring streams, all along the Sierra, and northward beneath cold skies by way of the mountain chains of Oregon, Washington, British Columbia, and Alaska, to the Arctic regions; gradually descending, until at the north end of the continent it reaches the level of the sea; blooming as profusely and at about the same time on mossy frozen tundras as on the high Sierra moraines.

Bryanthus, the companion of cassiope, accompanies it as far north as southeastern Alaska, where together they weave thick plushy beds on rounded mountain tops above the glaciers. It grows mostly at slightly lower elevations; the upper margin of what may be called the bryanthus belt in the Sierra uniting with and overlapping the lower margin of the cassiope. The wide bell-shaped flowers are bright purple, about three fourths of an inch in diameter, hundreds to the square yard, the young branches, mostly erect, being covered with them. No Highlander in heather enjoys more luxurious rest than the Sierra mountaineer in a bed of blooming bryanthus. And imagine the show on calm dewy mornings, when there is a radiant globe in the throat of every flower, and smaller gems on the needle-shaped leaves, the sunbeams pouring through them.

In the same wild, cold region the tiny Vaccinium myrtillus, mixed with kalmia and dwarf willows, spreads thinner carpets, the down-pressed matted leaves profusely sprinkled with pink bells ; and on higher sandy slopes you will find several alpine species of eriogonum with gorgeous bossy masses of yellow bloom, and the lovely Arctic daisy with many blessed companions ; charming plants, gentle mountaineers, Nature's darlings, which seem always the finer the higher and stormier their homes.

Many interesting ferns are distributed over the Park from the foothills to a little above the timber line. The greater number are rock ferns, pellæa, cheilanthes, polypodium, adiantum, woodsia, cryptogramme, etc., with small tufted fronds, lining glens and gorges and fringing the cliffs and moraines. The most important of the larger species are woodwardia, aspidium, asplenium, and the common pteris. Woodwardia radicans is a superb fern five to eight feet high, growing in vaselike clumps where the ground is level, and on slopes in a regular thatch, frond over frond, like shingles on a roof. Its range in the Park is from the western boundary up to about five thousand feet, mostly on benches of the north walls of cañons watered by small outspread streams. It is far more abundant in the Coast Mountains beneath the noble redwoods, where it attains a height of ten to twelve feet. The aspidiums are mostly restricted to the moist parts of the lower forests, Asplenium filix-fœ-

mina to marshy streams. The hardy, broad-
shouldered Pteris aquilina, the commonest of
ferns, grows tall and graceful on sunny flats and
hillsides, at elevations between three thousand
and six thousand feet. Those who know it only
in the Eastern states can form no fair conception
of its stately beauty in the sunshine of the Sierra. On the level sandy floors of Yosemite
valleys it often attains a height of six to eight
feet in fields thirty or forty acres in extent, the
magnificent fronds outspread in a nearly horizontal position, forming a ceiling beneath which
one may walk erect in delightful mellow shade.
No other fern does so much for the color glory
of autumn, with its browns and reds and yellows
changing and interblending. Even after lying
dead all winter beneath the snow it spreads a
lively brown mantle over the desolate ground,
until the young fronds with a noble display of
faith and hope come rolling up into the light
through the midst of the beautiful ruins. A
few weeks suffice for their development, then,
gracefully poised each in its place, they manage
themselves in every exigency of weather as if
they had passed through a long course of train-
ing. I have seen solemn old sugar pines thrown
into momentary confusion by the sudden onset
of a storm, tossing their arms excitedly as if
scarce awake, and wondering what had happened,
but I never noticed surprise or embarrassment in
the behavior of this noble pteris.

Of five species of pellæa in the Park, the handsome andromedæfolia, growing in brushy foothills with Adiantum emarginatum, is the largest. P. Breweri, the hardiest and at the same time the most fragile of the genus, grows in dense tufts among rocks on storm-beaten mountain sides along the upper margin of the fern line. It is a charming little fern, four or five inches high, has shining bronze-colored stalks which are about as brittle as glass, and pale green pinnate fronds. Its companions on the lower part of its range are Cryptogramme acrostichoides and Phegopteris alpestris, the latter soft and tender, not at all like a rock fern, though it grows on rocks where the snow lies longest. P. Bridgesii, with blue-green, narrow, simply pinnate fronds, is about the same size as Breweri and ranks next to it as a mountaineer, growing in fissures and around boulders on glacier pavements. About a thousand feet lower we find the smaller and more abundant P. densa, on ledges and boulder-strewn fissured pavements, watered until late in summer by oozing currents from snow-banks or thin outspread streams from moraines, growing in close sods, — its little bright green triangular tripinnate fronds, about an inch in length, as innumerable as leaves of grass. P. ornithopus has twice or thrice pinnate fronds, is dull in color, and dwells on hot rocky hillsides among chaparral.

Three species of Cheilanthes, — Californica, gracillima, and myriophylla, with beautiful two to four pinnate fronds, an inch to five inches long, adorn the stupendous walls of the cañons, however dry and sheer. The exceedingly delicate and interesting Californica is rare, the others abundant at from three thousand to seven thousand feet elevation, and are often accompanied by the little gold fern, Gymnogramme triangularis, and rarely by the curious little Botrychium simplex, the smallest of which are less than an inch high.

The finest of all the rock ferns is *Adiantum pedatum*, lover of waterfalls and the lightest waftings of irised spray. No other Sierra fern is so constant a companion of white spray-covered streams, or tells so well their wild thundering music. The homes it loves best are cave-like hollows beside the main falls, where it can float its plumes on their dewy breath, safely sheltered from the heavy spray-laden blasts. Many of these moss-lined chambers, so cool, so moist, and brightly colored with rainbow light, contain thousands of these happy ferns, clinging to the emerald walls by the slightest holds, reaching out the most wonderfully delicate fingered fronds on dark glossy stalks, sensitive, tremulous, all alive, in an attitude of eager attention ; throbbing in unison with every motion and tone of the resounding waters, compliant to their faintest impulses, moving each division of the frond separately at times as if fingering the music, playing on invisible keys.

Considering the lilies as you go up the mountains, the first you come to is L. Pardalinum, with large orange-yellow, purple-spotted flowers big enough for babies' bonnets. It is seldom found higher than thirty-five hundred feet above the sea, grows in magnificent groups of fifty to a hundred or more, in romantic waterfall dells in the pine woods shaded by overarching maple and willow, alder and dogwood, with bushes in front of the embowering trees for a border, and ferns and sedges in front of the bushes; while the bed of black humus in which the bulbs are set is carpeted with mosses and liverworts. These richly furnished lily gardens are the pride of the falls on the lower tributaries of the Tuolumne and Merced rivers, falls not like those of Yosemite valleys, — coming from the sky with rock-shaking thunder tones, — but small, with low, kind voices cheerily singing in calm leafy bowers, self-contained, keeping their snowy skirts well about them, yet furnishing plenty of spray for the lilies.

The Washington lily (*L. Washingtonianum*) is white, deliciously fragrant, moderate in size, with three to ten flowered racemes. The largest I ever measured was eight feet high, the raceme two feet long, with fifty-two flowers, fifteen of them open ; the others had faded or were still in the bud. This famous lily is distributed over the sunny portions of the sugar-pine woods, never in large garden companies like pardalinum, but widely scattered, standing up to the waist in dense ceanothus and manzanita chaparral, waving its lovely flowers above the blooming wilderness of brush, and giving their fragrance to the breeze. These stony, thorny jungles are about the last places in the mountains in which one would look for lilies. But though they toil not nor spin, like other people under adverse circumstances, they have to do the best they can. Because their large bulbs are good to eat they are dug up by Indians and bears; therefore, like hunted animals, they seek refuge in the chaparral, where among the boulders and tough tangled roots they are comparatively safe. This is the favorite Sierra lily, and it is now growing in all the best parks and gardens of the world.

The showiest gardens in the Park lie imbedded in the silver fir forests on the top of the main dividing ridges or hang like gayly colored scarfs down their sides. Their wet places are in great part taken up by veratrum, a robust broad-leaved plant determined to be seen, and habenaria and spiranthes; the drier parts by tall columbines, larkspurs, castilleias, lupines, hosackias, erigerons, valerian, etc., standing deep in grass, with violets here and there around the borders. But the finest feature of these forest gardens is Lilium parvum. It varies greatly in size, the tallest being from six to nine feet high, with splendid racemes of ten to fifty small orange-colored flowers, which rock and wave with great dignity above the other flowers in the infrequent winds that fall over the protecting wall of trees. Though rather frail-looking it is strong, reaching prime vigor and beauty eight thousand feet above the sea, and in some places venturing as high as eleven thousand.

Calochortus, or Mariposa tulip, is a unique genus of many species confined to the California side of the continent ; charming plants, somewhat resembling the tulips of Europe, but far finer. The richest calochortus region lies below the western boundary of the Park; still five or six species are included. C. Nuttallii is common on moraines in the forests of the two-leaved pine; and C. cæruleus and nudus, very slender, lowly species, may be found in moist garden spots near Yosemite. C. albus, with pure white flowers, growing in shady places among the foothill shrubs, is, I think, the very loveliest of all the lily family, — a spotless soul, plant saint, that every one must love and so be made better. It puts the wildest mountaineer on his good behavior. With this plant the whole world would seem rich though none other existed. Next after Calochortus, Brodiæa is the most interesting genus.

Nearly all the many species have beautiful showy
heads of blue, lilac, and yellow flowers, enriching
the gardens of the lower pine region. Other
liliaceous plants likely to attract attention are
the blue-flowered camassia, the bulbs of which
are prized as food by Indians; fritillaria, smila-
cina, chloragalum, and the twining climbing stro-
pholirion.

The common orchidaceous plants are corallo-
rhiza, goodyera, spiranthes, and habenaria. Cy-
pripedium montanum, the only moccasin flower
I have seen in the Park, is a handsome, thought-
ful-looking plant living beside cool brooks. The
large oval lip is white, delicately veined with
purple; the other petals and sepals purple, strap-
shaped, and elegantly curved and twisted.

To tourists the most attractive of all the flowers of the forest is the snow plant (*Sarcodes san-
guinea*). It is a bright red, fleshy, succulent
pillar that pushes up through the dead needles
in the pine and fir woods like a gigantic aspara-
gus shoot. The first intimation of its coming is
a loosening and upbulging of the brown stratum
of decomposed needles on the forest floor, in the
cracks of which you notice fiery gleams; presently a blunt dome-shaped head an inch or two
in diameter appears, covered with closely imbri-
cated scales and bracts. In a week or so it
grows to a height of six to twelve inches. Then
the long fringed bracts spread and curl aside,

allowing the twenty or thirty five-lobed bell-shaped flowers to open and look straight out from the fleshy axis. It is said to grow up through the snow; on the contrary it always waits until the ground is warm, though with other early flowers it is occasionally buried or half buried for a day or two by spring storms. The entire plant — flowers, bracts, stem, scales, and roots — is red. But notwithstanding its glowing color and beautiful flowers, it is singularly unsympathetic and cold. Everybody admires it as a wonderful curiosity, but nobody loves it. Without fragrance, rooted in decaying vegetable matter, it stands beneath the pines and firs lonely, silent, and about as rigid as a graveyard monument.

Down in the main cañons adjoining the azalea and rose gardens there are fine beds of herbaceous plants, — tall mints and sunflowers, iris, œnothera, brodiæa, and bright beds of erythræa on the ferny meadows. Bolandera, sedum, and airy, feathery, purple-flowered heuchera adorn mossy nooks near falls, the shading trees wreathed and festooned with wild grapevines and clematis; while lightly shaded flats are covered with gilia and eunanus of many species, hosackia, arnica, chænactis, gayophytum, gnaphalium, monardella, etc.

Thousands of the most interesting gardens in the Park are never seen, for they are small and

lie far up on ledges and terraces of the sheer
cañon walls, wherever a strip of soil, however
narrow and shallow, can rest. The birds, winds,
and down-washing rains have planted them with
all sorts of hardy mountain flowers, and where
there is sufficient moisture they flourish in profusion. Many of them are watered by little
streams that seem lost on the tremendous precipices, clinging to the face of the rock in lacelike
strips, and dripping from ledge to ledge, too
silent to be called falls, pathless wanderers from
the upper meadows, which for centuries have
been seeking a way down to the rivers they belong to, without having worn as yet any appreciable channel, mostly evaporated or given to the
plants they meet before reaching the foot of the
cliffs. To these unnoticed streams the finest of
the cliff gardens owe their luxuriance and freshness of beauty. In the larger ones ferns and
showy flowers flourish in wonderful profusion,
— woodwardia, columbine, collomia, castilleia,
draperia, geranium, erythræa, pink and scarlet
mimulus, hosackia, saxifrage, sunflowers and
daisies, with azalea, spiræa, and calycanthus, a
few specimens of each that seem to have been
culled from the large gardens above and beneath
them. Even lilies are occasionally found in these
irrigated cliff gardens, swinging their bells over
the giddy precipices, seemingly as happy as their
relatives down in the waterfall dells. Most of

the cliff gardens, however, are dependent on summer showers, and though from the shallowness of the soil beds they are often dry, they still display a surprising number of bright flowers, — scarlet zauschneria, purple bush penstemon, mints, gilias, and bosses of glowing golden bahia. Nor is there any lack of commoner plants; the homely yarrow is often found in them, and sweet clover and honeysuckle for the bees.

In the upper cañons, where the walls are inclined at so low an angle that they are loaded with moraine material, through which perennial streams percolate in broad diffused currents, there are long wavering garden beds, that seem to be descending through the forest like cascades, their fluent lines suggesting motion, swaying from side to side of the forested banks, surging up here and there over island-like boulder piles, or dividing and flowing around them. In some of these floral cascades the vegetation is chiefly sedges and grasses ruffled with willows; in others, showy flowers like those of the lily gardens on the main divides. Another curious and picturesque series of wall gardens are made by thin streams that ooze slowly from moraines and slip gently over smooth glaciated slopes. From particles of sand and mud they carry, a pair of lobe-shaped sheets of soil an inch or two thick are gradually formed, one of them hanging down from the brow of the slope, the other leaning up from the foot of it, like stalactite and stalagmite, the soil being held together by the flowery, moisture-loving plants growing in it.

Along the rocky parts of the cañon bottoms between lake basins, where the streams flow fast over glacier-polished granite, there are rows of pothole gardens full of ferns, daisies, golden-rods, and other common plants of the neigh-borhood nicely arranged like bouquets, and standing out in telling relief on the bare shining rock banks. And all the way up the cañons to the Summit mountains, wherever there is soil of any sort, there is no lack of flowers, however short the summer may be. Within eight or ten feet of a snow bank lingering beneath a shadow, you may see belated ferns unrolling their fronds in September, and sedges hurrying up their brown spikes on ground that has been free from snow only eight or ten days, and likely to be covered again within a few weeks; the winter in the coolest of these shadow gardens being about eleven months long, while spring, summer, and autumn are hurried and crowded into one month. Again, under favorable conditions, alpine gar-dens three or four thousand feet higher than the last are in their prime in June. Between the Summit peaks at the head of the cañons sur-prising effects are produced where the sunshine falls direct on rocky slopes and reverberates among boulders. Toward the end of August, in one of these natural hothouses on the north shore of a glacier lake 11,500 feet above the sea, I found a luxuriant growth of hairy lupines, thistles, goldenrods, shrubby potentilla, spraguea, and the mountain epilobium with thousands of purple flowers an inch wide, while the opposite shore, at a distance of only three hundred yards, was bound in heavy avalanche snow, — flowery summer on one side, winter on the other. And I know a bench garden on the north wall of Yosemite in which a few flowers are in bloom all winter; the massive rocks about it storing up sunshine enough in summer to melt the snow about as fast as it falls. When tired of the confinement of my cabin I used to camp out in it in January, and never failed to find flowers, and butterflies also, except during snowstorms and a few days after.

From Yosemite one can easily walk in a day to the top of Mount Hoffman, a massive gray mountain that rises in the centre of the Park, with easy slopes adorned with castellated piles and crests on the south side, rugged precipices banked with perpetual snow on the north. Most of the broad summit is comparatively level and smooth, and covered with crystals of quartz, mica, hornblende, feldspar, garnet, zircon, tour- maline, etc., weathered out and strewn loosely as if sown broadcast; their radiance so dazzling in some places as to fairly hide the multitude of

small flowers that grow among them; myriads
of keen lance rays infinitely fine, white or colored,
making an almost continuous glow over all the
ground, with here and there throbbing, spangling
lilies of light, on the larger gems.   At first sight
only these crystal sunflowers are noticed, but
looking closely you discover minute gilias,
ivesias, eunanus, phloxes, etc., in thousands,
showing more petals than leaves; and larger
plants in hollows and on the borders of rills, —
lupines, potentillas, daisies, harebells, mountain
columbine, astragalus, fringed with heathworts.
You wander about from garden to garden enchanted, as if walking among stars, gathering
the brightest gems, each and all apparently doing
their best with eager enthusiasm, as if everything
depended on faithful shining; and considering
the flowers basking in the glorious light, many
of them looking like swarms of small moths and
butterflies that were resting after long dances in
the sunbeams.   Now your attention is called to
colonies of woodchucks and pikas, the mounds in
front of their burrows glittering like heaps of
jewelry, — romantic ground to live in or die in.
Now you look abroad over the vast round landscape bounded by the down-curving sky, nearly
all the Park in it displayed like a map, — forests,
meadows, lakes, rock waves, and snowy mountains.
Northward lies the basin of Yosemite Creek,
paved with bright domes and lakes like larger crys-

tals ; eastward, the meadowy, billowy Tuolumne region and the Summit peaks in glorious array ; southward, Yosemite ; and westward, the boundless forests. On no other mountain that I know of are you more likely to linger. It is a magnificent camp ground. Clumps of dwarf pine furnish rosiny roots and branches for fuel, and the rills pure water. Around your camp fire the flowers seem to be looking eagerly at the light, and the crystals shine unweariedly, making fine company as you lie at rest in the very heart of the vast, serene, majestic night.

The finest of the glacier meadow gardens lie at an elevation of about nine thousand feet, imbedded in the upper pine forests like lakes of light. They are smooth and level, a mile or two long, and the rich, well-drained ground is completely covered with a soft, silky, plushy sod enameled with flowers, not one of which is in the least weedy or coarse. In some places the sod is so crowded with showy flowers that the grasses are scarce noticed, in others they are rather sparingly scattered ; while every leaf and flower seems to have its winged representative in the swarms of happy flower-like insects that enliven the air above them.

With the winter snowstorms wings and petals are folded, and for more than half the year the meadows are snow-buried ten or fifteen feet deep. In June they begin to thaw out, small patches of

the dead sloppy sod appear, gradually increasing
in size until they are free and warm again, face
to face with the sky; myriads of growing points
push through the steaming mould, frogs sing
cheeringly, soon joined by the birds, and the
merry insects come back as if suddenly raised
from the dead. Soon the ground is green with
mosses and liverworts and dotted with small
fungi, making the first crop of the season. Then
the grass leaves weave a new sod, and the exceedingly slender panicles rise above it like a
purple mist, speedily followed by potentilla,
ivesia, bossy orthocarpus, yellow and purple, and
a few pentstemons. Later come the daisies and
goldenrods, asters and gentians. Of the last
there are three species, small and fine, with varying tones of blue, and in glorious abundance,
coloring extensive patches where the sod is shal-
lowest. Through the midst flows a stream only
two or three feet wide, silently gliding as if careful not to disturb the hushed calm of the solitude,
its banks embossed by the common sod bent
down to the water's edge, and trimmed with mosses
and violets; slender grass panicles lean over like
miniature pine trees, and here and there on the
driest places small mats of heathworts are neatly
spread, enriching without roughening the bossy
down-curling sod. In spring and summer the
weather is mostly crisp, exhilarating sunshine,
though magnificent mountain ranges of cumuli

are often upheaved about noon, their shady hollows tinged with purple ineffably fine, their snowy sun-beaten bosses glowing against the sky, casting cooling shadows for an hour or two, then dissolving in a quick washing rain. But for days in succession there are no clouds at all, or only faint wisps and pencilings scarcely discernible.

Toward the end of August the sunshine grows hazy, announcing the coming of Indian summer, the outlines of the landscapes are softened and mellowed, and more and more plainly are the mountains clothed with light, white tinged with pale purple, richest in the morning and evening. The warm, brooding days are full of life and thoughts of life to come, ripening seeds with next summer in them or a hundred summers. The nights are unspeakably impressive and calm ; frost crystals of wondrous beauty grow on the grass, — each carefully planned and finished as if intended to endure forever. The sod becomes yellow and brown, but the late asters and gentians, carefully closing their flowers at night, do not seem to feel the frost ; no nipped, wilted plants of any kind are to be seen ; even the early snowstorms fail to blight them. At last the precious seeds are ripe, all the work of the season is done, and the sighing pines tell the coming of winter and rest.

Ascending the range you find that many of

the higher meadows slope considerably, from
the amount of loose material washed into their
basins; and sedges and rushes are mixed with
the grasses or take their places, though all are
still more or less flowery and bordered with
heathworts, sibbaldea, and dwarf willows. Here
and there you come to small bogs, the wettest
smooth and adorned with parnassia and butter-
cups, others tussocky and ruffled like bits of
Arctic tundra, their mosses and lichens inter-
woven with dwarf shrubs. On boulder piles the
red iridescent oxyria abounds, and on sandy,
gravelly slopes several species of shrubby, yellow-flowered eriogonum, some of the plants, less
than a foot high, being very old, a century or
more, as is shown by the rings made by the
annual whorls of leaves on the big roots. Above
these flower-dotted slopes the gray, savage wilderness of crags and peaks seems lifeless and bare.
Yet all the way up to the tops of the highest
mountains, commonly supposed to be covered
with eternal snow, there are bright garden spots
crowded with flowers, their warm colors calling
to mind the sparks and jets of fire on polar volcanoes rising above a world of ice. The principal mountain-top plants are phloxes, drabas,
saxifrages, silene, cymopterus, hulsea, and polemonium, growing in detached stripes and mats,
— the highest streaks and splashes of the summer wave as it breaks against these wintry

heights. The most beautiful are the phloxes (douglasii and cæspitosum), and the red-flowered silene, with innumerable flowers hiding the leaves. Though herbaceous plants, like the trees and shrubs, are dwarfed as they ascend, two of these mountain dwellers, Hulsea algida and Polemonium confertum, are notable exceptions. The yellow-flowered hulsea is eight to twelve inches high, stout, erect, — the leaves, three to six inches long, secreting a rosiny, fragrant gum, standing up boldly on the grim lichen-stained crags, and never looking in the least tired or discouraged. Both the ray and disk flowers are yellow; the heads are nearly two inches wide, and are eagerly sought for by roving bee mountaineers. The polemonium is quite as luxuriant and tropical-looking as its companion, about the same height, glandular, fragrant, its blue flowers closely packed in eight or ten heads, twenty to forty in a head. It is never far from hulsea, growing at elevations of between eleven and thirteen thousand feet wherever a little hollow or crevice favorably situated with a handful of wind-driven soil can be found.

From these frosty Arctic sky gardens you may descend in one straight swoop to the abronia, mentzelia, and œnothera gardens of Mono, where the sunshine is warm enough for palms.

But the greatest of all the gardens is the belt of forest trees, profusely covered in the spring with blue and purple, red and yellow blossoms, each tree with a gigantic panicle of flowers fifty to a hundred feet long. Yet strange to say they are seldom noticed. Few travel through the woods when they are in bloom, the flowers of some of the showiest species opening before the snow is off the ground. Nevertheless, one would think the news of such gigantic flowers would quickly spread, and travelers from all the world would make haste to the show. Eager inquiries are made for the bloomtime of rhodo-dendron-covered mountains and for the bloom-time of Yosemite streams, that they may be en-joyed in their prime; but the far grander outburst of tree bloom covering a thousand mountains — who inquires about that? That the pistillate flowers of the pines and firs should escape the eyes of careless lookers is less to be wondered at, since they mostly grow aloft on the topmost branches, and can hardly be seen from the foot of the trees. Yet even these make a magnificent show from the top of an overlooking ridge when the sunbeams are pouring through them. But the far more numerous staminate flowers of the pines in large rosy clusters, and those of the silver firs in countless thousands on the under side of the branches, cannot be hid, stand where you may. The mountain hemlock also is glori-ously colored with a profusion of lovely blue and purple flowers, a spectacle to gods and men.

A single pine or hemlock or silver fir in the prime of its beauty about the middle of June is well worth the pains of the longest journey; how much more broad forests of them thousands of miles long!

One of the best ways to see tree flowers is to climb one of the tallest trees and to get into close tingling touch with them, and then look abroad. Speaking of the benefits of tree climbing, Thoreau says: "I found my account in climbing a tree once. It was a tall white pine, on the top of a hill; and though I got well pitched, I was well paid for it, for I discovered new mountains in the horizon which I had never seen before. I might have walked about the foot of the tree for threescore years and ten, and yet I certainly should never have seen them. But, above all, I discovered around me, — it was near the middle of June, — on the ends of the topmost branches, a few minute and delicate red conelike blossoms, the fertile flower of the white pine looking heavenward. I carried straightway to the village the topmost spire, and showed it to stranger jurymen who walked the streets, — for it was court week, — and to farmers and lumbermen and woodchoppers and hunters, and not one had ever seen the like before, but they wondered as at a star dropped down."

The same marvelous blindness prevails here, although the blossoms are a thousandfold more

abundant and telling. Once when I was collect-
ing flowers of the red silver fir near a summer
tourist resort on the mountains above Lake Tahoe, I carried a handful of flowery branches to
the boarding house, where they quickly attracted
a wondering, admiring crowd of men, women,
and children. " Oh, where did you get these? "
they cried. " How pretty they are — mighty
handsome — just too lovely for anything — where
do they grow? " " On the commonest trees
about you," I replied. " You are now standing
beside one of them, and it is in full bloom ; look
up." And I pointed to a blossom-laden Abies
magnifica, about a hundred and twenty feet high,
in front of the house, used as a hitching post.
And seeing its beauty for the first time, their
wonder could hardly have been greater or more
sincere had their silver fir hitching post blossomed
for them at that moment as suddenly as Aaron's
rod.

    The mountain hemlock extends an almost con-
tinuous belt along the Sierra and northern ranges
to Prince William's Sound, accompanied part of
the way by the pines ; our two silver firs, to
Mount Shasta, thence the fir belt is continued
through Oregon, Washington, and British Columbia by four other species, Abies nobilis, grandis,
amabilis, and lasiocarpa ; while the magnificent
Sitka spruce, with large, bright, purple flowers,
adorns the coast region from California to Cook's

Inlet and Kodiak. All these, interblending, form one flowery belt — one garden blooming in June, rocking its myriad spires in the hearty weather, bowing and swirling, enjoying clouds and the winds and filling them with balsam ; covering thousands of miles of the wildest mountains, clothing the long slopes by the sea, crowning bluffs and headlands and innumerable islands, and, fringing the banks of the glaciers, one wild wavering belt of the noblest flowers in the world, worth a lifetime of love work to know it.

CHAPTER VI

AMONG THE ANIMALS OF THE YOSEMITE

THE Sierra bear, brown or gray, the sequoia of the animals, tramps over all the park, though few travelers have the pleasure of seeing him. On he fares through the majestic forests and cañons, facing all sorts of weather, rejoicing in his strength, everywhere at home, harmonizing with the trees and rocks and shaggy chaparral. Happy fellow! his lines have fallen in pleasant places, — lily gardens in silver-fir forests, miles of bushes in endless variety and exuberance of bloom over hill-waves and valleys and along the banks of streams, cañons full of music and waterfalls, parks fair as Eden, — places in which one might expect to meet angels rather than bears.

In this happy land no famine comes nigh him. All the year round his bread is sure, for some of the thousand kinds that he likes are always in season and accessible, ranged on the shelves of the mountains like stores in a pantry. From one to another, from climate to climate, up and down he climbs, feasting on each in turn, — en-

joying as great variety as if he traveled to far-off
countries north and south. To him almost every
thing is food except granite. Every tree helps
to feed him, every bush and herb, with fruits and
flowers, leaves and bark ; and all the animals he
can catch, — badgers, gophers, ground squirrels,
lizards, snakes, etc., and ants, bees, wasps, old
and young, together with their eggs and larvæ
and nests. Craunched and hashed, down all go
to his marvelous stomach, and vanish as if cast
into a fire. What digestion ! A sheep or a
wounded deer or a pig he eats warm, about as
quickly as a boy eats a buttered muffin ; or should
the meat be a month old, it still is welcomed with
tremendous relish. After so gross a meal as
this, perhaps the next will be strawberries and
clover, or raspberries with mushrooms and nuts,
or puckery acorns and chokecherries. And as
if fearing that anything eatable in all his domin-
ions should escape being eaten, he breaks into
cabins to look after sugar, dried apples, bacon, etc.
Occasionally he eats the mountaineer's bed ; but
when he has had a full meal of more tempting
dainties he usually leaves it undisturbed, though
he has been known to drag it up through a hole
in the roof, carry it to the foot of a tree, and lie
down on it to enjoy a siesta. Eating everything,
never is he himself eaten except by man, and
only man is an enemy to be feared. " B'ar meat,"
said a hunter from whom I was seeking informa-

tion, " b'ar meat is the best meat in the mountains; their skins make the best beds, and their
grease the best butter. Biscuit shortened with
b'ar grease goes as far as beans; a man will
walk all day on a couple of them biscuit."

In my first interview with a Sierra bear we
were frightened and embarrassed, both of us,
but the bear's behavior was better than mine.
When I discovered him, he was standing in a
narrow strip of meadow, and I was concealed behind a tree on the side of it. After studying his
appearance as he stood at rest, I rushed toward
him to frighten him, that I might study his gait
in running. But, contrary to all I had heard
about the shyness of bears, he did not run at all;
and when I stopped short within a few steps of
him, as he held his ground in a fighting attitude,
my mistake was monstrously plain. I was then
put on my good behavior, and never afterward
forgot the right manners of the wilderness.

This happened on my first Sierra excursion in
the forest to the north of Yosemite Valley. I
was eager to meet the animals, and many of them
came to me as if willing to show themselves and
make my acquaintance; but the bears kept out
of my way.

An old mountaineer, in reply to my questions,
told me that bears were very shy, all save grim
old grizzlies, and that I might travel the mountains for years without seeing one, unless I gave

my mind to them and practiced the stealthy ways of hunters. Nevertheless, it was only a few weeks after I had received this information that I met the one mentioned above, and obtained instruction at first-hand.

I was encamped in the woods about a mile back of the rim of Yosemite, beside a stream that falls into the valley by the way of Indian Cañon. Nearly every day for weeks I went to the top of the North Dome to sketch ; for it commands a general view of the valley, and I was anxious to draw every tree and rock and waterfall. Carlo, a St. Bernard dog, was my companion, — a fine, intelligent fellow that belonged to a hunter who was compelled to remain all summer on the hot plains, and who loaned him to me for the season for the sake of having him in the mountains, where he would be so much better off. Carlo knew bears through long experience, and he it was who led me to my first interview, though he seemed as much surprised as the bear at my unhunter-like behavior. One morning in June, just as the sunbeams began to stream through the trees, I set out for a day's sketching on the dome ; and before we had gone half a mile from camp Carlo snuffed the air and looked cautiously ahead, lowered his bushy tail, drooped his ears, and began to step softly like a cat, turning every few yards and looking me in the face with a telling expression, saying plainly enough, " There is a bear a little way ahead." I walked carefully in the indicated direction, until I approached a small flowery meadow that I was familiar with, then crawled to the foot of a tree on its margin, bearing in mind what I had been told about the shyness of bears. Looking out cautiously over the instep of the tree, I saw a big, burly cinnamon bear about thirty yards off, half erect, his paws resting on the trunk of a fir that had fallen into the meadow, his hips almost buried in grass and flowers. He was listening attentively and trying to catch the scent, showing that in some way he was aware of our approach. I watched his gestures, and tried to make the most of my opportunity to learn what I could about him, fearing he would not stay long. He made a fine picture, standing alert in the sunny garden walled in by the most beautiful firs in the world.

After examining him at leisure, noting the sharp muzzle thrust inquiringly forward, the long shaggy hair on his broad chest, the stiff ears nearly buried in hair, and the slow, heavy way in which he moved his head, I foolishly made a rush on him, throwing up my arms and shouting to frighten him, to see him run. He did not mind the demonstration much; only pushed his head farther forward, and looked at me sharply as if asking, "What now? If you want to fight, I'm ready." Then I began to fear that on me would fall the work of running. But I was afraid to

run, lest he should be encouraged to pursue me ;
therefore I held my ground, staring him in the
face within a dozen yards or so, putting on as
bold a look as I could, and hoping the influence
of the human eye would be as great as it is said
to be.   Under these strained relations the interview seemed to last a long time.   Finally, the bear,
seeing how still I was, calmly withdrew his huge
paws from the log, gave me a piercing look, as if
warning me not to follow him, turned, and walked
slowly up the middle of the meadow into the forest ; stopping every few steps and looking back
to make sure that I was not trying to take him
at a disadvantage in a rear attack.   I was glad
to part with him, and greatly enjoyed the vanishing view as he waded through the lilies and
columbines.

Thenceforth I always tried to give bears re-
spectful notice of my approach, and they usually kept well out of my way.   Though they
often came around my camp in the night, only
once afterward, as far as I know, was I very
near one of them in daylight.   This time it was
a grizzly I met ; and as luck would have it, I
was even nearer to him than I had been to the
big cinnamon.   Though not a large specimen,
he seemed formidable enough at a distance of
less than a dozen yards.   His shaggy coat was
well grizzled, his head almost white.   When I
first caught sight of him he was eating acorns

under a Kellogg oak, at a distance of perhaps
seventy-five yards, and I tried to slip past without disturbing him.   But he had either heard
my steps on the gravel or caught my scent, for
he came straight toward me, stopping every rod
or so to look and listen : and as I was afraid to
be seen running, I crawled on my hands and
knees a little way to one side and hid behind a
libocedrus, hoping he would pass me unnoticed.
He soon came up opposite me, and stood looking ahead, while I looked at him, peering past
the bulging trunk of the tree.   At last, turning his head, he caught sight of mine, stared
sharply a minute or two, and then, with fine
dignity,   disappeared   in   a   manzanita-covered
earthquake talus.

Considering how heavy and broad-footed bears
are, it is wonderful how little harm they do in
the wilderness.   Even in the well-watered gardens of the middle region, where the flowers
grow tallest, and where during warm weather the
bears wallow and roll, no evidence of destruction is visible.   On the contrary, under nature's
direction, the massive beasts act as gardeners.
On the forest floor, carpeted with needles and
brush, and on the tough sod of glacier meadows,
bears make no mark ; but around the sandy margin of lakes their magnificent tracks form grand
lines of embroidery.   Their well-worn trails extend along the main cañons on either side, and

though dusty in some places make no scar on the landscape. They bite and break off the branches of some of the pines and oaks to get the nuts, but this pruning is so light that few mountaineers ever notice it ; and though they interfere with the orderly lichen-veiled decay of fallen trees, tearing them to pieces to reach the colonies of ants that inhabit them, the scattered ruins are quickly pressed back into harmony by snow and rain and over-leaning vegetation.

The number of bears that make the Park their home may be guessed by the number that have been killed by the two best hunters, Duncan and old David Brown. Duncan began to be known as a bear-killer about the year 1865. He was then roaming the woods, hunting and prospecting on the south fork of the Merced. A friend told me that he killed his first bear near his cabin at Wawona ; that after mustering courage to fire he fled, without waiting to learn the effect of his shot. Going back in a few hours he found poor Bruin dead, and gained courage to try again. Duncan confessed to me, when we made an excursion together in 1875, that he was at first mortally afraid of bears, but after killing a half dozen he began to keep count of his victims, and became ambitious to be known as a great bear-hunter. In nine years he had killed forty-nine, keeping count by notches cut on one of the timbers of his cabin on the shore of Cres-

cent Lake, near the south boundary of the Park.
He said the more he knew about bears, the more
he respected them and the less he feared them.
But at the same time he grew more and more
cautious, and never fired until he had every advantage, no matter how long he had to wait and
how far he had to go before he got the bear just
right as to the direction of the wind, the distance, and the way of escape in case of accident;
making allowance also for the character of the
animal, old or young, cinnamon or grizzly. For
old grizzlies, he said, he had no use whatever,
and he was mighty careful to avoid their acquaintance. He wanted to kill an even hundred;
then he was going to confine himself to safer
game. There was not much money in bears,
anyhow, and a round hundred was enough for
glory.

I have not seen or heard of him lately, and do
not know how his bloody count stands. On my
excursions, I occasionally passed his cabin. It
was full of meat and skins hung in bundles from
the rafters, and the ground about it was strewn
with bones and hair, — infinitely less tidy than
a bear's den. He went as hunter and guide
with a geological survey party for a year or two,
and was very proud of the scientific knowledge
he picked up. His admiring fellow mountaineers, he said, gave him credit for knowing not
only the botanical names of all the trees and

bushes, but also the "botanical names of the bears."

The most famous hunter of the region was David Brown, an old pioneer, who early in the gold period established his main camp in a little forest glade on the north fork of the Merced, which is still called "Brown's Flat." No finer solitude for a hunter and prospector could be found; the climate is delightful all the year, and the scenery of both earth and sky is a perpetual feast. Though he was not much of a "scenery fellow," his friends say that he knew a pretty place when he saw it as well as any one, and liked mightily to get on the top of a commanding ridge to "look off."

When out of provisions, he would take down his old-fashioned long-barreled rifle from its deer-horn rest over the fireplace and set out in search of game. Seldom did he have to go far for venison, because the deer liked the wooded slopes of Pilot Peak ridge, with its open spots where they could rest and look about them, and enjoy the breeze from the sea in warm weather, free from troublesome flies, while they found hiding-places and fine aromatic food in the deer-brush chaparral. A small, wise dog was his only companion, and well the little mountaineer understood the object of every hunt, whether deer or bears, or only grouse hidden in the fir-tops. In deer-hunting Sandy had little to do, trotting behind

his master as he walked noiselessly through the
fragrant woods, careful not to step heavily on
dry twigs, scanning open spots in the chaparral
where the deer feed in the early morning and
toward sunset, peering over ridges and swells as
new outlooks were reached, and along alder and
willow fringed flats and streams, until he found
a young buck, killed it, tied its legs together,
threw it on his shoulder, and so back to camp.
But when bears were hunted, Sandy played an
important part as leader, and several times saved
his master's life; and it was as a bear-hunter that
David Brown became famous. His method, as
I had it from a friend who had passed many an
evening in his cabin listening to his long stories
of adventure, was simply to take a few pounds
of flour and his rifle, and go slowly and silently
over hill and valley in the loneliest part of the
wilderness, until little Sandy came upon the
fresh track of a bear, then follow it to the death,
paying no heed to time. Wherever the bear
went he went, however rough the ground, led by
Sandy, who looked back from time to time to see
how his master was coming on, and regulated his
pace accordingly, never growing weary or allowing any other track to divert him. When high
ground was reached a halt was made, to scan
the openings in every direction, and perchance
Bruin would be discovered sitting upright on
his haunches, eating manzanita berries; pulling

down the fruit-laden branches with his paws and pressing them together, so as to get substantial mouthfuls, however mixed with leaves and twigs. The time of year enabled the hunter to determine approximately where the game would be found : in spring and early summer, in lush grass and clover meadows and in berry tangles along the banks of streams, or on pea-vine and lupine clad slopes; in late summer and autumn, beneath the pines, eating the cones cut off by the squirrels, and in oak groves at the bottom of cañons, munching acorns, manzanita berries, and cherries; and after snow had fallen, in alluvial bottoms, feeding on ants and yellow-jacket wasps. These food places were always cautiously approached, so as to avoid the chance of sudden encounters.

"Whenever," said the hunter, "I saw a bear before he saw me, I had no trouble in killing him. I just took lots of time to learn what he was up to and how long he would be likely to stay, and to study the direction of the wind and the lay of the land. Then I worked round to leeward of him, no matter how far I had to go; crawled and dodged to within a hundred yards, near the foot of a tree that I could climb, but which was too small for a bear to climb. There I looked well to the priming of my rifle, took off my boots so as to climb quickly if necessary, and, with my rifle in rest and Sandy behind me, waited until my bear stood right, when I made a sure, or at least a good shot back of the fore leg. In case he showed fight, I got up the tree I had in mind, before he could reach me. But bears are slow and awkward with their eyes, and being to windward they could not scent me, and often I got in a second shot before they saw the smoke. Usually, however, they tried to get away when they were hurt, and I let them go a good safe while before I ventured into the brush after them. Then Sandy was pretty sure to find them dead; if not, he barked bold as a lion to draw attention, or rushed in and nipped them behind, enabling me to get to a safe distance and watch a chance for a finishing shot.

"Oh yes, bear-hunting is a mighty interesting business, and safe enough if followed just right, though, like every other business, especially the wild kind, it has its accidents, and Sandy and I have had close calls at times. Bears are nobody's fools, and they know enough to let men alone as a general thing, unless they are wounded, or cornered, or have cubs. In my opinion, a hungry old mother would catch and eat a man, if she could; which is only fair play, anyhow, for we eat them. But nobody, as far as I know, has been eaten up in these rich mountains. Why they never tackle a fellow when he is lying asleep I never could understand. They could gobble us mighty handy, but I suppose it's nature to respect a sleeping man."

Sheep-owners and their shepherds have killed a great many bears, mostly by poison and traps of various sorts. Bears are fond of mutton, and levy heavy toll on every flock driven into the mountains. They usually come to the corral at night, climb in, kill a sheep with a stroke of the paw, carry it off a little distance, eat about half of it, and return the next night for the other half; and so on all summer, or until they are themselves killed. It is not, however, by direct killing, but by suffocation through crowding against the corral wall in fright, that the greatest losses are incurred. From ten to fifteen sheep are found dead, smothered in the corral, after every attack; or the walls are broken, and the flock is scattered far and wide. A flock may escape the attention of these marauders for a week or two in the spring; but after their first taste of the fine mountain-fed meat the visits are persistently kept up, in spite of all precautions. Once I spent a night with two Portuguese shepherds, who were greatly troubled with bears, from two to four or five visiting them almost every night. Their camp was near the middle of the Park, and the wicked bears, they said, were getting worse and worse. Not waiting now until dark, they came out of the brush in broad daylight, and boldly carried off as many sheep as they liked. One evening, before sundown, a bear, followed by two cubs,

came for an early supper, as the flock was being
slowly driven toward the camp. Joe, the elder
of the shepherds, warned by many exciting experiences, promptly climbed a tall tamarack pine,
and left the freebooters to help themselves;
while Antone, calling him a coward, and declaring that he was not going to let bears eat up his
sheep before his face, set the dogs on them, and
rushed toward them with a great noise and a
stick. The frightened cubs ran up a tree, and
the mother ran to meet the shepherd and dogs.
Antone stood astonished for a moment, eying
the oncoming bear; then fled faster than Joe
had, closely pursued. He scrambled to the roof
of their little cabin, the only refuge quickly
available; and fortunately, the bear, anxious
about her young, did not climb after him, —
only held him in mortal terror a few minutes,
glaring and threatening, then hastened back to
her cubs, called them down, went to the frightened, huddled flock, killed a sheep, and feasted
in peace. Antone piteously entreated cautious
Joe to show him a good safe tree, up which he
climbed like a sailor climbing a mast, and held on
as long as he could with legs crossed, the slim
pine recommended by Joe being nearly branchless. " So you, too, are a bear coward as well
as Joe," I said, after hearing the story. " Oh,
I tell you," he replied, with grand solemnity,
" bear face close by look awful; she just as soon

eat me as not. She do so as eef all my sheeps b'long every one to her own self. I run to bear no more. I take tree every time."

After this the shepherds corraled the flock about an hour before sundown, chopped large quantities of dry wood and made a circle of fires around the corral every night, and one with a gun kept watch on a stage built in a pine by the side of the cabin, while the other slept. But after the first night or two this fire fence did no good, for the robbers seemed to regard the light as an advantage, after becoming used to it.

On the night I spent at their camp the show made by the wall of fire when it was blazing in its prime was magnificent, — the illumined trees round about relieved against solid darkness, and the two thousand sheep lying down in one gray mass, sprinkled with gloriously brilliant gems, the effect of the firelight in their eyes. It was nearly midnight when a pair of the freebooters arrived. They walked boldly through a gap in the fire circle, killed two sheep, carried them out, and vanished in the dark woods, leaving ten dead in a pile, trampled down and smothered against the corral fence; while the scared watcher in the tree did not fire a single shot, saying he was afraid he would hit some of the sheep, as the bears got among them before he could get a good sight.

In the morning I asked the shepherds why

they did not move the flock to a new pasture. "Oh, no use!" cried Antone. "Look my dead sheeps. We move three four time before, all the same bear come by the track. No use. To-morrow we go home below. Look my dead sheeps. Soon all dead."

Thus were they driven out of the mountains more than a month before the usual time. After Uncle Sam's soldiers, bears are the most effective forest police, but some of the shepherds are very successful in killing them. Altogether, by hunters, mountaineers, Indians, and sheepmen, probably five or six hundred have been killed within the bounds of the Park, during the last thirty years. But they are not in danger of extinction. Now that the Park is guarded by soldiers, not only has the vegetation in great part come back to the desolate ground, but all the wild animals are increasing in numbers. No guns are allowed in the Park except under certain restrictions, and after a permit has been obtained from the officer in charge. This has stopped the barbarous slaughter of bears, and especially of deer, by shepherds, hunters, and hunting tourists, who, it would seem, can find no pleasure without blood.

The Sierra deer — the blacktail — spend the winters in the brushy and exceedingly rough region just below the main timber-belt, and are less accessible to hunters there than when they are passing through the comparatively open forests to and from their summer pastures near the summits of the range. They go up the mountains early in the spring as the snow melts, not waiting for it all to disappear; reaching the high Sierra about the first of June, and the coolest recesses at the base of the peaks a month or so later. I have tracked them for miles over compacted snow from three to ten feet deep.

Deer are capital mountaineers, making their way into the heart of the roughest mountains; seeking not only pasturage, but a cool climate, and safe hidden places in which to bring forth their young. They are not supreme as rock-climbing animals; they take second rank, yielding the first to the mountain sheep, which dwell above them on the highest crags and peaks. Still, the two meet frequently; for the deer climbs all the peaks save the lofty summits above the glaciers, crossing piles of angular boulders, roaring swollen streams, and sheer-walled cañons by fords and passes that would try the nerves of the hardiest mountaineers, — climbing with graceful ease and reserve of strength that cannot fail to arouse admiration. Everywhere some species of deer seems to be at home, — on rough or smooth ground, lowlands or highlands, in swamps and barrens and the densest woods, in varying climates, hot or cold, over all the continent; maintaining glorious health, never making an awkward step. Standing, lying down, walking, feeding, running even for life, it is always invincibly graceful, and adds beauty and animation to every landscape, — a charming animal, and a great credit to nature.

I never see one of the common blacktail deer, the only species in the Park, without fresh admiration; and since I never carry a gun I see them well : lying beneath a juniper or dwarf pine, among the brown needles on the brink of some cliff or the end of a ridge commanding a wide outlook; feeding in sunny openings among chaparral, daintily selecting aromatic leaves and twigs ; leading their fawns out of my way, or making them lie down and hide ; bounding past through the forest, or curiously advancing and retreating again and again.

One morning when I was eating breakfast in a little garden spot on the Kaweah, hedged around with chaparral, I noticed a deer's head thrust through the bushes, the big beautiful eyes gazing at me. I kept still, and the deer ventured forward a step, then snorted and withdrew. In a few minutes she returned, and came into the open garden, stepping with infinite grace, followed by two others. After showing themselves for a moment, they bounded over the hedge with sharp, timid snorts and vanished. But curiosity brought them back with still another, and all four came into my garden, and, satisfied that I meant them no ill, began to feed, actually eating breakfast with me, like tame, gentle sheep around a shepherd, — rare company, and the most graceful in movements and attitudes. I eagerly watched them while they fed on ceanothus and wild cherry, daintily culling single leaves here and there from the side of the hedge, turning now and then to snip a few leaves of mint from the midst of the garden flowers. Grass they did not eat at all. No wonder the contents of the deer's stomach are eaten by the Indians.

While exploring the upper cañon of the north fork of the San Joaquin, one evening, the sky threatening rain, I searched for a dry bed, and made choice of a big juniper that had been pushed down by a snow avalanche, but was resting stubbornly on its knees high enough to let me lie under its broad trunk. Just below my shelter there was another juniper on the very brink of a precipice, and, examining it, I found a deer-bed beneath it, completely protected and concealed by drooping branches, — a fine refuge and lookout as well as resting-place. About an hour before dark I heard the clear, sharp snorting of a deer, and looking down on the brushy, rocky cañon bottom, discovered an anxious doe that no doubt had her fawns concealed near by. She bounded over the chaparral and up the farther slope of the wall, often stopping to look

back and listen, — a fine picture of vivid, eager
alertness. I sat perfectly still, and as my shirt
was colored like the juniper bark I was not easily
seen. After a little she came cautiously toward
me, sniffing the air and grazing, and her movements, as she descended the cañon side over
boulder piles and brush and fallen timber, were
admirably strong and beautiful; she never
strained or made apparent efforts, although
jumping high here and there. As she drew
nigh she sniffed anxiously, trying the air in different directions until she caught my scent;
then bounded off, and vanished behind a small
grove of firs. Soon she came back with the same
caution and insatiable curiosity, — coming and
going five or six times. While I sat admiring
her, a Douglas squirrel, evidently excited by her
noisy alarms, climbed a boulder beneath me, and
witnessed her performances as attentively as I
did, while a frisky chipmunk, too restless or hungry for such shows, busied himself about his
supper in a thicket of shadbushes, the fruit of
which was then ripe, glancing about on the
slender twigs lightly as a sparrow.

Toward the end of the Indian summer, when
the young are strong, the deer begin to gather
in little bands of from six to fifteen or twenty,
and on the approach of the first snowstorm they
set out on their march down the mountains to
their winter quarters; lingering usually on warm

hillsides and spurs eight or ten miles below the summits, as if loath to leave. About the end of November, a heavy, far-reaching storm drives them down in haste along the dividing ridges between the rivers, led by old experienced bucks whose knowledge of the topography is wonderful.

It is when the deer are coming down that the Indians set out on their grand fall hunt. Too lazy to go into the recesses of the mountains away from trails, they wait for the deer to come out, and then waylay them. This plan also has the advantage of finding them in bands. Great preparations are made. Old guns are mended, bullets moulded, and the hunters wash themselves and fast to some extent, to insure good luck, as they say. Men and women, old and young, set forth together. Central camps are made on the well-known highways of the deer, which are soon red with blood. Each hunter comes in laden, old crones as well as maidens smiling on the luckiest. All grow fat and merry. Boys, each armed with an antlered head, play at buck-fighting, and plague the industrious women, who are busily preparing the meat for transportation, by stealing up behind them and throwing fresh hides over them. But the Indians are passing away here as everywhere, and their red camps on the mountains are fewer every year.

There are panthers, foxes, badgers, porcupines, and coyotes in the Park, but not in large numbers. I have seen coyotes well back in the range at the head of the Tuolumne Meadows as early as June 1st, before the snow was gone, feeding on marmots; but they are far more numerous on the inhabited lowlands around ranches, where they enjoy life on chickens, turkeys, quail eggs, ground squirrels, hares, etc., and all kinds of fruit. Few wild sheep, I fear, are left hereabouts; for, though safe on the high peaks, they are driven down the eastern slope of the mountains when the deer are driven down the western, to ridges and outlying spurs where the snow does not fall to a great depth, and there they are within reach of the cattlemen's rifles.

The two squirrels of the Park, the Douglas and the California gray, keep all the woods lively. The former is far more abundant and more widely distributed, being found all the way up from the foothills to the dwarf pines on the Summit peaks. He is the most influential of the Sierra animals, though small, and the brightest of all the squirrels I know, — a squirrel of squirrels, quick mountain vigor and valor condensed, purely wild, and as free from disease as a sunbeam. One cannot think of such an animal ever being weary or sick. He claims all the woods, and is inclined to drive away even men as intruders. How he scolds, and what faces he makes! If

not so comically small he would be a dreadful
fellow. The gray, Sciurus fossor, is the handsomest, I think, of all the large American
squirrels. He is something like the Eastern
gray, but is brighter and clearer in color, and
more lithe and slender. He dwells in the oak
and pine woods up to a height of about five
thousand feet above the sea, is rather common in
Yosemite Valley, Hetch-Hetchy, Kings River
Cañon, and indeed in all the main cañons and
Yosemites, but does not like the high fir-covered
ridges. Compared with the Douglas, the gray
is more than twice as large; nevertheless, he
manages to make his way through the trees with
less stir than his small, peppery neighbor, and is
much less influential in every way. In the
spring, before the pine-nuts and hazel-nuts are
ripe, he examines last year's cones for the few
seeds that may be left in them between the half-
open scales, and gleans fallen nuts and seeds on
the ground among the leaves, after making sure
that no enemy is nigh. His fine tail floats, now
behind, now above him, level or gracefully
curled, light and radiant as dry thistledown.
His body seems hardly more substantial than his
tail. The Douglas is a firm, emphatic bolt of
life, fiery, pungent, full of brag and show and
fight, and his movements have none of the ele-
gant deliberation of the gray. They are so
quick and keen they almost sting the onlooker,

and the acrobatic harlequin gyrating show he makes of himself turns one giddy to see. The gray is shy and oftentimes stealthy, as if half expecting to find an enemy in every tree and bush and behind every log; he seems to wish to be let alone, and manifests no desire to be seen, or admired, or feared. He is hunted by the Indians, and this of itself is cause enough for caution. The Douglas is less attractive for game, and probably increasing in numbers in spite of every enemy. He goes his ways bold as a lion, up and down and across, round and round, the happiest, merriest of all the hairy tribe, and at the same time tremendously earnest and solemn, sunshine incarnate, making every tree tingle with his electric toes. If you prick him, you cannot think he will bleed. He seems above the chance and change that beset common mortals, though in busily gathering burs and nuts he shows that he has to work for a living, like the rest of us. I never found a dead Douglas. He gets into the world and out of it without being noticed; only in prime is he seen, like some little plants that are visible only when in bloom.

The little striped Tamias quadrivittatus is one of the most amiable and delightful of all the mountain tree-climbers. A brighter, cheerier chipmunk does not exist. He is smarter, more arboreal and squirrel-like, than the familiar Eastern species, and is distributed as widely on the

Sierra as the Douglas. Every forest, however dense or open, every hilltop and cañon, however brushy or bare, is cheered and enlivened by this happy little animal. You are likely to notice him first on the lower edge of the coniferous belt, where the Sabine and yellow pines meet; and thence upward, go where you may, you will find him every day, even in winter, unless the weather is stormy. He is an exceedingly interesting little fellow, full of odd, quaint ways, confiding, thinking no evil; and without being a squirrel — a true shadow-tail — he lives the life of a squirrel, and has almost all squirrelish accomplishments without aggressive quarrelsomeness.

I never weary of watching him as he frisks about the bushes, gathering seeds and berries; poising on slender twigs of wild cherry, shad, chinquapin, buckthorn, bramble; skimming along prostrate trunks or over the grassy, needle-strewn forest floor; darting from boulder to boulder on glacial pavements and the tops of the great domes. When the seeds of the conifers are ripe, he climbs the trees and cuts off the cones for a winter store, working diligently, though not with the tremendous lightning energy of the Douglas, who frequently drives him out of the best trees. Then he lies in wait, and picks up a share of the burs cut off by his domineering cousin, and stores them beneath logs and in hollows. Few of the Sierra animals are so well liked as this little airy, fluffy half squirrel, half spermophile.   So gentle, confiding, and busily cheery and happy, he takes one's heart and keeps his place among the best-loved of the mountain darlings.   A diligent collector of seeds, nuts, and berries, of course he is well fed, though never in the least dumpy with fat.   On the contrary, he looks like a mere fluff of fur, weighing but little more than a field mouse, and of his frisky, birdlike liveliness without haste there is no end.   Douglas can bark with his mouth closed, but little quad always opens his when he talks or sings.   He has a considerable variety of notes which correspond with his movements, some of them sweet and liquid, like water dripping into a pool with tinkling sound.   His eyes are black and animated, shining like dew.   He seems dearly to like teasing a dog, venturing within a few feet of it, then frisking away with a lively chipping and low squirrelish churring ; beating time to his music, such as it is, with his tail, which at each chip and churr describes a half circle.   Not even Douglas is surer footed or takes greater risks.   I have seen him running about on sheer Yosemite cliffs, holding on with as little effort as a fly and as little thought of danger, in places where, if he had made the least slip, he would have fallen thousands of feet.   How fine it would be could mountaineers move about on precipices with the same sure grip !

Before the pine-nuts are ripe, grass seeds and those of the many species of ceanothus, with strawberries, raspberries, and the soft red thimbleberries of Rubus nutkanus, form the bulk of his food, and a neater eater is not to be found in the mountains. Bees powdered with pollen, poking their blunt noses into the bells of flowers, are comparatively clumsy and boorish. Frisking along some fallen pine or fir, when the grass seeds are ripe, he looks about him, considering which of the tufts he sees is likely to have the best, runs out to it, selects what he thinks is sure to be a good head, cuts it off, carries it to the top of the log, sits upright and nibbles out the grain without getting awns in his mouth, turning the head round, holding it and fingering it as if playing on a flute; then skips for another and another, bringing them to the same dining-log.

The woodchuck (*Arctomys monax*) dwells on high bleak ridges and boulder piles; and a very different sort of mountaineer is he, — bulky, fat, aldermanic, and fairly bloated at times by hearty indulgence in the lush pastures of his airy home. And yet he is by no means a dull animal. In the midst of what we regard as storm-beaten desolation, high in the frosty air, beside the glaciers he pipes and whistles right cheerily and lives to a good old age. If you are as early a riser as he is, you may oftentimes see him come blinking out of his burrow to meet the first beams of the morning and take a sunbath on some favorite flat-topped boulder. Afterward, well warmed, he goes to breakfast in one of his garden hollows, eats heartily like a cow in clover until comfortably swollen, then goes a-visiting, and plays and loves and fights.

In the spring of 1875, when I was exploring the peaks and glaciers about the head of the middle fork of the San Joaquin, I had crossed the range from the head of Owen River, and one morning, passing around a frozen lake where the snow was perhaps ten feet deep, I was surprised to find the fresh track of a woodchuck plainly marked, the sun having softened the surface. What could the animal be thinking of, coming out so early while all the ground was snow-buried? The steady trend of his track showed he had a definite aim, and fortunately it was toward a mountain thirteen thousand feet high that I meant to climb. So I followed to see if I could find out what he was up to. From the base of the mountain the track pointed straight up, and I knew by the melting snow that I was not far behind him. I lost the track on a crumbling ridge, partly projecting through the snow, but soon discovered it again. Well toward the summit of the mountain, in an open spot on the south side, nearly inclosed by disintegrating pinnacles among which the sun heat reverberated, making an isolated patch of warm climate, I found a nice garden, full of rock cress, phlox, silene, draba, etc., and a few grasses; and in this garden I overtook the wanderer, enjoying a fine fresh meal, perhaps the first of the season. How did he know the way to this one garden spot, so high and far off, and what told him that it was in bloom while yet the snow was ten feet deep over his den? For this it would seem he would need more botanical, topographical, and climatological knowledge than most mountaineers are possessed of.

The shy, curious mountain beaver, Haplodon, lives on the heights, not far from the woodchuck. He digs canals and controls the flow of small streams under the sod. And it is startling when one is camped on the edge of a sloping meadow near the homes of these industrious mountaineers, to be awakened in the still night by the sound of water rushing and gurgling under one's head in a newly formed canal. Pouched gophers also have a way of awakening nervous campers that is quite as exciting as the Haplodon's paln; that is, by a series of firm upward pushes when they are driving tunnels and shoving up the dirt. One naturally cries out, " Who's there?" and then discovering the cause, " All right. Go on. Good-night," and goes to sleep again.

The haymaking pika, bob-tailed spermophile, and wood-rat are also among the most interest-

ing of the Sierra animals. The last Neotoma
is scarcely at all like the common rat, is nearly
twice as large, has a delicate, soft, brownish fur,
white on the belly, large ears thin and translucent, eyes full and liquid and mild in expression, nose blunt and squirrelish, slender
claws sharp as needles, and as his limbs are
strong he can climb about as well as a squirrel;
while no rat or squirrel has so innocent a look,
is so easily approached, or in general expresses
so much confidence in one's good intentions.
He seems too fine for the thorny thickets he in-
habits, and his big, rough hut is as unlike himself as possible. No other animal in these
mountains makes nests so large and striking in
appearance as his. They are built of all kinds
of sticks (broken branches, and old rotten moss-
grown chunks and green twigs, smooth or
thorny, cut from the nearest bushes), mixed with
miscellaneous rubbish and curious odds and ends,
— bits of cloddy earth, stones, bones, bits of
deer-horn, etc.: the whole simply piled in conical
masses on the ground in chaparral thickets.
Some of these cabins are five or six feet high,
and occasionally a dozen or more are grouped
together; less, perhaps, for society's sake than
for advantages of food and shelter.

Coming through deep, stiff chaparral in the
heart of the wilderness, heated and weary in
forcing a way, the solitary explorer, happening

into one of these curious neotoma villages, is startled at the strange sight, and may imagine he is in an Indian village, and feel anxious as to the reception he will get in a place so wild. At first, perhaps, not a single inhabitant will be seen, or at most only two or three seated on the tops of their huts as at the doors, observing the stranger with the mildest of mild eyes. The nest in the centre of the cabin is made of grass and films of bark chewed to tow, and lined with feathers and the down of various seeds. The thick, rough walls seem to be built for defense against enemies — fox, coyote, etc. — as well as for shelter, and the delicate creatures in their big, rude homes, suggest tender flowers, like those of Salvia carduacea, defended by thorny involucres.

Sometimes the home is built in the forks of an oak, twenty or thirty feet from the ground, and even in garrets. Among housekeepers who have these bushmen as neighbors or guests they are regarded as thieves, because they carry away and pile together everything transportable (knives, forks, tin cups, spoons, spectacles, combs, nails, kindling-wood, etc., as well as eatables of all sorts), to strengthen their fortifications or to shine among rivals. Once, far back in the high Sierra, they stole my snow-goggles, the lid of my teapot, and my aneroid barometer; and one stormy night, when encamped under a prostrate cedar, I was awakened

by a gritting sound on the granite, and by the
light of my fire I discovered a handsome neotoma beside me, dragging away my ice-hatchet,
pulling with might and main by a buckskin
string on the handle. I threw bits of bark at
him and made a noise to frighten him, but he
stood scolding and chattering back at me, his fine
eyes shining with an air of injured innocence.

A great variety of lizards enliven the warm
portions of the Park. Some of them are more
than a foot in length, others but little larger
than grasshoppers. A few are snaky and repulsive at first sight, but most of the species are
handsome and attractive, and bear acquaintance
well; we like them better the farther we see into
their charming lives. Small fellow mortals, gentle and guileless, they are easily tamed, and have
beautiful eyes, expressing the clearest innocence,
so that, in spite of prejudices brought from cool,
lizardless countries, one must soon learn to like
them. Even the horned toad of the plains and
foothills, called horrid, is mild and gentle, with
charming eyes, and so are the snakelike species
found in the underbrush of the lower forests.
These glide in curves with all the ease and grace
of snakes, while their small, undeveloped limbs
drag for the most part as useless appendages.
One specimen that I measured was fourteen
inches long, and as far as I saw it made no use
whatever of its diminutive limbs.

Most of them glint and dart on the sunny rocks and across open spaces from bush to bush, swift as dragonflies and humming-birds, and about as brilliantly colored. They never make a long-sustained run, whatever their object, but dart direct as arrows for a distance of ten or twenty feet, then suddenly stop, and as suddenly start again. These stops are necessary as rests, for they are short-winded, and when pursued steadily are soon run out of breath, pant piti- fully, and may easily be caught where no retreat in bush or rock is quickly available.

If you stay with them a week or two and be- have well, these gentle saurians, descendants of an ancient race of giants, will soon know and trust you, come to your feet, play, and watch your every motion with cunning curiosity. You will surely learn to like them, not only the bright ones, gorgeous as the rainbow, but the little ones, gray as lichened granite, and scarcely bigger than grasshoppers ; and they will teach you that scales may cover as fine a nature as hair or feathers or anything tailored.

There are many snakes in the cañons and lower forests, but they are mostly handsome and harmless. Of all the tourists and travelers who have visited Yosemite and the adjacent moun- tains, not one has been bitten by a snake of any sort, while thousands have been charmed by them. Some of them vie with the lizards in beauty of color and dress patterns. Only the rattlesnake is venomous, and he carefully keeps his venom to himself as far as man is concerned, unless his life is threatened.

Before I learned to respect rattlesnakes I killed two, the first on the San Joaquin plain. He was coiled comfortably around a tuft of bunch-grass, and I discovered him when he was between my feet as I was stepping over him. He held his head down and did not attempt to strike, although in danger of being trampled. At that time, thirty years ago, I imagined that rattlesnakes should be killed wherever found. I had no weapon of any sort, and on the smooth plain there was not a stick or a stone within miles; so I crushed him by jumping on him, as the deer are said to do. Looking me in the face he saw I meant mischief, and quickly cast himself into a coil, ready to strike in defense. I knew he could not strike when traveling, therefore I threw handfuls of dirt and grass sods at him, to tease him out of coil. He held his ground a few minutes, threatening and strik-ing, and then started off to get rid of me. I ran forward and jumped on him; but he drew back his head so quickly my heel missed, and he also missed his stroke at me. Persecuted, tormented, again and again he tried to get away, bravely striking out to protect himself; but at last my heel came squarely down, sorely wounding him, and a few more brutal stampings crushed him. I felt degraded by the killing business, farther from heaven, and I made up my mind to try to be at least as fair and charitable as the snakes themselves, and to kill no more save in self-defense.

The second killing might also, I think, have been avoided, and I have always felt somewhat sore and guilty about it. I had built a little cabin in Yosemite, and for convenience in getting water, and for the sake of music and society, I led a small stream from Yosemite Creek into it. Running along the side of the wall it was not in the way, and it had just fall enough to ripple and sing in low, sweet tones, making delightful company, especially at night when I was lying awake. Then a few frogs came in and made merry with the stream, — and one snake, I suppose to catch the frogs.

Returning from my long walks, I usually brought home a large handful of plants, partly for study, partly for ornament, and set them in a corner of the cabin, with their stems in the stream to keep them fresh. One day, when I picked up a handful that had begun to fade, I uncovered a large coiled rattler that had been hiding behind the flowers. Thus suddenly brought to light face to face with the rightful owner of the place, the poor reptile was desperately embarrassed, evidently realizing that he had no right in the cabin. It was not only fear that he showed, but a good deal of downright bashfulness and embarrassment, like that of a more than half honest person caught under suspicious circumstances behind a door. Instead of striking or threatening to strike, though coiled and ready, he slowly drew his head down as far as he could, with awkward, confused kinks in his neck and a shamefaced expression, as if wishing the ground would open and hide him. I have looked into the eyes of so many wild animals that I feel sure I did not mistake the feelings of this unfortunate snake. I did not want to kill him, but I had many visitors, some of them children, and I oftentimes came in late at night; so I judged he must die.

Since then I have seen perhaps a hundred or more in these mountains, but I have never intentionally disturbed them, nor have they disturbed me to any great extent, even by accident, though in danger of being stepped on. Once, while I was on my knees kindling a fire, one glided under the arch made by my arm. He was only going away from the ground I had selected for a camp, and there was not the slightest danger, because I kept still and allowed him to go in peace. The only time I felt myself in serious danger was when I was coming out of the Tuolumne Cañon by a steep side cañon toward the head of Yosemite Creek. On an earthquake talus, a boulder in my way presented a front so high that I could just reach the upper edge of it while standing on the next below it. Drawing myself up, as soon as my head was above the flat top of it I caught sight of a coiled rattler. My hands had alarmed him, and he was ready for me; but even with this provocation, and when my head came in sight within a foot of him, he did not strike. The last time I sauntered through the big cañon I saw about two a day. One was not coiled, but neatly folded in a narrow space between two cobblestones on the side of the river, his head below the level of them, ready to shoot up like a Jack-in-the-box for frogs or birds. My foot spanned the space above within an inch or two of his head, but he only held it lower. In making my way through a particularly tedious tangle of buckthorn, I parted the branches on the side of an open spot and threw my bundle of bread into it; and when, with my arms free, I was pushing through after it, I saw a small rattlesnake dragging his tail from beneath my bundle. When he caught sight of me he eyed me angrily, and with an air of righteous indignation seemed to be asking why I had thrown that stuff on him. He was so small that I was inclined to slight him, but he struck out so angrily that I drew back, and approached the opening from the other side. But he had been listening, and when I looked through the brush I found him confronting me, still with a come-in-if-you-dare expression. In vain I tried to explain that I only wanted my bread; he stoutly held the ground in front of it; so I went back a dozen rods and kept still for half an hour, and when I returned he had gone.

One evening, near sundown, in a very rough, boulder-choked portion of the cañon, I searched long for a level spot for a bed, and at last was glad to find a patch of flood-sand on the river-bank, and a lot of driftwood close by for a camp-fire. But when I threw down my bundle, I found two snakes in possession of the ground. I might have passed the night even in this snake den without danger, for I never knew a single instance of their coming into camp in the night; but fearing that, in so small a space, some late comers, not aware of my presence, might get stepped on when I was replenishing the fire, to avoid possible crowding I encamped on one of the earthquake boulders.

There are two species of Crotalus in the Park, and when I was exploring the basin of Yosemite Creek I thought I had discovered a new one. I saw a snake with curious divided appendages on its head. Going nearer, I found that the strange headgear was only the feet of a frog. Cutting a switch, I struck the snake lightly until he disgorged the poor frog, or rather allowed it to

ONE OF THE KINGS RIVER FOUNTAINS

back out. On its return to the light from one
of the very darkest of death valleys, it blinked a
moment with a sort of dazed look, then plunged
into a stream, apparently happy and well.

Frogs abound in all the bogs, marshes, pools,
and lakes, however cold and high and isolated.
How did they manage to get up these high
mountains? Surely not by jumping. Long and
dry excursions through weary miles of boulders
and brush would be trying to frogs. Most likely
their stringy spawn is carried on the feet of ducks,
cranes, and other waterbirds. Anyhow, they are
most thoroughly distributed, and flourish fa-
mously. What a cheery, hearty set they are,
and how bravely their krink and tronk concerts
enliven the rocky wilderness!

None of the high-lying mountain lakes or
branches of the rivers above sheer falls had fish
of any sort until stocked by the agency of man.
In the high Sierra, the only river in which trout
exist naturally is the middle fork of Kings River.
There are no sheer falls on this stream; some of
the rapids, however, are so swift and rough, even
at the lowest stage of water, that it is surprising
any fish can climb them. I found trout in
abundance in this fork up to seventy-five hundred
feet. They also run quite high on the Kern.
On the Merced they get no higher than Yosemite
Valley, four thousand feet, all the forks of the
river being barred there by sheer falls, and on

the main Tuolumne they are stopped by a fall
below Hetch-Hetchy, still lower than Yosemite.
Though these upper waters are inaccessible to
the fish, one would suppose their eggs might
have been planted there by some means. Nature
has so many ways of doing such things. In this
case she waited for the agency of man, and now
many of these hitherto fishless lakes and streams
are full of fine trout, stocked by individual enter-
prise, Walton clubs, etc., in great part under the
auspices of the United States Fish Commission.
A few trout carried into Hetch-Hetchy in a common water-bucket have multiplied wonderfully
fast. Lake Tenaya, at an elevation of over eight
thousand feet, was stocked eight years ago by
Mr. Murphy, who carried a few trout from Yosemite. Many of the small streams of the eastern slope have also been stocked with trout trans-
ported over the passes in tin cans on the backs
of mules. Soon, it would seem, all the streams
of the range will be enriched by these lively fish,
and will become the means of drawing thousands
of visitors into the mountains. Catching trout
with a bit of bent wire is a rather trivial business,
but fortunately people fish better than they know.
In most cases it is the man who is caught.
Trout-fishing regarded as bait for catching men,
for the saving of both body and soul, is important, and deserves all the expense and care be-
stowed on it.

CHAPTER VII

TRAVELERS in the Sierra forests usually complain of the want of life. " The trees," they say, " are fine, but the empty stillness is deadly; there are no animals to be seen, no birds. We have not heard a song in all the woods." And no wonder! They go in large parties with mules and horses; they make a great noise; they are dressed in outlandish, unnatural colors; every animal shuns them. Even the frightened pines would run away if they could. But Nature-lovers, devout, silent, open-eyed, looking and listening with love, find no lack of inhabitants in these mountain mansions, and they come to them gladly. Not to mention the large animals or the small insect people, every waterfall has its ouzel and every tree its squirrel or tamias or bird : tiny nuthatch threading the furrows of the bark, cheerily whispering to itself as it deftly pries off loose scales and examines the curled edges of lichens; or Clarke crow or jay examining the cones; or some singer — oriole, tanager, warbler — resting, feeding, attending to domestic affairs.

Hawks and eagles sail overhead, grouse walk in happy flocks below, and song sparrows sing in every bed of chaparral. There is no crowding, to be sure. Unlike the low Eastern trees, those of the Sierra in the main forest belt average nearly two hundred feet in height, and of course many birds are required to make much show in them, and many voices to fill them. Nevertheless, the whole range, from foothills to snowy summits, is shaken into song every summer; and though low and thin in winter, the music never ceases.

The sage cock (*Centrocercus urophasianus*) is the largest of the Sierra game-birds and the king of American grouse. It is an admirably strong, hardy, handsome, independent bird, able with comfort to bid defiance to heat, cold, drought, hunger, and all sorts of storms, living on whatever seeds or insects chance to come in its way, or simply on the leaves of sage-brush, everywhere abundant on its desert range. In winter, when the temperature is oftentimes below zero, and heavy snowstorms are blowing, he sits beneath a sage bush and allows himself to be covered, poking his head now and then through the snow to feed on the leaves of his shelter. Not even the Arctic ptarmigan is hardier in braving frost and snow and wintry darkness. When in full plumage he is a beautiful bird, with a long, firm, sharp-pointed tail, which in walking is slightly raised and swings sidewise back and

forth with each step. The male is handsomely
marked with black and white on the neck, back,
and wings, weighs five or six pounds, and measures about thirty inches in length. The female
is clad mostly in plain brown, and is not so large.
They occasionally wander from the sage plains
into the open nut-pine and juniper woods, but
never enter the main coniferous forest. It is
only in the broad, dry, half-desert sage plains
that they are quite at home, where the weather
is blazing hot in summer, cold in winter. If any
one passes through a flock, all squat on the gray
ground and hold their heads low, hoping to escape observation; but when approached within
a rod or so, they rise with a magnificent burst of
wing-beats, looking about as big as turkeys and
making a noise like a whirlwind.

On the 28th of June, at the head of Owen's
Valley, I caught one of the young that was then
just able to fly. It was seven inches long, of a
uniform gray color, blunt-billed, and when cap-
tured cried lustily in a shrill piping voice, clear
in tone as a boy's small willow whistle. I have
seen flocks of from ten to thirty or forty on the
east margin of the Park, where the Mono Desert
meets the gray foothills of the Sierra; but since
cattle have been pastured there they are becoming rarer every year.

Another magnificent bird, the blue or dusky
grouse, next in size to the sage cock, is found all

through the main forest belt, though not in great
numbers. They like best the heaviest silver-fir
woods near garden and meadow openings, where
there is but little underbrush to cover the approach of enemies. When a flock of these brave
birds, sauntering and feeding on the sunny, flowery levels of some hidden meadow or Yosemite
valley far back in the heart of the mountains,
see a man for the first time in their lives, they
rise with hurried notes of surprise and excitement
and alight on the lowest branches of the trees,
wondering what the wanderer may be, and showing great eagerness to get a good view of the
strange vertical animal. Knowing nothing of
guns, they allow you to approach within a half
dozen paces, then quietly hop a few branches
higher or fly to the next tree without a thought
of concealment, so that you may observe them as
long as you like, near enough to see the fine
shading of their plumage, the feathers on their
toes, and the innocent wonderment in their beautiful wild eyes. But in the neighborhood of
roads and trails they soon become shy, and when
disturbed fly into the highest, leafiest trees, and
suddenly become invisible, so well do they know
how to hide and keep still and make use of their
protective coloring. Nor can they be easily dis-
lodged ere they are ready to go. In vain the
hunter goes round and round some tall pine or
fir into which he has perhaps seen a dozen enter,

gazing up through the branches, straining his eyes while his gun is held ready; not a feather can he see unless his eyes have been sharpened by long experience and knowledge of the blue grouse's habits. Then, perhaps, when he is thinking that the tree must be hollow and that the birds have all gone inside, they burst forth with a startling whir of wing-beats, and after gaining full speed go skating swiftly away through the forest arches in a long, silent, wavering slide, with wings held steady.

During the summer they are most of the time on the ground, feeding on insects, seeds, berries, etc., around the margins of open spots and rocky moraines, playing and sauntering, taking sun baths and sand baths, and drinking at little pools and rills during the heat of the day. In winter they live mostly in the trees, depending on buds for food, sheltering beneath dense overlapping branches at night and during storms on the lee-side of the trunk, sunning themselves on the southside limbs in fine weather, and sometimes diving into the mealy snow to flutter and wallow, apparently for exercise and fun.

I have seen young broods running beneath the firs in June at a height of eight thousand feet above the sea. On the approach of danger, the mother with a peculiar cry warns the helpless midgets to scatter and hide beneath leaves and twigs, and even in plain open places it is almost impossible to discover them. In the meantime the mother feigns lameness, throws herself at your feet, kicks and gasps and flutters, to draw your attention from the chicks. The young are generally able to fly about the middle of July; but even after they can fly well they are usually advised to run and hide and lie still, no matter how closely approached, while the mother goes on with her loving, lying acting, apparently as desperately concerned for their safety as when they were featherless infants. Sometimes, however, after carefully studying the circumstances, she tells them to take wing; and up and away in a blurry birr and whir they scatter to all points of the compass, as if blown up with gunpowder, dropping cunningly out of sight three or four hundred yards off, and keeping quiet until called, after the danger is supposed to be past. If you walk on a little way without manifesting any inclination to hunt them, you may sit down at the foot of a tree near enough to see and hear the happy reunion. One touch of nature makes the whole world kin; and it is truly wonderful how love-telling the small voices of these birds are, and how far they reach through the woods into one another's hearts and into ours. The tones are so perfectly human and so full of anxious affection, few mountaineers can fail to be touched by them.

They are cared for until full grown. On the

20th of August, as I was passing along the margin of a garden spot on the head-waters of the San Joaquin, a grouse rose from the ruins of an old juniper that had been uprooted and brought down by an avalanche from a cliff overhead. She threw herself at my feet, limped and fluttered and gasped, showing, as I thought, that she had a nest and was raising a second brood. Looking for the eggs, I was surprised to see a strong-winged flock nearly as large as the mother fly up around me.

Instead of seeking a warmer climate when the winter storms set in, these hardy birds stay all the year in the high Sierra forests, and I have never known them to suffer in any sort of weather. Able to live on the buds of pine, spruce, and fir, they are forever independent in the matter of food supply, which gives so many of us trouble, dragging us here and there away from our best work. How gladly I would live on pine buds, however pitchy, for the sake of this grand independence! With all his superior resources, man makes more distracting difficulty concerning food than any other of the family.

The mountain quail, or plumed partridge (*Oreortyx pictus plumiferus*) is common in all the upper portions of the Park, though nowhere in numbers. He ranges considerably higher than the grouse in summer, but is unable to endure the heavy storms of winter. When his food is buried, he descends the range to the brushy foothills, at a height of from two thousand to three thousand feet above the sea; but like every true mountaineer, he is quick to follow the spring back into the highest mountains. I think he is the very handsomest and most interesting of all the American partridges, larger and handsomer than the famous Bob White, or even the fine California valley quail, or the Massena partridge of Arizona and Mexico. That he is not so regarded, is because as a lonely mountaineer he is not half known.

His plumage is delicately shaded, brown above, white and rich chestnut below and on the sides, with many dainty markings of black and white and gray here and there, while his beautiful head plume, three or four inches long, nearly straight, composed of two feathers closely folded so as to appear as one, is worn jauntily slanted backward like a single feather in a boy's cap, giving him a very marked appearance. They wander over the lonely mountains in family flocks of from six to fifteen, beneath ceanothus, manzanita, and wild cherry thickets, and over dry sandy flats, glacier meadows, rocky ridges, and beds of Bryanthus around glacier lakes, especially in autumn, when the berries of the upper gardens are ripe, uttering low clucking notes to enable them to keep together. When they are so suddenly disturbed that they are afraid they cannot escape the danger by running into thickets, they rise with a fine hearty whir and scatter in the brush over an area of half a square mile or so, a few of them diving into leafy trees. But as soon as the danger is past, the parents with a clear piping note call them together again. By the end of July the young are two thirds grown and fly well, though only dire necessity can compel them to try their wings. In gait, gestures, habits, and general behavior they are like domestic chickens, but infinitely finer, searching for insects and seeds, looking to this side and that, scratching among fallen leaves, jumping up to pull down grass heads, and clucking and muttering in low tones.

Once when I was seated at the foot of a tree on the head-waters of the Merced, sketching, I heard a flock up the valley behind me, and by their voices gradually sounding nearer I knew that they were feeding toward me. I kept still, hoping to see them. Soon one came within three or four feet of me, without noticing me any more than if I were a stump or a bulging part of the trunk against which I was leaning, my clothing being brown, nearly like the bark. Presently along came another and another, and it was delightful to get so near a view of these handsome chickens perfectly undisturbed, observe their manners, and hear their low peaceful notes. At last one of them caught my eye,

gazed in silent wonder for a moment, then uttered a peculiar cry, which was followed by a lot
of hurried muttered notes that sounded like
speech.   The others, of course, saw me as soon
as the alarm was sounded, and joined the wonder talk, gazing and chattering, astonished but
not frightened.   Then all with one accord ran
back with the news to the rest of the flock.
" What is it? what is it?   Oh, you never saw
the like," they seemed to be saying.   " Not a
deer, or a wolf, or a bear; come see, come see."
" Where? where? "   " Down there by that
tree."   Then they approached cautiously, past
the tree, stretching their necks, and looking up
in turn as if knowing from the story told them
just where I was.   For fifteen or twenty minutes
they kept coming and going, venturing within
a few feet of me, and discussing the wonder in
charming chatter.   Their curiosity at last satisfied, they began to scatter and feed again, going
back in the direction they had come from;
while I, loath to part with them, followed noiselessly, crawling beneath the bushes, keeping
them in sight for an hour or two, learning their
habits, and finding out what seeds and berries
they liked best.

The valley quail is not a mountaineer, and
seldom enters the Park except at a few of the
lowest places on the western boundary.   It belongs to the brushy foothills and plains, orchards

and wheatfields, and is a hundred times more numerous than the mountain quail. It is a beautiful bird, about the size of the Bob White, and has a handsome crest of four or five feathers an inch long, recurved, standing nearly erect at times or drooping forward. The loud calls of these quails in the spring — Pe-check-ah, Pe-check-a, Hoy, Hoy — are heard far and near over all the lowlands. They have vastly increased in numbers since the settlement of the country, notwithstanding the immense numbers killed every season by boys and pot-hunters as well as the regular leggined sportsmen from the towns; for man's destructive action is more than counterbalanced by increased supply of food from cultivation, and by the destruction of their enemies — coyotes, skunks, foxes, hawks, owls, etc. — which not only kill the old birds, but plunder their nests. Where coyotes and skunks abound, scarce one pair in a hundred is successful in raising a brood. So well aware are these birds of the protection afforded by man, even now that the number of their wild enemies has been greatly diminished, that they prefer to nest near houses, notwithstanding they are so shy. Four or five pairs rear their young around our cottage every spring. One year a pair nested in a straw pile within four or five feet of the stable door, and did not leave the eggs when the men led the horses back and forth within a foot or two. For many seasons a pair nested in a tuft of pampas grass in the garden ; another pair in an ivy vine on the cottage roof, and when the young were hatched, it was interesting to see the parents getting the fluffy dots down. They were greatly excited, and their anxious calls and directions to their many babes attracted our attention. They had no great difficulty in persuading the young birds to pitch themselves from the main roof to the porch roof among the ivy, but to get them safely down from the latter to the ground, a distance of ten feet, was most distressing. It seemed impossible the frail soft things could avoid being killed. The anxious parents led them to a point above a spiræa bush, that reached nearly to the eaves, which they seemed to know would break the fall. Anyhow they led their chicks to this point, and with infinite coaxing and encouragement got them to tumble themselves off. Down they rolled and sifted through the soft leaves and panicles to the pavement, and, strange to say, all got away unhurt except one that lay as if dead for a few minutes. When it revived, the joyful parents, with their brood fairly launched on the journey of life, proudly led them down the cottage hill, through the garden, and along an osage orange hedge into the cherry orchard. These charming birds even enter towns and villages, where the gardens are of good size and guns are forbidden, sometimes going several miles to feed, and returning every evening to their roosts in ivy or brushy trees and shrubs.

Geese occasionally visit the Park, but never stay long. Sometimes on their way across the range, a flock wanders into Hetch-Hetchy or Yosemite to rest or get something to eat, and if shot at, are often sorely bewildered in seeking a way out. I have seen them rise from the meadow or river, wheel round in a spiral until a height of four or five hundred feet was reached, then form ranks and try to fly over the wall. But Yosemite magnitudes seem to be as deceptive to geese as to men, for they would suddenly find themselves against the cliffs not a fourth of the way to the top. Then turning in confusion, and screaming at the strange heights, they would try the opposite side, and so on until exhausted they were compelled to rest, and only after discovering the river cañon could they make their escape. Large, harrow-shaped flocks may often be seen crossing the range in the spring, at a height of at least fourteen thousand feet. Think of the strength of wing required to sustain so heavy a bird in air so thin. At this elevation it is but little over half as dense as at the sea level. Yet they hold bravely on in beautifully dressed ranks, and have breath enough to spare for loud honking. After the crest of the Sierra is passed it is only a smooth slide down the sky to

the waters of Mono, where they may rest as long
as they like.

Ducks of five or six species, among which are
the mallard and wood duck, go far up into the
heart of the mountains in the spring, and of
course come down in the fall with the families
they have reared. A few, as if loath to leave
the mountains, pass the winter in the lower valleys of the Park at a height of three thousand to
four thousand feet, where the main streams are
never wholly frozen over, and snow never falls to
a great depth or lies long. In summer they are
found up to a height of eleven thousand feet on
all the lakes and branches of the rivers except
the smallest, and those beside the glaciers incum-
bered with drifting ice and snow. I found mal-
lards and wood ducks at Lake Tenaya, June 1,
before the ice-covering was half melted, and a
flock of young ones in Bloody Cañon Lake, June
20. They are usually met in pairs, never in large
flocks. No place is too wild or rocky or solitary
for these brave swimmers, no stream too rapid.
In the roaring, resounding cañon torrents, they
seem as much at home as in the tranquil reaches
and lakes of the broad glacial valleys. Aban-
doning themselves to the wild play of the waters,
they go drifting confidingly through blinding,
thrashing spray, dancing on boulder-dashed
waves, tossing in beautiful security on rougher
water than is usually encountered by sea birds
when storms are blowing.

A mother duck with her family of ten little ones, waltzing round and round in a pot-hole ornamented with foam bells, huge rocks leaning over them, cascades above and below and beside them, made one of the most interesting bird pictures I ever saw.

I have never found the great northern diver in the Park lakes. Most of them are inaccessible to him. He might plump down into them, but would hardly be able to get out of them, since, with his small wings and heavy body, a wide expanse of elbow room is required in rising. Now and then one may be seen in the lower Sierra lakes to the northward about Lassens Butte and Shasta, at a height of four thousand to five thousand feet, making the loneliest places lonelier with the wildest of wild cries.

Plovers are found along the sandy shores of nearly all the mountain lakes, tripping daintily on the water's edge, picking up insects; and it is interesting to learn how few of these familiar birds are required to make a solitude cheerful.

Sandhill cranes are sometimes found in comparatively small marshes, mere dots in the mighty forest. In such spots, at an elevation of from six thousand to eight thousand feet above the sea, they are occasionally met in pairs as early as the end of May, while the snow is still deep in the surrounding fir and sugar-pine woods. And on sunny days in autumn, large

flocks may be seen sailing at a great height
above the forests, shaking the crisp air into rolling waves with their hearty koor-r-r, koor-r-r,
uck-uck, soaring in circles for hours together on
their majestic wings, seeming to float without
effort like clouds, eying the wrinkled landscape
outspread like a map mottled with lakes and glaciers and meadows and streaked with shadowy
cañons and streams, and surveying every frog
marsh and sandy flat within a hundred miles.

Eagles and hawks are oftentimes seen above the
ridges and domes.   The greatest height at which
I have observed them was about twelve thousand
feet, over the summits of Mount Hoffman, in
the middle region of the Park.   A few pairs
had their nests on the cliffs of this mountain,
and could be seen every day in summer, hunting
marmots, mountain beavers, pikas, etc.   A pair
of golden eagles have made their home in Yosemite ever since I went there thirty years ago.
Their nest is on the Nevada Fall Cliff, opposite
the Liberty Cap.   Their screams are rather
pleasant to hear in the vast gulfs between the
granite cliffs, and they help the owls in keeping
the echoes busy.

But of all the birds of the high Sierra, the
strangest, noisiest, and most notable is the Clarke
crow (*Nucifraga columbiana*).   He is a foot
long and nearly two feet in extent of wing, ashy
gray in general color, with black wings, white

YOSEMITE NATIONAL PARK FROM GLACIER POINT

tail, and a strong, sharp bill, with which he digs
into the pine cones for the seeds on which he
mainly subsists. He is quick, boisterous, jerky,
and irregular in his movements and speech,
and makes a tremendously loud and showy ad-
vertisement of himself, — swooping and diving
in deep curves across gorges and valleys from
ridge to ridge, alighting on dead spars, looking
warily about him, and leaving his dry springy
perches, trembling from the vigor of his kick as
he launches himself for a new flight, screaming
from time to time loud enough to be heard more
than a mile in still weather. He dwells far back
on the high stormbeaten margin of the forest,
where the mountain pine, juniper, and hemlock
grow wide apart on glacier pavements and domes
and rough crumbling ridges, and the dwarf pine
makes a low crinkled growth along the flanks
of the Summit peaks. In so open a region, of
course, he is well seen. Everybody notices him,
and nobody at first knows what to make of him.
One guesses he must be a woodpecker; another a
crow or some sort of jay, another a magpie. He
seems to be a pretty thoroughly mixed and fer-
mented compound of all these birds, has all their
strength, cunning, shyness, thievishness, and
wary, suspicious curiosity combined and condensed. He flies like a woodpecker, hammers
dead limbs for insects, digs big holes in pine
cones to get at the seeds, cracks nuts held be-

tween his toes, cries like a crow or Stellar jay, —
but in a far louder, harsher, and more forbidding
tone of voice, — and besides his crow caws and
screams, has a great variety of small chatter talk,
mostly uttered in a fault-finding tone.   Like the
magpie, he steals articles that can be of no use to
him.   Once when I made my camp in a grove
at Cathedral Lake, I chanced to leave a cake of
soap on the shore where I had been washing, and
a few minutes afterward I saw my soap flying
past me through the grove, pushed by a Clarke
crow.

In winter, when the snow is deep, the cones of
the mountain pines are empty, and the juniper,
hemlock, and dwarf pine orchard buried, he comes
down to glean seeds in the yellow pine forests,
startling the grouse with his loud screams.   But
even in winter, in calm weather, he stays in his
high mountain home, defying the bitter frost.
Once I lay snowbound through a three days'
storm at the timber-line on Mount Shasta; and
while the roaring snow-laden blast swept by, one
of these brave birds came to my camp, and began
hammering at the cones on the topmost branches
of half-buried pines, without showing the slightest distress.   I have seen Clarke crows feeding
their young as early as June 19, at a height of
more than ten thousand feet, when nearly the
whole landscape was snow-covered.

They are excessively shy, and keep away from

the traveler as long as they think they are observed; but when one goes on without seeming
to notice them, or sits down and keeps still, their
curiosity speedily gets the better of their caution, and they come flying from tree to tree,
nearer and nearer, and watch every motion. Few,
I am afraid, will ever learn to like this bird, he is
so suspicious and self-reliant, and his voice is so
harsh that to most ears the scream of the eagle
will seem melodious compared with it. Yet the
mountaineer who has battled and suffered and
struggled must admire his strength and endurance, — the way he faces the mountain weather,
cleaves the icy blasts, cares for his young, and
digs a living from the stern wilderness.

Higher yet than Nucifraga dwells the little
dun-headed sparrow (*Leucosticte tephrocotis*).
From early spring to late autumn he is to be
found only on the snowy, icy peaks at the head
of the glacier cirques and cañons. His feeding
grounds in spring are the snow sheets between
the peaks, and in midsummer and autumn the
glaciers. Many bold insects go mountaineering
almost as soon as they are born, ascending the
highest summits on the mild breezes that blow
in from the sea every day during steady weather;
but comparatively few of these adventurers find
their way down or see a flower bed again. Getting tired and chilly, they alight on the snow
fields and glaciers, attracted perhaps by the

glare, take cold, and die. There they lie as if
on a white cloth purposely outspread for them,
and the dun sparrows find them a rich and varied
repast requiring no pursuit, — bees and butterflies on ice, and many spicy beetles, a perpetual
feast, on tables big for guests so small, and in
vast banqueting halls ventilated by cool breezes
that ruffle the feathers of the fairy brownies.
Happy fellows, no rivals come to dispute possession with them.   No other birds, not even hawks,
as far as I have noticed, live so high.   They
see people so seldom, they flutter around the explorer with the liveliest curiosity, and come down
a little way, sometimes nearly a mile, to meet him
and conduct him into their icy homes.

When I was exploring the Merced group,
climbing up the grand cañon between the Merced
and Red mountains into the fountain amphi-
theatre of an ancient glacier, just as I was approaching the small active glacier that leans back
in the shadow of Merced Mountain, a flock of
twenty or thirty of these little birds, the first I
had seen, came down the cañon to meet me, flying low, straight toward me as if they meant to
fly in my face.   Instead of attacking me or passing by, they circled round my head, chirping
and fluttering for a minute or two, then turned
and escorted me up the cañon, alighting on the
nearest rocks on either hand, and flying ahead a
few yards at a time to keep even with me.

I have not discovered their winter quarters. Probably they are in the desert ranges to the eastward, for I never saw any of them in Yosemite, the winter refuge of so many of the mountain birds.

Humming-birds are among the best and most conspicuous of the mountaineers, flashing their ruby throats in countless wild gardens far up the higher slopes, where they would be least expected. All one has to do to enjoy the company of these mountain-loving midgets is to display a showy blanket or handkerchief.

The arctic bluebird is another delightful mountaineer, singing a wild, cheery song and " carrying the sky on his back " over all the gray ridges and domes of the subalpine region.

A fine, hearty, good-natured lot of woodpeckers dwell in the Park, and keep it lively all the year round. Among the most notable of these are the magnificent log cock (*Ceophlœus pileatus*), the prince of Sierra woodpeckers, and only second in rank, as far as I know, of all the woodpeckers of the world; the Lewis woodpecker, large, black, glossy, that flaps and flies like a crow, does but little hammering, and feeds in great part on wild cherries and berries; and the carpenter, who stores up great quantities of acorns in the bark of trees for winter use. The last-named species is a beautiful bird, and far more common than the others. In the woods of the West he represents the Eastern red-head. Bright, cheerful, industrious, not in the least shy, the carpenters give delightful animation to the open Sierra forests at a height of from three thousand to fifty-five hundred feet, especially in autumn, when the acorns are ripe. Then no squirrel works harder at his pine-nut harvest than these woodpeckers at their acorn harvest, drilling holes in the thick, corky bark of the yellow pine and incense cedar, in which to store the crop for winter use, — a hole for each acorn, so nicely adjusted as to size that when the acorn, point foremost, is driven in, it fits so well that it cannot be drawn out without digging around it. Each acorn is thus carefully stored in a dry bin, perfectly protected from the weather, — a most laborious method of stowing away a crop, a granary for each kernel. Yet the birds seem never to weary at the work, but go on so diligently that they seem determined to save every acorn in the grove. They are never seen eating acorns at the time they are storing them, and it is commonly believed that they never eat them or intend to eat them, but that the wise birds store them and protect them from the depredations of squirrels and jays, solely for the sake of the worms they are supposed to contain. And because these worms are too small for use at the time the acorns drop, they are shut up like lean calves and steers, each in a

separate stall with abundance of food, to grow
big and fat by the time they will be most wanted,
that is, in winter, when insects are scarce and
stall-fed worms most valuable. So these woodpeckers are supposed to be a sort of cattle-raisers,
each with a drove of thousands, rivaling the ants
that raise grain and keep herds of plant lice
for milk cows. Needless to say the story is
not true, though some naturalists, even, believe
it. When Emerson was in the Park, having
heard the worm story and seen the great pines
plugged full of acorns, he asked (just to pump
me, I suppose), " Why do the woodpeckers take
the trouble to put acorns into the bark of the
trees ? " " For the same reason," I replied,
" that bees store honey and squirrels nuts."
" But they tell me, Mr. Muir, that woodpeckers
don't eat acorns." " Yes, they do," I said, " I
have seen them eating them. During snowstorms they seem to eat little besides acorns. I
have repeatedly interrupted them at their meals,
and seen the perfectly sound, half-eaten acorns.
They eat them in the shell as some people eat
eggs." " But what about the worms ?" " I
suppose," I said, " that when they come to a
wormy one they eat both worm and acorn.
Anyhow, they eat the sound ones when they
can't find anything they like better, and from
the time they store them until they are used they
guard them, and woe to the squirrel or jay

caught stealing." Indians, in times of scarcity, frequently resort to these stores and chop them out with hatchets; a bushel or more may be gathered from a single cedar or pine.

The common robin, with all his familiar notes and gestures, is found nearly everywhere throughout the Park, — in shady dells beneath dogwoods and maples, along the flowery banks of the streams, tripping daintily about the margins of meadows in the fir and pine woods, and far beyond on the shores of glacier lakes and the slopes of the peaks. How admirable the constitution and temper of this cheery, graceful bird, keeping glad health over so vast and varied a range. In all America he is at home, flying from plains to mountains, up and down, north and south, away and back, with the seasons and supply of food. Oftentimes in the High Sierra, as you wander through the solemn woods, awe-stricken and silent, you will hear the reassuring voice of this fellow wanderer ringing out sweet and clear as if saying, " Fear not, fear not. Only love is here." In the severest solitudes he seems as happy as in gardens and apple orchards.

The robins enter the Park as soon as the snow melts, and go on up the mountains, gradually higher, with the opening flowers, until the topmost glacier meadows are reached in June and July. After the short summer is done, they

descend like most other summer visitors in concord with the weather, keeping out of the first
heavy snows as much as possible, while lingering
among the frost-nipped wild cherries on the
slopes just below the glacier meadows. Thence
they go to the lower slopes of the forest region,
compelled to make haste at times by heavy all-
day storms, picking up seeds or benumbed insects by the way; and at last all, save a few that
winter in Yosemite valleys, arrive in the vine-
yards and orchards and stubble-fields of the lowlands in November, picking up fallen fruit and
grain, and awakening old-time memories among
the white-headed pioneers, who cannot fail to
recognize the influence of so homelike a bird.
They are then in flocks of hundreds, and make
their way into the gardens of towns as well as
into the parks and fields and orchards about the
bay of San Francisco, where many of the wanderers are shot for sport and the morsel of meat
on their breasts. Man then seems a beast of
prey. Not even genuine piety can make the
robin-killer quite respectable. Saturday is the
great slaughter day in the bay region. Then
the city pot-hunters, with a rag-tag of boys, go
forth to kill, kept in countenance by a sprinkling
of regular sportsmen arrayed in self-conscious
majesty and leggins, leading dogs and carrying
hammerless, breech-loading guns of famous
makers. Over the fine landscapes the killing

goes forward with shameful enthusiasm. After
escaping countless dangers, thousands fall, big
bagfuls are gathered, many are left wounded to
die slowly, no Red Cross Society to help them.
Next day, Sunday, the blood and leggins vanish
from the most devout of the bird-butchers, who
go to church, carrying gold-headed canes instead
of guns. After hymns, prayers, and sermon
they go home to feast, to put God's song birds
to use, put them in their dinners instead of in
their hearts, eat them, and suck the pitiful little
drumsticks. It is only race living on race, to
be sure, but Christians singing Divine Love need
not be driven to such straits while wheat and
apples grow and the shops are full of dead cattle.
Song birds for food! Compared with this, making kindlings of pianos and violins would be
pious economy.

The larks come in large flocks from the hills
and mountains in the fall, and are slaughtered
as ruthlessly as the robins. Fortunately, most
of our song birds keep back in leafy hidings,
and are comparatively inaccessible.

The water ouzel, in his rocky home amid
foaming waters, seldom sees a gun, and of all
the singers I like him the best. He is a plainly
dressed little bird, about the size of a robin, with
short, crisp, but rather broad wings, and a tail
of moderate length, slanted up, giving him, with
his nodding, bobbing manners, a wrennish look.

He is usually seen fluttering about in the spray of falls and the rapid cascading portions of the main branches of the rivers. These are his favorite haunts; but he is often seen also on comparatively level reaches and occasionally on the shores of mountain lakes, especially at the beginning of winter, when heavy snowfalls have blurred the streams with sludge. Though not a water-bird in structure, he gets his living in the water, and is never seen away from the immediate margin of streams. He dives fearlessly into rough, boiling eddies and rapids to feed at the bottom, flying under water seemingly as easily as in the air. Sometimes he wades in shallow places, thrusting his head under from time to time in a nodding, frisky way that is sure to attract attention. His flight is a solid whir of wing-beats like that of a partridge, and in going from place to place along his favorite string of rapids he follows the windings of the stream, and usually alights on some rock or snag on the bank or out in the current, or rarely on the dry limb of an overhanging tree, perching like a tree bird when it suits his convenience. He has the oddest, neatest manners imaginable, and all his gestures as he flits about in the wild, dashing waters bespeak the utmost cheerfulness and confidence. He sings both winter and summer, in all sorts of weather, — a sweet, fluty melody, rather low, and much less keen and accentuated than from the brisk vigor of his movements one would be led to expect.

How romantic and beautiful is the life of this brave little singer on the wild mountain streams, building his round bossy nest of moss by the side of a rapid or fall, where it is sprinkled and kept fresh and green by the spray ! No wonder he sings well, since all the air about him is music ; every breath he draws is part of a song, and he gets his first music lessons before he is born ; for the eggs vibrate in time with the tones of the waterfalls. Bird and stream are inseparable, songful and wild, gentle and strong, — the bird ever in danger in the midst of the stream's mad whirlpools, yet seemingly immortal. And so I might go on, writing words, words, words ; but to what purpose ? Go see him and love him, and through him as through a window look into Nature's warm heart.

CHAPTER VIII

THE FOUNTAINS AND STREAMS OF THE YOSEM-ITE NATIONAL PARK

" Come let 's to the fields, the meads, and the mountains,
The forests invite us, the streams and the fountains."
Carlyle, *Translations*, vol. iii.

THE joyful, songful streams of the Sierra are among the most famous and interesting in the world, and draw the admiring traveler on and on through their wonderful cañons, year after year, unwearied. After long wanderings with them, tracing them to their fountains, learning their history and the forms they take in their wild works and ways throughout the different seasons of the year, we may then view them together in one magnificent show, outspread over all the range like embroidery, their silvery branches interlacing on a thousand mountains, singing their way home to the sea : the small rills, with hard roads to travel, dropping from ledge to ledge, pool to pool, like chains of sweet-toned bells, slipping gently over beds of pebbles and sand, resting in lakes, shining, spangling, shimmering, lapping the shores with whispering ripples, and shaking over-

leaning bushes and grass; the larger streams
and rivers in the cañons displaying noble purity
and beauty with ungovernable energy, rushing
down smooth inclines in wide foamy sheets fold
over fold, springing up here and there in magnificent whirls, scattering crisp clashing spray for
the sunbeams to iris, bursting with hoarse rever-
berating roar through rugged gorges and boulder
dams, booming in falls, gliding, glancing with
cool soothing murmuring, through long forested
reaches richly embowered, — filling the grand
cañons with glorious song, and giving life to all
the landscape.

The present rivers of the Sierra are still young,
and have made but little mark as yet on the
grand cañons prepared for them by the ancient
glaciers. Only a very short geological time ago
they all lay buried beneath the glaciers they
drained, singing in low smothered or silvery
ringing tones in crystal channels, while the summer weather melted the ice and snow of the surface or gave showers. At first only in warm
weather was any part of these buried rivers displayed in the light of day; for as soon as frost
prevailed the surface rills vanished, though the
streams beneath the ice and in the body of it
flowed on all the year.

When, toward the close of the glacial period,
the ice mantle began to shrink and recede from
the lowlands, the lower portions of the rivers were

developed, issuing from cavelike openings on the melting margin and growing longer as the ice withdrew ; while for many a century the tributaries and upper portions of the trunks remained covered. In the fullness of time these also were set free in the sunshine, to take their places in the newborn landscapes ; each tributary with its smaller branches being gradually developed like the main trunks, as the climatic changes went on. At first all of them were muddy with glacial detritus, and they became clear only after the glaciers they drained had receded beyond lake basins in which the sediments were dropped.

This early history is clearly explained by the present rivers of southeastern Alaska. Of those draining glaciers that discharge into arms of the sea, only the rills on the surface of the ice, and upboiling, eddying, turbid currents in the tide water in front of the terminal ice wall, are visible. Where glaciers, in the first stage of decadence, have receded from the shore, short sections of the trunks of the rivers that are to take their places may be seen rushing out from caverns and tunnels in the melting front, — rough, roaring, detritus-laden torrents, foaming and tumbling over outspread terminal moraines to the sea, perhaps without a single bush or flower to brighten their raw, shifting banks. Again, in some of the warmer cañons and valleys from which the trunk glaciers have been melted, the

main trunks of the rivers are well developed, and
their banks planted with fine forests, while their
upper branches, lying high on the snowy mountains, are still buried beneath shrinking residual
glaciers ; illustrating every stage of development,
from icy darkness to light, and from muddiness
to crystal clearness.

Now that the hard grinding sculpture work of
the glacial period is done, the whole bright band
of Sierra rivers run clear all the year, except when
the snow is melting fast in the warm spring
weather, and during extraordinary winter floods
and the heavy thunderstorms of summer called
cloud-bursts.   Even then they are not muddy
above the foothill mining region, unless the moraines have been loosened and the vegetation destroyed by sheep ; for the rocks of the upper
basins are clean, and the most able streams find
but little to carry save the spoils of the forests,
— trees, branches, flakes of bark, cones, leaves,
pollen dust, etc., — with scales of mica, sand
grains, and boulders, which are rolled along the
bottom of the steep parts of the main channels.
Short sections of a few of the highest tributaries
heading in glaciers are of course turbid with
finely ground rock mud, but this is dropped in
the first lakes they enter.

On the northern part of the range, mantled
with porous fissured volcanic rocks, the fountain
waters sink and flow below the surface for con-

siderable distances, groping their way in the
dark like the draining streams of glaciers, and
at last bursting forth in big generous springs,
filtered and cool and exquisitely clear. Some of
the largest look like lakes, their waters welling
straight up from the bottom of deep rock basins
in quiet massive volume giving rise to young
rivers. Others issue from horizontal clefts in
sheer bluffs, with loud tumultuous roaring that
may be heard half a mile or more. Magnificent
examples of these great northern spring fountains, twenty or thirty feet deep and ten to
nearly a hundred yards wide, abound on the
main branches of the Feather, Pitt, McCloud,
and Fall rivers.

The springs of the Yosemite Park, and the
high Sierra in general, though many times more
numerous, are comparatively small, oozing from
moraines and snowbanks in thin, flat irregular
currents which remain on the surface or near it,
the rocks of the south half of the range being
mostly flawless impervious granite ; and since
granite is but slightly soluble, the streams are
particularly pure. Nevertheless, though they
are all clear, and in the upper and main central
forest regions delightfully lively and cool, they
vary somewhat in color and taste as well as temperature, on account of differences, however
slight, in exposure, and in the rocks and vegetation with which they come in contact. Some

are more exposed than others to winds and sunshine in their falls and thin plumelike cascades;
the amount of dashing, mixing, and airing the
waters of each receive varies considerably; and
there is always more or less variety in the kind
and quantity of the vegetation they flow through,
and in the time they lie in shady or sunny lakes
and bogs.

The water of one of the branches of the north
fork of Owens River, near the southeastern boundary of the Park, at an elevation of ninety-five
hundred feet above the sea, is the best I ever
found. It is not only delightfully cool and
bright, but brisk, sparkling, exhilarating, and so
positively delicious to the taste that a party of
friends I led to it twenty-five years ago still
praise it, and refer to it as " that wonderful
champagne water;" though, comparatively, the
finest wine is a coarse and vulgar drink. The
party camped about a week in a pine grove on
the edge of a little round sedgy meadow through
which the stream ran bank full, and drank its
icy water on frosty mornings, before breakfast,
and at night about as eagerly as in the heat of
the day; lying down and taking massy draughts
direct from the brimming flood, lest the touch
of a cup might disturb its celestial flavor. On
one of my excursions I took pains to trace this
stream to its head springs. It is mostly derived
from snow that lies in heavy drifts and avalanche

heaps on or near the axis of the range. It flows
first in flat sheets over coarse sand or shingle
derived from a granite ridge and the metamor-
phic slates of Red Mountain. Then, gathering
its many small branches, it runs through beds of
moraine material, and a series of lakelets and
meadows and frosty juicy bogs bordered with
heathworts and linked together by short bouldery reaches. Below these, growing strong with
tribute drawn from many a snowy fountain on
either side, the glad stream goes dashing and
swirling through clumps of the white-barked
pine, and tangled willow and alder thickets enriched by the fragrant herbaceous vegetation
usually found about them. And just above the
level camp meadow it is chafed and churned and
beaten white over and over again in crossing a
talus of big earthquake boulders, giving it a
very thorough airing. But to what the peculiar
indefinable excellence of this water is due I don't
know; for other streams in adjacent cañons are
aired in about the same way, and draw traces of
minerals and plant essences from similar sources.
The best mineral water yet discovered in the
Park flows from the Tuolumne soda springs,
on the north side of the Big Meadow. Mountaineers like it and ascribe every healing virtue
to it, but in no way can any of these waters be
compared with the Owens River champagne.

It is a curious fact that the waters of some

of the Sierra lakes and streams are invisible,
or nearly so, under certain weather conditions.
This is noticed by mountaineers, hunters, and
prospectors, wide-awake, sharp-eyed observers,
little likely to be fooled by fine whims. One of
these mountain men, whom I had nursed while a
broken leg was mending, always gratefully reported the wonders he found. Once, returning
from a trip on the head waters of the Tuolumne,
he came running eagerly, crying: "Muir, I've
found the queerest lake in the mountains! It's
high up where nothing grows; and when it isn't
shiny you can't see it, and you walk right into it
as if there was nothing there. The first you
know of that lake you are in it, and get tripped
up by the water, and hear the splash." The
waters of Illilouette Creek are nearly invisible in
the autumn; so that, in following the channel,
jumping from boulder to boulder after a shower,
you will frequently drag your feet in the apparently surfaceless pools.

Excepting a few low, warm slopes, fountain
snow usually covers all the Yosemite Park from
November or December to May, most of it until
June or July, while on the coolest parts of the
north slopes of the mountains, at a height of
eleven to thirteen thousand feet, it is perpetual.
It seldom lies at a greater depth than two or
three feet on the lower margin, ten feet over the
middle forested region, or fifteen to twenty feet

in the shadowy cañons and cirques among the peaks of the Summit, except where it is drifted, or piled in avalanche heaps at the foot of long converging slopes to form perennial fountains.

The first crop of snow crystals that whitens the mountains and refreshes the streams usually falls in September or October, in the midst of charming Indian summer weather, often while the goldenrods and gentians are in their prime; but these Indian summer snows, like some of the late ones that bury the June gardens, vanish in a day or two, and garden work goes on with accelerated speed. The grand winter storms that load the mountains with enduring fountain snow seldom set in before the end of November. The fertile clouds, descending, glide about and hover in brooding silence, as if thoughtfully examining the forests and streams with reference to the work before them; then small flakes or single crystals appear, glinting and swirling in zigzags and spirals; and soon the thronging feathery masses fill the sky and make darkness like night, hurrying wandering mountaineers to their winter quarters. The first fall is usually about two to four feet deep. Then, with intervals of bright weather, not very cold, storm succeeds storm, heaping snow on snow, until from thirty to fifty or sixty feet has fallen; but on account of heavy settling and compacting, and the waste from evaporation and melting, the depth in the middle region, as stated above, rarely exceeds ten feet. Evaporation never wholly ceases, even in the coldest weather, and the sunshine between storms melts the surface more or less. Waste from melting also goes on at the bottom from summer heat stored in the rocks, as is shown by the rise of the streams after the first general storm, and their steady sustained flow all winter.

In the deep sugar-pine and silver-fir woods, up to a height of eight thousand feet, most of the snow lies where it falls, in one smooth universal fountain, until set free in the streams. But in the lighter forests of the two-leaved pine, and on the bleak slopes above the timber line, there is much wild drifting during storms accompanied by high winds, and for a day or two after they have fallen, when the temperature is low, and the snow dry and dusty. Then the trees, bending in the darkening blast, roar like feeding lions; the frozen lakes are buried; so also are the streams, which now flow in dark tunnels, as if another glacial period had come. On high ridges, where the winds have a free sweep, magnificent over-curling cornices are formed, which, with the avalanche piles, last as fountains almost all summer; and when an exceptionally high wind is blowing from the north, the snow, rolled, drifted, and ground to dust, is driven up the converging northern slopes of the peaks and sent flying for miles in the form of bright wavering banners,

YOSEMITE WOODS

displayed in wonderful clearness and beauty against the sky.

The greatest storms, however, are usually followed by a deep, peculiar silence, especially profound and solemn in the forests; and the noble trees stand hushed and motionless, as if under a spell, until the morning sunbeams begin to sift through their laden spires. Then the snow, shifting and falling from the top branches, strikes the lower ones in succession, and dislodges bossy masses all the way down. Thus each tree is enveloped in a hollow conical avalanche of fairy fineness, silvery white, irised on the outside; while the relieved branches spring up and wave with startling effect in the general stillness, as if moving of their own volition. These beautiful tree avalanches, hundreds of which may be seen falling at once on fine mornings after storms, pile their snow in raised rings around corresponding hollows beneath the trees, making the forest mantle somewhat irregular, but without greatly influencing its duration and the flow of the streams.

The large storm avalanches are most abundant on the Summit peaks of the range. They descend the broad, steep slopes, as well as narrow gorges and couloirs, with grand roaring and booming, and glide in graceful curves out on the glaciers they so bountifully feed.

Down in the main cañons of the middle region

broad masses are launched over the brows of cliffs three or four thousand feet high, which, worn to dust by friction in falling so far through the air, oftentimes hang for a minute or two in front of the tremendous precipices like gauzy half-transparent veils, gloriously beautiful when the sun is shining through them. Most of the cañon avalanches, however, flow in regular channels, like the cascades of tributary streams. When the snow first gives way on the upper slopes of their basins a dull muffled rush and rumble is heard, which, increasing with heavy deliberation, seems to draw rapidly nearer with appalling intensity of tone. Presently the wild flood comes in sight, bounding out over bosses and sheer places, leaping from bench to bench, spreading and narrowing and throwing off clouds of whirling diamond dust like a majestic foamy cataract. Compared with cascades and falls, avalanches are short-lived, and the sharp clashing sounds so common in dashing water are usually wanting; but in their deep thunder tones and pearly purple-tinged whiteness, and in dress, gait, gestures, and general behavior, they are much alike.

Besides these common storm avalanches there are two other kinds, the annual and the century, which still further enrich the scenery, though their influence on fountains is comparatively small. Annual avalanches are composed of heavy com-

pacted snow which has been subjected to frequent
alternations of frost and thaw. They are developed on cañon and mountain sides, the greater
number of them, at elevations of from nine to
ten thousand feet, where the slopes are so inclined that the dry snows of winter accumulate
and hold fast until the spring thaws sap their
foundations and make them slippery. Then away
in grand style go the ponderous icy masses,
adorned with crystalline spray without any
cloudy snow dust; some of the largest descending more than a mile with even, sustained energy
and directness like thunderbolts. The grand century avalanches, that mow wide swaths through
the upper forests, occur on shady mountain sides
about ten to twelve thousand feet high, where,
under ordinary conditions, the snow accumulated
from winter to winter lies at rest for many years,
allowing trees fifty to a hundred feet high to
grow undisturbed on the slopes below them. On
their way through the forests they usually make
a clean sweep, stripping off the soil as well as the
trees, clearing paths two or three hundred yards
wide from the timber line to the glacier meadows,
and piling the uprooted trees, head downward,
in windrows along the sides like lateral moraines.
Scars and broken branches on the standing trees
bordering the gaps record the side depth of the
overwhelming flood; and when we come to count
the annual wood rings of the uprooted trees, we

learn that some of these colossal avalanches occur only once in about a century, or even at still wider intervals.

Few mountaineers go far enough, during the snowy months, to see many avalanches, and fewer still know the thrilling exhilaration of riding on them. In all my wild mountaineering I have enjoyed only one avalanche ride; and the start was so sudden, and the end came so soon, I thought but little of the danger that goes with this sort of travel, though one thinks fast at such times. One calm, bright morning in Yosemite, after a hearty storm had given three or four feet of fresh snow to the mountains, being eager to see as many avalanches as possible, and gain wide views of the peaks and forests arrayed in their new robes, before the sunshine had time to change or rearrange them, I set out early to climb by a side cañon to the top of a commanding ridge a little over three thousand feet above the valley. On account of the looseness of the snow that blocked the cañon I knew the climb would be trying, and estimated it might require three or four hours. But it proved far more difficult than I had foreseen. Most of the way I sank waist-deep, in some places almost out of sight; and after spending the day to within half an hour of sundown in this loose, baffling snow work, I was still several hundred feet below the summit. Then my hopes were reduced to get-

ting up in time for the sunset, and a quick,
sparkling home-going beneath the stars.   But I
was not to get top views of any sort that day ;
for deep trampling near the cañon head, where
the snow was strained, started an avalanche, and
I was swished back down to the foot of the
cañon as if by enchantment.   The plodding,
wallowing ascent of about a mile had taken all
day, the undoing descent perhaps a minute.
When the snow suddenly gave way, I instinctively threw myself on my back and spread my
arms, to try to keep from sinking.   Fortunately,
though the grade of the cañon was steep, it was
not interrupted by step levels or precipices big
enough to cause outbounding or free plunging.
On no part of the rush was I buried.   I was only
moderately imbedded on the surface or a little
below it, and covered with a hissing back-stream-
ing veil of dusty snow particles ; and as the
whole mass beneath or about me joined in the
flight I felt no friction, though tossed here and
there, and lurched from side to side.   And when
the torrent swedged and came to rest, I found
myself on the top of the crumpled pile, without
a single bruise or scar.   Hawthorne says that
steam has spiritualized travel, notwithstanding
the smoke, friction, smells, and clatter of boat
and rail riding.   This flight in a milky way of
snow flowers was the most spiritual of all my
travels ; and, after many years, the mere thought
of it is still an exhilaration.

In the spring, after all the avalanches are down and the snow is melting fast, it is glorious to hear the streams sing out on the mountains. Every fountain swelling, countless rills hurry together to the rivers at the call of the sun, — beginning to run and sing soon after sunrise, increasing until toward sundown, then gradually failing through the cold frosty hours of the night. Thus the volume of the upper rivers, even in flood time, is nearly doubled during the day, rising and falling as regularly as the tides of the sea. At the height of flood, in the warmest June weather, they seem fairly to shout for joy, and clash their upleaping waters together like clapping of hands; racing down the cañons with white manes flying in glorious exuberance of strength, compelling huge sleeping boulders to wake up and join in the dance and song to swell their chorus.

Then the plants also are in flood; the hidden sap singing into leaf and flower, responding as faithfully to the call of the sun as the streams from the snow, gathering along the outspread roots like rills in their channels on the mountains, rushing up the stems of herb and tree, swirling in their myriad cells like streams in potholes, spreading along the branches and breaking into foamy bloom, while fragrance, like a finer music, rises and flows with the winds.

About the same may be said of the spring

gladness of blood when the red streams surge and sing in accord with the swelling plants and rivers, inclining animals and everybody to travel in hurrahing crowds like floods, while exhilarating melody in color and fragrance, form and motion, flows to the heart through all the quickening senses.

In early summer the streams are in bright prime, running crystal clear, deep and full, but not overflowing their banks, — about as deep through the night as the day, the variation so marked in spring being now too slight to be noticed. Nearly all the weather is cloudless sunshine, and everything is at its brightest, — lake, river, garden, and forest, with all their warm, throbbing life. Most of the plants are in full leaf and flower; the blessed ousels have built their mossy huts, and are now singing their sweetest songs on spray-sprinkled ledges beside the waterfalls.

In tranquil, mellow autumn, when the year's work is about done, when the fruits are ripe, birds and seeds out of their nests, and all the landscape is glowing like a benevolent countenance at rest, then the streams are at their lowest ebb, — their wild rejoicing soothed to thoughtful calm. All the smaller tributaries whose branches do not reach back to the perennial fountains of the Summit peaks shrink to whispering, tinkling currents. The snow of their

basins gone, they are now fed only by small moraine springs, whose waters are mostly evaporated in passing over warm pavements, and in
feeling their way from pool to pool through the
midst of boulders and sand. Even the main
streams are so low they may be easily forded,
and their grand falls and cascades, now gentle
and approachable, have waned to sheets and webs
of embroidery, falling fold over fold in new and
ever changing beauty.

Two of the most songful of the rivers, the
Tuolumne and Merced, water nearly all the Park,
spreading their branches far and wide, like broad-
headed oaks ; and the highest branches of each
draw their sources from one and the same fountain on Mount Lyell, at an elevation of about
thirteen thousand feet above the sea. The crest
of the mountain, against which the head of the
glacier rests, is worn to a thin blade full of joints,
through which a part of the glacial water flows
southward, giving rise to the highest trickling
affluents of the Merced ; while the main drainage, flowing northward, gives rise to those of the
Tuolumne. After diverging for a distance of
ten or twelve miles, these twin rivers flow in a
general westerly direction, descending rapidly
for the first thirty miles, and rushing in glorious
apron cascades and falls from one Yosemite valley
to another. Below the Yosemites they descend
in gray rapids and swirling, swaying reaches,

TUOLUMNE CASCADE, YOSEMITE

through the chaparral-clad cañons of the foothills and across the golden California plain, to
their confluence with the San Joaquin, where,
after all their long wanderings, they are only
about ten miles apart.

The main cañons are from fifty to seventy
miles long, and from two to four thousand feet
deep, carved in the solid flank of the range.
Though rough in some places and hard to travel,
they are the most delightful of roads, leading
through the grandest scenery, full of life and
motion, and offering most telling lessons in earth
sculpture. The walls, far from being unbroken,
featureless cliffs, seem like ranges of separate
mountains, so deep and varied is their sculpture; rising in lordly domes, towers, round-
browed outstanding headlands, and clustering
spires, with dark, shadowy side cañons between.
But, however wonderful in height and mass and
fineness of finish, no anomalous curiosities are
presented, no "freaks of nature."   All stand
related in delicate rhythm, a grand glacial rock
song.

Among the most interesting and influential
of the secondary features of cañon scenery are
the great avalanche taluses, that lean against the
walls at intervals of a mile or two.   In the middle Yosemite region they are usually from three
to five hundred feet high, and are made up of
huge, angular, well-preserved, unshifting boul-

ders, overgrown with gray lichens, trees, shrubs, and delicate flowering plants. Some of the largest of the boulders are forty or fifty feet cube, weighing from five to ten thousand tons ; and where the cleavage joints of the granite are exceptionally wide apart a few blocks may be found nearly a hundred feet in diameter. These wonderful boulder piles are distributed throughout all the cañons of the range, completely choking them in some of the narrower portions, and no mountaineer will be likely to forget the savage roughness of the roads they make. Even the swift, overbearing rivers, accustomed to sweep everything out of their way, are in some places bridled and held in check by them. Foaming, roaring, in glorious majesty of flood, rushing off long rumbling trains of ponderous blocks without apparent effort, they are not able to move the largest, which, withstanding all assaults for centuries, are left at rest in the channels like islands, with gardens on their tops, fringed with foam below, with flowers above.

On some points concerning the origin of these taluses I was long in doubt. Plainly enough they were derived from the cliffs above them, the size of each talus being approximately measured by a scar on the wall, the rough angular surface of which contrasts with the rounded, glaciated, unfractured parts. I saw also that, instead of being slowly accumulated material,

weathered off, boulder by boulder, in the ordinary way, almost every talus had been formed
suddenly, in a single avalanche, and had not been
increased in size during the last three or four
centuries; for trees three or four hundred years
old were growing on them, some standing at the
top close to the wall, without a bruise or broken
branch, showing that scarcely a single boulder
had fallen among them since they were planted.
Furthermore, all the taluses throughout the range
seemed, by the trees and lichens growing on
them, to be of the same age. All the phenomena
pointed straight to a grand ancient earthquake.
But I left the question open for years, and went on
from cañon to cañon, observing again and again;
measuring the heights of taluses throughout
the range on both flanks, and the variations in
the angles of their surface slopes; studying the
way their boulders were assorted and related
and brought to rest, and the cleavage joints of
the cliffs from whence they were derived, cautious
about making up my mind. Only after I had
seen one made did all doubt as to their formation
vanish.

In Yosemite Valley, one morning about two
o'clock, I was aroused by an earthquake; and
though I had never before enjoyed a storm of this
sort, the strange, wild thrilling motion and rumbling could not be mistaken, and I ran out of my
cabin, near the Sentinel Rock, both glad and

frightened, shouting, " A noble earthquake! "
feeling sure I was going to learn something.
The shocks were so violent and varied, and succeeded one another so closely, one had to balance
in walking as if on the deck of a ship among the
waves, and it seemed impossible the high cliffs
should escape being shattered.   In particular, I
feared that the sheer-fronted Sentinel Rock,
which rises to a height of three thousand feet,
would be shaken down, and I took shelter back
of a big pine, hoping I might be protected from
outbounding boulders, should any come so far.
I was now convinced that an earthquake had
been the maker of the taluses, and positive
proof soon came. It was a calm moonlight night,
and no sound was heard for the first minute or
two save a low muffled underground rumbling
and a slight rustling of the agitated trees, as if,
in wrestling with the mountains, Nature were
holding her breath.   Then, suddenly, out of the
strange silence and strange motion there came a
tremendous roar.   The Eagle Rock, a short distance up the valley, had given way, and I saw it
falling in thousands of the great boulders I had
been studying so long, pouring to the valley
floor in a free curve luminous from friction,
making a terribly sublime and beautiful spectacle, — an arc of fire fifteen hundred feet span,
as true in form and as steady as a rainbow, in the
midst of the stupendous roaring rock storm.   The

sound was inconceivably deep and broad and earnest, as if the whole earth, like a living creature, had at last found a voice and were calling to her sister planets. It seemed to me that if all the thunder I ever heard were condensed into one roar it would not equal this rock roar at the birth of a mountain talus. Think, then, of the roar that arose to heaven when all the thousands of ancient cañon taluses throughout the length and breadth of the range were simultaneously given birth.

The main storm was soon over, and, eager to see the new-born talus, I ran up the valley in the moonlight and climbed it before the huge blocks, after their wild fiery flight, had come to complete rest. They were slowly settling into their places, chafing, grating against one another, groaning, and whispering; but no motion was visible except in a stream of small fragments pattering down the face of the cliff at the head of the talus. A cloud of dust particles, the smallest of the boulders, floated out across the whole breadth of the valley and formed a ceiling that lasted until after sunrise; and the air was loaded with the odor of crushed Douglas spruces, from a grove that had been mowed down and mashed like weeds.

Sauntering about to see what other changes had been made, I found the Indians in the middle of the valley, terribly frightened, of course, fear-

ing the angry spirits of the rocks were trying to
kill them.   The few whites wintering in the valley were assembled in front of the old Hutchings
Hotel, comparing notes and meditating flight to
steadier ground, seemingly as sorely frightened as
the Indians.   It is always interesting to see people
in dead earnest, from whatever cause, and earthquakes make everybody earnest.   Shortly after
sunrise, a low blunt muffled rumbling, like distant
thunder, was followed by another series of
shocks, which, though not nearly so severe as
the first, made the cliffs and domes tremble like
jelly, and the big pines and oaks thrill and swish
and wave their branches with startling effect.
Then the groups of talkers were suddenly hushed,
and the solemnity on their faces was sublime.
One in particular of these winter neighbors, a
rather thoughtful, speculative man, with whom I
had often conversed, was a firm believer in the
cataclysmic origin of the valley; and I now
jokingly remarked that his wild tumble-down-
and-engulfment hypothesis might soon be proved,
since these underground rumblings and shakings
might be the forerunners of another Yosemite-
making cataclysm, which would perhaps double
the depth of the valley by swallowing the floor,
leaving the ends of the wagon roads and trails
three or four thousand feet in the air.   Just then
came the second series of shocks, and it was fine
to see how awfully silent and solemn he became.

His belief in the existence of a mysterious abyss, into which the suspended floor of the valley and all the domes and battlements of the walls might at any moment go roaring down, mightily troubled him. To cheer and tease him into another view of the case, I said : " Come, cheer up ; smile a little and clap your hands, now that kind Mother Earth is trotting us on her knee to amuse us and make us good." But the well-meant joke seemed irreverent and utterly failed, as if only prayerful terror could rightly belong to the wild beauty-making business. Even after all the heavier shocks were over, I could do nothing to reassure him. On the contrary, he handed me the keys of his little store, and, with a companion of like mind, fled to the lowlands. In about a month he returned ; but a sharp shock occurred that very day, which sent him flying again.

The rocks trembled more or less every day for over two months, and I kept a bucket of water on my table to learn what I could of the movements. The blunt thunder-tones in the depths of the mountains were usually followed by sudden jarring, horizontal thrusts from the northward, often succeeded by twisting, upjolting movements. Judging by its effects, this Yosemite, or Inyo earthquake, as it is sometimes called, was gentle as compared with the one that gave rise to the grand talus system of the range and did so much

for the cañon scenery.   Nature, usually so delib-
erate in her operations, then created, as we have
seen, a new set of features, simply by giving the
mountains a shake, — changing not only the high
peaks and cliffs, but the streams.   As soon as
these rock avalanches fell every stream began to
sing new songs ; for in many places thousands of
boulders were hurled into their channels, roughening and half damming them, compelling the
waters to surge and roar in rapids where before
they were gliding smoothly.   Some of the streams
were completely dammed, driftwood, leaves, etc.,
filling the interstices between the boulders, thus
giving rise to lakes and level reaches ; and these,
again, after being gradually filled in, to smooth
meadows, through which the streams now silently
meander ; while at the same time some of the
taluses took the places of old meadows and groves.
Thus rough places were made smooth, and smooth
places rough.   But on the whole, by what at
first sight seemed pure confusion and ruin, the
landscapes were enriched ; for gradually every
talus, however big the boulders composing it,
was covered with groves and gardens, and made
a finely proportioned and ornamental base for the
sheer cliffs.   In this beauty work, every boulder
is prepared and measured and put in its place
more thoughtfully than are the stones of temples.
If for a moment you are inclined to regard these
taluses as mere draggled, chaotic dumps, climb

to the top of one of them, tie your mountain
shoes firmly over the instep, and with braced
nerves run down without any haggling, puttering
hesitation, boldly jumping from boulder to boulder with even speed. You will then find your
feet playing a tune, and quickly discover the
music and poetry of rock piles, — a fine lesson ;
and all nature's wildness tells the same story.
Storms of every sort, torrents, earthquakes, cataclysms, " convulsions of nature," etc., however
mysterious and lawless at first sight they may
seem, are only harmonious notes in the song of
creation, varied expressions of God's love.

CHAPTER IX

THE SEQUOIA AND GENERAL GRANT NATIONAL PARKS

THE Big Tree (*Sequoia gigantea*) is Nature's forest masterpiece, and, so far as I know, the greatest of living things. It belongs to an ancient stock, as its remains in old rocks show, and has a strange air of other days about it, a thoroughbred look inherited from the long ago — the auld lang syne of trees. Once the genus was common, and with many species flourished in the now desolate Arctic regions, in the interior of North America, and in Europe, but in long, eventful wanderings from climate to climate only two species have survived the hardships they had to encounter, the gigantea and sempervirens, the former now restricted to the western slopes of the Sierra, the other to the Coast Mountains, and both to California, excepting a few groves of Redwood which extend into Oregon. The Pacific Coast in general is the paradise of conifers. Here nearly all of them are giants, and display a beauty and magnificence unknown elsewhere. The climate is mild, the ground never freezes,

and moisture and sunshine abound all the
year.   Nevertheless it is not easy to account for
the colossal size of the Sequoias.   The largest
are about three hundred feet high and thirty feet
in diameter.   Who of all the dwellers of the
plains and prairies and fertile home forests of
round-headed oak and maple, hickory and elm,
ever dreamed that earth could bear such growths,
— trees that the familiar pines and firs seem to
know nothing about, lonely, silent, serene, with
a physiognomy almost godlike; and so old, thousands of them still living had already counted
their years by tens of centuries when Columbus
set sail from Spain and were in the vigor of youth
or middle age when the star led the Chaldean
sages to the infant Saviour's cradle!   As far as
man is concerned they are the same yesterday,
to-day, and forever, emblems of permanence.

No description can give any adequate idea of
their singular majesty, much less of their beauty.
Excepting the sugar-pine, most of their neighbors with pointed tops seem to be forever shouting Excelsior, while the Big Tree, though soaring
above them all, seems satisfied, its rounded head,
poised lightly as a cloud, giving no impression
of trying to go higher.   Only in youth does it
show like other conifers a heavenward yearning,
keenly aspiring with a long quick-growing top.
Indeed the whole tree for the first century or two,
or until a hundred to a hundred and fifty feet

high, is arrowhead in form, and, compared with
the solemn rigidity of age, is as sensitive to the
wind as a squirrel tail.   The lower branches are
gradually dropped as it grows older, and the
upper ones thinned out until comparatively few
are left.   These, however, are developed to great
size, divide again and again, and terminate in
bossy rounded masses of leafy branchlets, while
the head becomes dome-shaped.   Then poised in
fullness of strength and beauty, stern and solemn
in mien, it glows with eager, enthusiastic life,
quivering to the tip of every leaf and branch
and far-reaching root, calm as a granite dome,
the first to feel the touch of the rosy beams of
the morning, the last to bid the sun good-night.

Perfect specimens, unhurt by running fires or
lightning, are singularly regular and symmetrical
in general form, though not at all conventional,
showing infinite variety in sure unity and harmony of plan.   The immensely strong, stately
shafts, with rich purplish brown bark, are free of
limbs for a hundred and fifty feet or so, though
dense tufts of sprays occur here and there, producing an ornamental effect, while long parallel
furrows give a fluted columnar appearance.   It
shoots forth its limbs with equal boldness in every
direction, showing no weather side.   On the old
trees the main branches are crooked and rugged,
and strike rigidly outward mostly at right angles
from the trunk, but there is always a certain

measured restraint in their reach which keeps
them within bounds. No other Sierra tree has
foliage so densely massed or outline so finely,
firmly drawn and so obediently subordinate to
an ideal type. A particularly knotty, angular,
ungovernable-looking branch, five to eight feet in
diameter and perhaps a thousand years old, may
occasionally be seen pushing out from the trunk
as if determined to break across the bounds of the
regular curve, but like all the others, as soon as the
general outline is approached the huge limb dissolves into massy bosses of branchlets and sprays,
as if the tree were growing beneath an invisible
bell glass against the sides of which the branches
were moulded, while many small, varied depar-
tures from the ideal form give the impression of
freedom to grow as they like.

Except in picturesque old age, after being
struck by lightning and broken by a thousand
snowstorms, this regularity of form is one of the
Big Tree's most distinguishing characteristics.
Another is the simple sculptural beauty of the
trunk and its great thickness as compared with its
height and the width of the branches, many of
them being from eight to ten feet in diameter at a
height of two hundred feet from the ground, and
seeming more like finely modeled and sculptured
architectural columns than the stems of trees,
while the great strong limbs are like rafters sup-
porting the magnificent dome head.

The root system corresponds in magnitude with the other dimensions of the tree, forming a flat far-reaching spongy network two hundred feet or more in width without any taproot, and the instep is so grand and fine, so suggestive of endless strength, it is long ere the eye is released to look above it. The natural swell of the roots, though at first sight excessive, gives rise to buttresses no greater than are required for beauty as well as strength, as at once appears when you stand back far enough to see the whole tree in its true proportions.   The fineness of the taper of the trunk is shown by its thickness at great heights — a diameter of ten feet at a height of two hundred being, as we have seen, not uncommon.   Indeed the boles of but few trees hold their thickness as well as Sequoia.   Resolute, consummate, determined in form, always beheld with wondering admiration, the Big Tree always seems unfamiliar, standing alone, unrelated, with peculiar physiognomy, awfully solemn and earnest.   Nevertheless, there is nothing alien in its looks.   The Madrona, clad in thin, smooth, red and yellow bark and big glossy leaves, seems, in the dark coniferous forests of Washington and Vancouver Island, like some lost wanderer from the magnolia groves of the South, while the Sequoia, with all its strangeness, seems more at home than any of its neighbors, holding the best right to the ground as the oldest, strong-

est inhabitant. One soon becomes acquainted
with new species of pine and fir and spruce as
with friendly people, shaking their outstretched
branches like shaking hands, and fondling their
beautiful little ones ; while the venerable aboriginal Sequoia, ancient of other days, keeps you
at a distance, taking no notice of you, speaking
only to the winds, thinking only of the sky,
looking as strange in aspect and behavior among
the neighboring trees as would the mastodon or
hairy elephant among the homely bears and deer.
Only the Sierra Juniper is at all like it, standing rigid and unconquerable on glacial pavements for thousands of years, grim, rusty, silent,
uncommunicative, with an air of antiquity about
as pronounced as that so characteristic of Sequoia.

The bark of full grown trees is from one to
two feet thick, rich cinnamon brown, purplish on
young trees and shady parts of the old, forming
magnificent masses of color with the underbrush
and beds of flowers. Toward the end of winter
the trees themselves bloom while the snow is
still eight or ten feet deep. The pistillate
flowers are about three eighths of an inch long,
pale green, and grow in countless thousands
on the ends of the sprays. The staminate are
still more abundant, pale yellow, a fourth of an
inch long; and when the golden pollen is ripe
they color the whole tree and dust the air and
the ground far and near.

The cones are bright grass-green in color, about two and a half inches long, one and a half wide, and are made up of thirty or forty strong, closely packed, rhomboidal scales with four to eight seeds at the base of each. The seeds are extremely small and light, being only from an eighth to a fourth of an inch long and wide, including a filmy surrounding wing, which causes them to glint and waver in falling and enables the wind to carry them considerable distances from the tree.

The faint lisp of snowflakes as they alight is one of the smallest sounds mortal can hear. The sound of falling Sequoia seeds, even when they happen to strike on flat leaves or flakes of bark, is about as faint. Very different is the bumping and thudding of the falling cones. Most of them are cut off by the Douglas squirrel and stored for the sake of the seeds, small as they are. In the calm Indian summer these busy harvesters with ivory sickles go to work early in the morning, as soon as breakfast is over, and nearly all day the ripe cones fall in a steady pattering, bumping shower. Unless harvested in this way they discharge their seeds and remain on the trees for many years. In fruitful seasons the trees are fairly laden. On two small specimen branches one and a half and two inches in diameter I counted four hundred and eighty cones. No other California conifer produces nearly so many

seeds, excepting perhaps its relative, the Redwood of the Coast Mountains. Millions are
ripened annually by a single tree, and the product
of one of the main groves in a fruitful year would
suffice to plant all the mountain ranges of the
world.

The dense tufted sprays make snug nesting
places for birds, and in some of the loftiest, leafiest towers of verdure thousands of generations
have been reared, the great solemn trees shedding
off flocks of merry singers every year from nests,
like the flocks of winged seeds from the cones.

The Big Tree keeps its youth far longer than
any of its neighbors. Most silver firs are old in
their second or third century, pines in their fourth
or fifth, while the Big Tree growing beside them
is still in the bloom of its youth, juvenile in every
feature at the age of old pines, and cannot be
said to attain anything like prime size and beauty
before its fifteen hundredth year, or under favorable circumstances become old before its three
thousandth. Many, no doubt, are much older
than this. On one of the Kings River giants,
thirty-five feet and eight inches in diameter ex-
clusive of bark, I counted upwards of four thousand annual wood-rings, in which there was no
trace of decay after all these centuries of mountain weather. There is no absolute limit to the
existence of any tree. Their death is due to accidents, not, as of animals, to the wearing out of

organs. Only the leaves die of old age, their
fall is foretold in their structure ; but the leaves
are renewed every year and so also are the other
essential organs — wood, roots, bark, buds.
Most of the Sierra trees die of disease. Thus
the magnificent silver firs are devoured by fungi,
and comparatively few of them live to see their
three hundredth birth year. But nothing hurts
the Big Tree. I never saw one that was sick or
showed the slightest sign of decay. It lives on
through indefinite thousands of years until
burned, blown down, undermined, or shattered
by some tremendous lightning stroke. No ordinary bolt ever seriously hurts Sequoia. In all my
walks I have seen only one that was thus killed out-
right. Lightning, though rare in the California
lowlands, is common on the Sierra. Almost every
day in June and July small thunderstorms re-
fresh the main forest belt. Clouds like snowy
mountains of marvelous beauty grow rapidly in
the calm sky about midday and cast cooling
shadows and showers that seldom last more than
an hour. Nevertheless these brief, kind storms
wound or kill a good many trees. I have seen
silver firs two hundred feet high split into long
peeled rails and slivers down to the roots, leaving not even a stump, the rails radiating like
the spokes of a wheel from a hole in the ground
where the tree stood. But the Sequoia, instead
of being split and slivered, usually has forty or

fifty feet of its brash knotty top smashed off in short chunks about the size of cord-wood, the beautiful rosy red ruins covering the ground in a circle a hundred feet wide or more. I never saw any that had been cut down to the ground or even to below the branches except one in the Stanislaus Grove, about twelve feet in diameter, the greater part of which was smashed to fragments, leaving only a leafless stump about seventy-five feet high. It is a curious fact that all the very old Sequoias have lost their heads by lightning. " All things come to him who waits." But of all living things Sequoia is perhaps the only one able to wait long enough to make sure of being struck by lightning. Thousands of years it stands ready and waiting, offering its head to every passing cloud as if inviting its fate, praying for heaven's fire as a blessing ; and when at last the old head is off, another of the same shape immediately begins to grow on. Every bud and branch seems excited, like bees that have lost their queen, and tries hard to repair the damage. Branches that for many centuries have been growing out horizontally at once turn upward and all their branchlets arrange themselves with reference to a new top of the same peculiar curve as the old one. Even the small subordinate branches halfway down the trunk do their best to push up to the top and help in this curious head-making.

The great age of these noble trees is even more
wonderful than their huge size, standing bravely
up, millennium in, millennium out, to all that
fortune may bring them, triumphant over tem-
pest and fire and time, fruitful and beautiful,
giving food and shelter to multitudes of small
fleeting creatures dependent on their bounty.
Other trees may claim to be about as large or as
old : Australian Gums, Senegal Baobabs, Mexican
Taxodiums, English Yews, and venerable Lebanon
Cedars, trees of renown, some of which are from
ten to thirty feet in diameter. We read of oaks
that are supposed to have existed ever since the
creation, but strange to say I can find no definite
accounts of the age of any of these trees, but
only estimates based on tradition and assumed
average rates of growth. No other known tree
approaches the Sequoia in grandeur, height and
thickness being considered, and none as far as I
know has looked down on so many centuries or
opens such impressive and suggestive views into
history. The majestic monument of the Kings
River Forest is, as we have seen, fully four thousand years old, and measuring the rings of annual
growth we find it was no less than twenty-seven
feet in diameter at the beginning of the Christian
era, while many observations lead me to expect
the discovery of others ten or twenty centuries
older. As to those of moderate age, there are
thousands, mere youths as yet, that —

" Saw the light that shone
On Mahomet's uplifted crescent,
On many a royal gilded throne
And deed forgotten in the present,
. . . saw the age of sacred trees
And Druid groves and mystic larches,
And saw from forest domes like these
The builder bring his Gothic arches."

Great trees and groves used to be venerated as sacred monuments and halls of council and worship. But soon after the discovery of the Calaveras Grove one of the grandest trees was cut down for the sake of a stump ! The laborious vandals had seen " the biggest tree in the world," then, forsooth, they must try to see the biggest stump and dance on it.

The growth in height for the first two centuries is usually at the rate of eight to ten inches a year. Of course all very large trees are old, but those equal in size may vary greatly in age on account of variations in soil, closeness or openness of growth, etc. Thus a tree about ten feet in diameter that grew on the side of a meadow was, according to my own count of the wood-rings, only two hundred and fifty-nine years old at the time it was felled, while another in the same grove, of almost exactly the same size but less favorably situated, was fourteen hundred and forty years old. The Calaveras tree cut for a dance floor was twenty-four feet in diameter and only thirteen hundred years old, another about the same size was a thousand years older.

The following Sequoia notes and measurements are copied from my notebooks : —

Diameter.		Height in	Age.
Feet.	Inches.	Feet.	Years.
0	1 3-4	10	7
0	5	24	20
0	5	25	41
0	6	25	66
0	6	28 1-2	39
0	8	25	29
0	11	45	71
1	0	60	71
3	2	156	260
6	0	192	240
7	3	195	339
7	3	255	506
7	6	240	493
7	7	207	424
9	0	243	259
9	3	222	280
10	6		1440
12			1825[1]
15			2150 [2]
24			1300
25			2300
35	8 inside bark		over 4000

[1] 6 feet in diameter at height of 200 feet.
[2] 7 feet in diameter at height of 200 feet.

Little, however, is to be learned in confused, hurried tourist trips, spending only a poor noisy hour in a branded grove with a guide. You should go looking and listening alone on long walks through the wild forests and groves in all the seasons of the year. In the spring the winds are balmy and sweet, blowing up and down over great beds of chaparral and through the woods now rich in softening balsam and rosin and the

scent of steaming earth. The sky is mostly sunshine, oftentimes tempered by magnificent clouds,
the breath of the sea built up into new mountain
ranges, warm during the day, cool at night, good
flower-opening weather. The young cones of
the Big Trees are showing in clusters, their flower
time already past, and here and there you may
see the sprouting of their tiny seeds of the pre-
vious autumn, taking their first feeble hold of the
ground and unpacking their tender whorls of
cotyledon leaves. Then you will naturally be led
on to consider their wonderful growth up and up
through the mountain weather, now buried in
snow bent and crinkled, now straightening in
summer sunshine like uncoiling ferns, shooting
eagerly aloft in youth's joyful prime, and towering serene and satisfied through countless years of
calm and storm, the greatest of plants and all
but immortal.

Under the huge trees up come the small plant
people, putting forth fresh leaves and blossoming
in such profusion that the hills and valleys
would still seem gloriously rich and glad were
all the grand trees away. By the side of melting snowbanks rise the crimson sarcodes, round-
topped and massive as the Sequoias themselves,
and beds of blue violets and larger yellow ones
with leaves curiously lobed; azalea and saxifrage, daisies and lilies on the mossy banks of
the streams; and a little way back of them, be-

neath the trees and on sunny spots on the hills around the groves, wild rose and rubus, spiræa and ribes, mitella, tiarella, campanula, monardella, forget-me-not, etc., many of them as worthy of lore immortality as the famous Scotch daisy, wanting only a Burns to sing them home to all hearts.

In the midst of this glad plant work the birds are busy nesting, some singing at their work, some silent, others, especially the big pileated woodpeckers, about as noisy as backwoodsmen building their cabins. Then every bower in the groves is a bridal bower, the winds murmur softly overhead, the streams sing with the birds, while from far-off waterfalls and thunder-clouds come deep rolling organ notes.

In summer the days go by in almost constant brightness, cloudless sunshine pouring over the forest roof, while in the shady depths there is the subdued light of perpetual morning. The new leaves and cones are growing fast and make a grand show, seeds are ripening, young birds learning to fly, and with myriads of insects glad as birds keep the air whirling, joy in every wing-beat, their humming and singing blending with the gentle ah-ing of the winds; while at evening every thicket and grove is enchanted by the tranquil chirping of the blessed hylas, the sweetest and most peaceful of sounds, telling the very heart-joy of earth as it rolls through the heavens.

In the autumn the sighing of the winds is softer than ever, the gentle ah-ah-ing filling the sky with a fine universal mist of music, the birds have little to say, and there is no appreciable stir or rustling among the trees save that caused by the harvesting squirrels. Most of the seeds are ripe and away, those of the trees mottling the sunny air, glinting, glancing through the midst of the merry insect people, rocks and trees, everything alike drenched in gold light, heaven's colors coming down to the meadows and groves, making every leaf a romance, air, earth, and water in peace beyond thought, the great brooding days opening and closing in divine psalms of color.

Winter comes suddenly, arrayed in storms, though to mountaineers silky streamers on the peaks and the tones of the wind give sufficient warning. You hear strange whisperings among the tree-tops, as if the giants were taking counsel together. One after another, nodding and swaying, calling and replying, spreads the news, until all with one accord break forth into glorious song, welcoming the first grand snowstorm of the year, and looming up in the dim clouds and snowdrifts like lighthouse towers in flying scud and spray. Studying the behavior of the giants from some friendly shelter, you will see that even in the glow of their wildest enthusiasm, when the storm roars loudest, they never lose

their god-like composure, never toss their arms
or bow or wave like the pines, but only slowly,
solemnly nod and sway, standing erect, making
no sign of strife, none of rest, neither in alliance
nor at war with the winds, too calmly, uncon-
sciously noble and strong to strive with or bid
defiance to anything. Owing to the density of
the leafy branchlets and great breadth of head
the Big Tree carries a much heavier load of
snow than any of its neighbors, and after a
storm, when the sky clears, the laden trees are
a glorious spectacle, worth any amount of cold
camping to see. Every bossy limb and crown
is solid white, and the immense height of the
giants becomes visible as the eye travels the
white steps of the colossal tower, each relieved
by a mass of blue shadow.

In midwinter the forest depths are as fresh
and pure as the crevasses and caves of glaciers.
Grouse, nuthatches, a few woodpeckers, and
other hardy birds dwell in the groves all winter,
and the squirrels may be seen every clear day
frisking about, lively as ever, tunneling to their
stores, never coming up empty-mouthed, diving
in the loose snow about as quickly as ducks in
water, while storms and sunshine sing to each
other.

One of the noblest and most beautiful of the
late winter sights is the blossoming of the Big Tree
like gigantic goldenrods and the sowing of their

pollen over all the forest and the snow-covered ground — a most glorious view of Nature's immortal virility and flower-love.

One of my own best excursions among the Sequoias was made in the autumn of 1875, when I explored the then unknown or little known Sequoia region south of the Mariposa Grove for comprehensive views of the belt, and to learn what I could of the peculiar distribution of the species and its history in general. In particular I was anxious to try to find out whether it had ever been more widely distributed since the glacial period; what conditions favorable or otherwise were affecting it; what were its relations to climate, topography, soil, and the other trees growing with it, etc.; and whether, as was generally supposed, the species was nearing extinction. I was already acquainted in a general way with the northern groves, but excepting some passing glimpses gained on excursions into the high Sierra about the head-waters of Kings and Kern rivers I had seen nothing of the south end of the belt.

Nearly all my mountaineering has been done on foot, carrying as little as possible, depending on camp-fires for warmth, that so I might be light and free to go wherever my studies might lead. On this Sequoia trip, which promised to be long, I was persuaded to take a small wild mule with me to carry provisions and a pair of blankets. The friendly owner of the animal, having noticed that I sometimes looked tired when I came down from the peaks to replenish my bread sack, assured me that his " little Brownie mule " was just what I wanted, tough as a knot, perfectly untirable, low and narrow, just right for squeezing through brush, able to climb like a chipmunk, jump from boulder to boulder like a wild sheep, and go anywhere a man could go. But tough as he was and accomplished as a climber, many a time in the course of our journey when he was jaded and hungry, wedged fast in rocks or struggling in chaparral like a fly in a spiderweb, his troubles were sad to see, and I wished he would leave me and find his way home alone.

We set out from Yosemite about the end of August, and our first camp was made in the well-known Mariposa Grove. Here and in the adjacent pine woods I spent nearly a week, carefully examining the boundaries of the grove for traces of its greater extension without finding any. Then I struck out into the majestic trackless forest to the southeastward, hoping to find new groves or traces of old ones in the dense silver fir and pine woods about the head of Big Creek, where soil and climate seemed most favorable to their growth, but not a single tree or old monument of any sort came to light until I climbed the high rock called Wamellow by the Indians. Here I obtained tell-

ing views of the fertile forest-filled basin of the
upper Fresno. Innumerable spires of the noble
yellow pine were displayed rising above one another on the braided slopes, and yet nobler sugar
pines with superb arms outstretched in the rich
autumn light, while away toward the southwest,
on the verge of the glowing horizon, I discovered the majestic dome-like crowns of Big Trees
towering high over all, singly and in close grove
congregations. There is something wonderfully
attractive in this king tree, even when beheld
from afar, that draws us to it with indescrib-
able enthusiasm; its superior height and massive smoothly rounded outlines proclaiming its
character in any company; and when one of
the oldest attains full stature on some commanding ridge it seems the very god of the
woods. I ran back to camp, packed Brownie,
steered over the divide and down into the heart
of the Fresno Grove. Then choosing a camp
on the side of a brook where the grass was good,
I made a cup of tea, and set off free among the
brown giants, glorying in the abundance of new
work about me. One of the first special things
that caught my attention was an extensive landslip. The ground on the side of a stream had
given way to a depth of about fifty feet and
with all its trees had been launched into the bottom of the stream ravine. Most of the trees —
pines, firs, incense cedar, and Sequoia — were still

standing erect and uninjured, as if unconscious
that anything out of the common had happened.
Tracing the ravine alongside the avalanche, I
saw many trees whose roots had been laid bare,
and in one instance discovered a Sequoia about
fifteen feet in diameter growing above an old
prostrate trunk that seemed to belong to a
former generation. This slip had occurred seven
or eight years ago, and I was glad to find that
not only were most of the Big Trees uninjured,
but that many companies of hopeful seedlings
and saplings were growing confidently on the
fresh soil along the broken front of the avalanche. These young trees were already eight or
ten feet high, and were shooting up vigorously,
as if sure of eternal life, though young pines,
firs, and libocedrus were runing a race with them
for the sunshine with an even start. Farther
down the ravine I counted five hundred and
thirty-six promising young Sequoias on a bed of
rough bouldery soil not exceeding two acres in
extent.

The Fresno Big Trees covered an area of
about four square miles, and while wandering
about surveying the boundaries of the grove,
anxious to see every tree, I came suddenly on a
handsome log cabin, richly embowered and so
fresh and unweathered it was still redolent of
gum and balsam like a newly felled tree. Strolling forward, wondering who could have built it,

I found an old, weary-eyed, speculative, gray-haired man on a bark stool by the door, reading a book. The discovery of his hermitage by a stranger seemed to surprise him, but when I explained that I was only a tree-lover sauntering along the mountains to study Sequoia, he bade me welcome, made me bring my mule down to a little slanting meadow before his door and camp with him, promising to show me his pet trees and many curious things bearing on my studies.

After supper, as the evening shadows were falling, the good hermit sketched his life in the mines, which in the main was like that of most other pioneer gold-hunters — a succession of intense experiences full of big ups and downs like the mountain topography. Since " '49 " he had wandered over most of the Sierra, sinking innumerable prospect holes like a sailor making soundings, digging new channels for streams, sifting gold-sprinkled boulder and gravel beds with unquenchable energy, life's noon the meanwhile passing unnoticed into late afternoon shadows. Then, health and gold gone, the game played and lost, like a wounded deer creeping into this forest solitude, he awaits the sundown call. How sad the undertones of many a life here, now the noise of the first big gold battles has died away! How many interesting wrecks lie drifted and stranded in hidden nooks of the gold region! Perhaps no other range contains the remains of so many rare and interesting men. The name of my hermit friend is John A. Nelder, a fine kind man, who in going into the woods has at last gone home; for he loves nature truly, and realizes that these last shadowy days with scarce a glint of gold in them are the best of all. Birds, squirrels, plants get loving, natural recognition, and delightful it was to see how sensitively he responds to the silent influences of the woods. His eyes brightened as he gazed on the trees that stand guard around his little home; squirrels and mountain quail came to his call to be fed, and he tenderly stroked the little snowbent sapling Sequoias, hoping they yet might grow straight to the sky and rule the grove. One of the greatest of his trees stands a little way back of his cabin, and he proudly led me to it, bidding me admire its colossal proportions and measure it to see if in all the forest there could be another so grand. It proved to be only twenty-six feet in diameter, and he seemed distressed to learn that the Mariposa Grizzly Giant was larger. I tried to comfort him by observing that his was the taller, finer formed, and perhaps the more favorably situated. Then he led me to some noble ruins, remnants of gigantic trunks of trees that he supposed must have been larger than any now standing, and though they had lain on the damp ground exposed to fire and the weather for centuries, the wood was perfectly sound. Sequoia timber is not only beautiful in color, rose red when fresh, and as easily worked as pine, but it is almost absolutely unperishable. Build a house of Big Tree logs on granite and that house will last about as long as its foundation. Indeed fire seems to be the only agent that has any appreciable effect on it. From one of these ancient trunk remnants I cut a specimen of the wood, which neither in color, strength, nor soundness could be distinguished from specimens cut from living trees, although it had certainly lain on the damp forest floor for more than three hundred and eighty years, probably more than thrice as long. The time in this instance was determined as follows : When the tree from which the specimen was derived fell it sunk itself into the ground, making a ditch about two hundred feet long and five or six feet deep; and in the middle of this ditch, where a part of the fallen trunk had been burned, a silver fir four feet in diameter and three hundred and eighty years old was growing, showing that the Sequoia trunk had lain on the ground three hundred and eighty years plus the unknown time that it lay before the part whose place had been taken by the fir was burned out of the way, and that which had elapsed ere the seed from which the monumental fir sprang fell into the prepared soil and took root. Now because Sequoia trunks are never wholly consumed in one forest fire and these fires recur only at considerable intervals, and because Sequoia ditches, after being cleared, are often left unplanted for centuries, it becomes evident that the trunk remnant in question may have been on the ground a thousand years or more.   Similar vestiges are common, and together with the root-bowls and long straight ditches of the fallen monarchs, throw a sure light back on the post-glacial history of the species, bearing on its distribution.   One of the most interesting features of this grove is the apparent ease and strength and comfortable independence in which the trees occupy their place in the general forest.   Seedlings, saplings, young and middle-aged trees are grouped promisingly around the old patriarchs, betraying no sign of approach to extinction.   On the contrary, all seem to be saying, " Everything is to our mind and we mean to live forever."   But, sad to tell, a lumber company was building a large mill and flume near by, assuring widespread destruction.

In the cones and sometimes in the lower portion of the trunk and roots there is a dark gritty substance which dissolves readily in water and yields a magnificent purple color.   It is a strong astringent, and is said to be used by the Indians as a big medicine.   Mr. Nelder showed me specimens of ink he had made from it, which I tried and found good, flowing freely and holding its color well. Indeed everything about the tree seems constant.

With these interesting trees, forming the largest
of the northern groves, I stopped only a week,
for I had far to go before the fall of the snow.
The hermit seemed to cling to me and tried to
make me promise to winter with him after the
season's work was done. Brownie had to be got
home, however, and other work awaited me,
therefore I could only promise to stop a day or
two on my way back to Yosemite and give him
the forest news.

The next two weeks were spent in the wide
basin of the San Joaquin, climbing innumerable ridges and surveying the far-extending sea
of pines and firs. But not a single Sequoia
crown appeared among them all, nor any trace
of a fallen trunk, until I had crossed the south
divide of the basin, opposite Dinky Creek, one of
the northmost tributaries of Kings River. On
this stream there is a small grove, said to have
been discovered a few years before my visit by
two hunters in pursuit of a wounded bear. Just
as I was fording one of the branches of Dinky
Creek I met a shepherd, and when I asked him
whether he knew anything about the Big Trees of
the neighborhood he replied, " I know all about
them, for I visited them only a few days ago and
pastured my sheep in the grove." He was fresh
from the East, and as this was his first summer in
the Sierra I was curious to learn what impression
the Sequoias had made on him. When I asked

whether it was true that the Big Trees were
really so big as people say, he warmly replied,
" Oh, yes sir, you bet. They 're whales. I never
used to believe half I heard about the awful size of
California trees, but they 're monsters and no mistake. One of them over here, they tell me, is the
biggest tree in the whole world, and I guess it is,
for it 's forty foot through and as many good
long paces around." He was very earnest, and in
fullness of faith offered to guide me to the grove
that I might not miss seeing this biggest tree.
A fair measurement four feet from the ground,
above the main swell of the roots, showed a
diameter of only thirty-two feet, much to the
young man's disgust. " Only thirty-two feet,"
he lamented, " only thirty-two, and I always
thought it was forty!" Then with a sigh of
relief, " No matter, that 's a big tree, anyway;
no fool of a tree, sir, that you can cut a plank
out of thirty feet broad, straight-edged, no bark,
all good wood, sound and solid. It would make
the brag white pine planks from old Maine look
like laths." A good many other fine specimens
are distributed along three small branches of the
creek, and I noticed several thrifty moderate-
sized Sequoias growing on a granite ledge, apparently as independent of deep soil as the pines and
firs, clinging to seams and fissures and sending
their roots far abroad in search of moisture.

The creek is very clear and beautiful, gliding

through tangles of shrubs and flower beds, gay
bee and butterfly pastures, the grove's own
stream, pure Sequoia water, flowing all the year,
every drop filtered through moss and leaves and
the myriad spongy rootlets of the giant trees.
One of the most interesting features of the grove
is a small waterfall with a flowery, ferny, clear
brimming pool at the foot of it. How cheerily
it sings the songs of the wilderness, and how
sweet its tones! You seem to taste as well as
hear them, while only the subdued roar of the
river in the deep cañon reaches up into the grove,
sounding like the sea and the winds. So charming a fall and pool in the heart of so glorious a
forest good pagans would have consecrated to
some lovely nymph.

Hence down into the main Kings River cañon,
a mile deep, I led and dragged and shoved my
patient, much-enduring mule through miles and
miles of gardens and brush, fording innumerable
streams, crossing savage rock slopes and taluses,
scrambling, sliding through gulches and gorges,
then up into the grand Sequoia forests of the
south side, cheered by the royal crowns displayed
on the narrow horizon. In a day and a half we
reached the Sequoia woods in the neighborhood
of the old Thomas' Mill Flat. Thence striking
off northeastward I found a magnificent forest
nearly six miles long by two in width, composed
mostly of Big Trees, with outlying groves as far

east as Boulder Creek. Here five or six days were spent, and it was delightful to learn from countless trees, old and young, how comfortably they were settled down in concordance with climate and soil and their noble neighbors.

Imbedded in these majestic woods there are numerous meadows, around the sides of which the Big Trees press close together in beautiful lines, showing their grandeur openly from the ground to their domed heads in the sky. The young trees are still more numerous and exuberant than in the Fresno and Dinky groves, standing apart in beautiful family groups, or crowding around the old giants. For every venerable lightning-stricken tree, there is one or more in all the glory of prime, and for each of these, many young trees and crowds of saplings. The young trees express the grandeur of their race in a way indefinable by any words at my command. When they are five or six feet in diameter and a hundred and fifty feet high, they seem like mere baby saplings as many inches in diameter, their juvenile habit and gestures completely veiling their real size, even to those who, from long experience, are able to make fair approximation in their measurements of common trees. One morning I noticed three airy, spiry, quick-growing babies on the side of a meadow, the largest of which I took to be about eight inches in diameter. On measuring it, I found to

my astonishment it was five feet six inches in
diameter, and about a hundred and forty feet
high.

On a bed of sandy ground fifteen yards square,
which had been occupied by four sugar pines,
I counted ninety-four promising seedlings, an
instance of Sequoia gaining ground from its
neighbors.   Here also I noted eighty-six young
Sequoias from one to fifty feet high on less than
half an acre of ground that had been cleared and
prepared for their reception by fire.   This was a
small bay burned into dense chaparral, showing
that fire, the great destroyer of tree life, is sometimes followed by conditions favorable for new
growths.   Sufficient fresh soil, however, is furnished for the constant renewal of the forest by
the fall of old trees without the help of any other
agent, — burrowing animals, fire, flood, landslip,
etc., — for the ground is thus turned and stirred
as well as cleared, and in every roomy, shady hollow beside the walls of upturned roots many
hopeful seedlings spring up.

The largest, and as far as I know the oldest, of
all the Kings River trees that I saw is the majestic stump, already referred to, about a hundred
and forty feet high, which above the swell of the
roots is thirty-five feet and eight inches inside the
bark, and over four thousand years old.   It was
burned nearly half through at the base, and I
spent a day in chopping off the charred surface,

cutting into the heart, and counting the wood-
rings with the aid of a lens.   I made out a little
over four thousand without difficulty or doubt,
but I was unable to get a complete count, owing
to confusion in the rings where wounds had been
healed over.   Judging by what is left of it, this
was a fine, tall, symmetrical tree nearly forty feet
in diameter before it lost its bark.   In the last
sixteen hundred and seventy-two years the increase in diameter was ten feet.   A short distance
south of this forest lies a beautiful grove, now
mostly included in the General Grant National
Park.   I found many shake-makers at work in
it, access to these magnificent woods having been
made easy by the old mill wagon road.   The Park
is only two miles square, and the largest of its
many fine trees is the General Grant, so named
before the date of my first visit, twenty-eight years
ago, and said to be the largest tree in the world,
though above the craggy bulging base the diameter is less than thirty feet.   The Sanger Lumber Company owns nearly all the Kings River
groves outside the Park, and for many years the
mills have been spreading desolation without any
advantage.

One of the shake-makers directed me to an
"old snag biggeren Grant."   It proved to be a
huge black charred stump thirty-two feet in diameter, the next in size to the grand monument
mentioned above.

YOUNG BIG TREE FELLED FOR SHINGLES

I found a scattered growth of Big Trees extending across the main divide to within a short distance of Hyde's Mill, on a tributary of Dry Creek. The mountain ridge on the south side of the stream was covered from base to summit with a most superb growth of Big Trees. What a picture it made! In all my wide forest wanderings I had seen none so sublime. Every tree of all the mighty host seemed perfect in beauty and strength, and their majestic domed heads, rising above one another on the mountain slope, were most imposingly displayed, like a range of bossy upswelling cumulus clouds on a calm sky.

In this glorious forest the mill was busy, forming a sore, sad centre of destruction, though small as yet, so immensely heavy was the growth. Only the smaller and most accessible of the trees were being cut. The logs, from three to ten or twelve feet in diameter, were dragged or rolled with long strings of oxen into a chute and sent flying down the steep mountain side to the mill flat, where the largest of them were blasted into manageable dimensions for the saws. And as the timber is very brash, by this blasting and careless felling on uneven ground, half or three fourths of the timber was wasted.

I spent several days exploring the ridge and counting the annual wood rings on a large number of stumps in the clearings, then replenished my bread sack and pushed on southward. All

the way across the broad rough basins of the
Kaweah and Tule rivers Sequoia ruled supreme,
forming an almost continuous belt for sixty or
seventy miles, waving up and down in huge
massy mountain billows in compliance with the
grand glacier-ploughed topography.

Day after day, from grove to grove, cañon to
cañon, I made a long, wavering way, terribly
rough in some places for Brownie, but cheery
for me, for Big Trees were seldom out of sight.
We crossed the rugged, picturesque basins of
Redwood Creek, the North Fork of the Kaweah,
and Marble Fork gloriously forested, and full of
beautiful cascades and falls, sheer and slanting,
infinitely varied with broad curly foam fleeces
and strips of embroidery in which the sunbeams
revel. Thence we climbed into the noble forest
on the Marble and Middle Fork Divide. After
a general exploration of the Kaweah basin, this
part of the Sequoia belt seemed to me the finest,
and I then named it " the Giant Forest." It extends, a magnificent growth of giants grouped in
pure temple groves, ranged in colonnades along
the sides of meadows, or scattered among the
other trees, from the granite headlands overlooking the hot foothills and plains of the San Joaquin
back to within a few miles of the old glacier
fountains at an elevation of 5000 to 8400 feet
above the sea.

When I entered this sublime wilderness the

day was nearly done, the trees with rosy, glowing countenances seemed to be hushed and thoughtful, as if waiting in conscious religious dependence on the sun, and one naturally walked softly and awe-stricken among them. I wandered on, meeting nobler trees where all are noble, subdued in the general calm, as if in some vast hall pervaded by the deepest sanctities and solemnities that sway human souls. At sundown the trees seemed to cease their worship and breathe free. I heard the birds going home. I too sought a home for the night on the edge of a level meadow where there is a long, open view between the evenly ranked trees standing guard along its sides. Then after a good place was found for poor Brownie, who had had a hard, weary day sliding and scrambling across the Marble Cañon, I made my bed and supper and lay on my back looking up to the stars through pillared arches finer far than the pious heart of man, telling its love, ever reared. Then I took a walk up the meadow to see the trees in the pale light. They seemed still more marvelously massive and tall than by day, heaving their colossal heads into the depths of the sky, among the stars, some of which appeared to be sparkling on their branches like flowers. I built a big fire that vividly illumined the huge brown boles of the nearest trees and the little plants and cones and fallen leaves at their feet, keeping up the show until I fell asleep to dream of boundless forests and trail-building for Brownie.

Joyous birds welcomed the dawn; and the squirrels, now their food cones were ripe and had to be quickly gathered and stored for winter, began their work before sunrise. My tea-and-bread-crumb breakfast was soon done, and leaving jaded Brownie to feed and rest I sauntered forth to my studies. In every direction Sequoia ruled the woods. Most of the other big conifers were present here and there, but not as rivals or companions. They only served to thicken and enrich the general wilderness. Trees of every age cover craggy ridges as well as the deep moraine-soiled slopes, and plant their magnificent shafts along every brookside and meadow. Bogs and meadows are rare or entirely wanting in the isolated groves north of Kings River; here there is a beautiful series of them lying on the broad top of the main dividing ridge, imbedded in the very heart of the mammoth woods as if for ornament, their smooth, plushy bosoms kept bright and fertile by streams and sunshine.

Resting awhile on one of the most beautiful of them when the sun was high, it seemed impossible that any other forest picture in the world could rival it. There lay the grassy, flowery lawn, three fourths of a mile long, smoothly outspread, basking in mellow autumn light, colored brown and yellow and purple, streaked with lines of green along the streams, and ruffled here and there with patches of ledum and scarlet vaccinium. Around the margin there is first a fringe of azalea and willow bushes, colored orange yellow, enlivened with vivid dashes of red cornel, as if painted. Then up spring the mighty walls of verdure three hundred feet high, the brown fluted pillars so thick and tall and strong they seem fit to uphold the sky ; the dense foliage, swelling forward in rounded bosses on the upper half, variously shaded and tinted, that of the young trees dark green, of the old yellowish. An aged lightning-smitten patriarch standing a little forward beyond the general line with knotty arms outspread was covered with gray and yellow lichens and surrounded by a group of saplings whose slender spires seemed to lack not a single leaf or spray in their wondrous perfection. Such was the Kaweah meadow picture that golden afternoon, and as I gazed every color seemed to deepen and glow as if the progress of the fresh sun-work were visible from hour to hour, while every tree seemed religious and conscious of the presence of God. A free man revels in a scene like this and time goes by unmeasured. I stood fixed in silent wonder or sauntered about shifting my points of view, studying the physiognomy of separate trees, and going out to the different color patches to see how they were put on and what they were made of, giving free ex-

pression to my joy, exulting in Nature's wild immortal vigor and beauty, never dreaming any
other human being was near.   Suddenly the
spell was broken by dull bumping, thudding
sounds, and a man and horse came in sight at
the farther end of the meadow, where they
seemed sadly out of place.   A good big bear or
mastodon or megatherium would have been more
in keeping with the old mammoth forest.   Nevertheless, it is always pleasant to meet one of our
own species after solitary rambles, and I stepped
out where I could be seen and shouted, when the
rider reined in his galloping mustang and waited
my approach.   He seemed too much surprised
to speak until, laughing in his puzzled face, I
said I was glad to meet a fellow mountaineer in
so lonely a place.   Then he abruptly asked,
"What are you doing?   How did you get
here?"   I explained that I came across the
cañons from Yosemite and was only looking at
the trees.   "Oh then, I know," he said, greatly
to my surprise, "you must be John Muir."   He
was herding a band of horses that had been
driven up a rough trail from the lowlands to feed
on these forest meadows.   A few handfuls of
crumb detritus was all that was left in my bread
sack, so I told him that I was nearly out of pro-
vision and asked whether he could spare me a
little flour.   "Oh yes, of course you can have
anything I 've got," he said.   "Just take my

track and it will lead you to my camp in a big
hollow log on the side of a meadow two or three
miles from here. I must ride after some strayed
horses, but I'll be back before night; in the
mean time make yourself at home." He galloped
away to the northward, I returned to my own
camp, saddled Brownie, and by the middle of the
afternoon discovered his noble den in a fallen
Sequoia hollowed by fire — a spacious loghouse
of one log, carbon-lined, centuries old yet sweet
and fresh, weather proof, earthquake proof,
likely to outlast the most durable stone castle,
and commanding views of garden and grove
grander far than the richest king ever enjoyed.
Brownie found plenty of grass and I found
bread, which I ate with views from the big
round, ever-open door. Soon the good Samaritan
mountaineer came in, and I enjoyed a famous
rest listening to his observations on trees, animals, adventures, etc., while he was busily preparing supper. In answer to inquiries concerning the distribution of the Big Trees he gave
a good deal of particular information of the
forest we were in, and he had heard that the
species extended a long way south, he knew not
how far. I wandered about for several days
within a radius of six or seven miles of the camp,
surveying boundaries, measuring trees, and
climbing the highest points for general views.
From the south side of the divide I saw telling

ranks of Sequoia-crowned headlands stretching
far into the hazy distance, and plunging vaguely
down into profound cañon depths foreshadowing
weeks of good work. I had now been out on
the trip more than a month, and I began to fear
my studies would be interrupted by snow, for
winter was drawing nigh. "Where there is n't
a way make a way," is easily said when no way
at the time is needed, but to the Sierra explorer
with a mule traveling across the cañon lines of
drainage the brave old phrase becomes heavy
with meaning. There are ways across the Sierra
graded by glaciers, well marked, and followed
by men and beasts and birds, and one of them
even by locomotives ; but none natural or artificial along the range, and the explorer who
would thus travel at right angles to the glacial
ways must traverse cañons and ridges extending
side by side in endless succession, roughened
by side gorges and gulches and stubborn chaparral, and defended by innumerable sheer-fronted
precipices. My own ways are easily made in any
direction, but Brownie, though one of the tough-
est and most skillful of his race, was oftentimes
discouraged for want of hands, and caused endless work. Wild at first, he was tame enough
now ; and when turned loose he not only refused
to run away, but as his troubles increased came
to depend on me in such a pitiful, touching way,
I became attached to him and helped him as if

A ONE-LOG HOUSE

he were a good-natured boy in distress, and then
the labor grew lighter. Bidding good-by to the
kind Sequoia cave-dweller, we vanished again in
the wilderness, drifting slowly southward, Sequoias on every ridge-top beckoning and pointing the way.

In the forest between the Middle and East
forks of the Kaweah, I met a great fire, and as
fire is the master scourge and controller of the
distribution of trees, I stopped to watch it and
learn what I could of its works and ways with
the giants. It came racing up the steep chapar-
ral-covered slopes of the East Fork cañon with
passionate enthusiasm in a broad cataract of
flames, now bending down low to feed on the
green bushes, devouring acres of them at a
breath, now towering high in the air as if looking abroad to choose a way, then stooping to
feed again, the lurid flapping surges and the
smoke and terrible rushing and roaring hiding
all that is gentle and orderly in the work. But
as soon as the deep forest was reached the ungovernable flood became calm like a torrent entering a lake, creeping and spreading beneath
the trees where the ground was level or sloped
gently, slowly nibbling the cake of compressed
needles and scales with flames an inch high, rising here and there to a foot or two on dry twigs
and clumps of small bushes and brome grass.
Only at considerable intervals were fierce bonfires

lighted, where heavy branches broken off by snow had accumulated, or around some venerable giant whose head had been stricken off by lightning.

I tethered Brownie on the edge of a little meadow beside a stream a good safe way off, and then cautiously chose a camp for myself in a big stout hollow trunk not likely to be crushed by the fall of burning trees, and made a bed of ferns and boughs in it. The night, however, and the strange wild fireworks were too beautiful and exciting to allow much sleep. There was no danger of being chased and hemmed in, for in the main forest belt of the Sierra, even when swift winds are blowing, fires seldom or never sweep over the trees in broad all-embracing sheets as they do in the dense Rocky Mountain woods and in those of the Cascade Mountains of Oregon and Washington. Here they creep from tree to tree with tranquil deliberation, allowing close observation, though caution is required in venturing around the burning giants to avoid falling limbs and knots and fragments from dead shattered tops. Though the day was best for study, I sauntered about night after night, learning what I could and admiring the wonderful show vividly displayed in the lonely darkness, the ground-fire advancing in long crooked lines gently grazing and smoking on the close-pressed leaves, springing up in thousands of little jets of pure flame on dry tassels and twigs, and tall spires and flat sheets with jagged flapping edges dancing here and there on grass tufts and bushes, big bonfires blazing in perfect storms of energy where heavy branches mixed with small ones lay smashed together in hundred cord piles, big red arches between spreading root-swells and trees growing close together, huge fire-mantled trunks on the hill slopes glowing like bars of hot iron, violet-colored fire running up the tall trees, tracing the furrows of the bark in quick quivering rills, and lighting magnificent torches on dry shattered tops, and ever and anon, with a tremendous roar and burst of light, young trees clad in low - descending feathery branches vanishing in one flame two or three hundred feet high.

One of the most impressive and beautiful sights was made by the great fallen trunks lying on the hillsides all red and glowing like colossal iron bars fresh from a furnace, two hundred feet long some of them, and ten to twenty feet thick. After repeated burnings have consumed the bark and sapwood, the sound charred surface, being full of cracks and sprinkled with leaves, is quickly overspread with a pure, rich, furred, ruby glow almost flameless and smokeless, producing a marvelous effect in the night. Another grand and interesting sight are the fires on the tops of the largest living trees flaming above the

green branches at a height of perhaps two hundred feet, entirely cut off from the ground-fires,
and looking like signal beacons on watch towers.
From one standpoint I sometimes saw a dozen or
more, those in the distance looking like great
stars above the forest roof.   At first I could not
imagine how these Sequoia lamps were lighted,
but the very first night, strolling about waiting
and watching, I saw the thing done again and
again.   The thick, fibrous bark of old trees is
divided by deep, nearly continuous furrows, the
sides of which are bearded with the bristling ends
of fibres broken by the growth swelling of the
trunk, and when the fire comes creeping around
the feet of the trees, it runs up these bristly furrows in lovely pale blue quivering, bickering rills
of flame with a low, earnest whispering sound to
the lightning-shattered top of the trunk, which,
in the dry Indian summer, with perhaps leaves
and twigs and squirrel-gnawed cone-scales and
seed-wings lodged in it, is readily ignited.   These
lamp-lighting rills, the most beautiful fire streams
I ever saw, last only a minute or two, but the big
lamps burn with varying brightness for days and
weeks, throwing off sparks like the spray of a
fountain, while ever and anon a shower of red
coals comes sifting down through the branches,
followed at times with startling effect by a big
burned-off chunk weighing perhaps half a ton.

The immense bonfires where fifty or a hundred

cords of peeled, split, smashed wood has been piled around some old giant by a single stroke of lightning is another grand sight in the night. The light is so great I found I could read common print three hundred yards from them, and the illumination of the circle of onlooking trees is indescribably impressive. Other big fires, roaring and booming like waterfalls, were blazing on the upper sides of trees on hillslopes, against which limbs broken off by heavy snow had rolled, while branches high overhead, tossed and shaken by the ascending air current, seemed to be writhing in pain. Perhaps the most startling phenomenon of all was the quick death of childlike Sequoias only a century or two of age. In the midst of the other comparatively slow and steady fire work one of these tall, beautiful saplings, leafy and branchy, would be seen blazing up suddenly, all in one heaving, booming, passionate flame reaching from the ground to the top of the tree and fifty to a hundred feet or more above it, with a smoke column bending forward and streaming away on the upper, free-flowing wind. To burn these green trees a strong fire of dry wood beneath them is required, to send up a current of air hot enough to distill inflammable gases from the leaves and sprays; then instead of the lower limbs gradually catching fire and igniting the next and next in succession, the whole tree seems to explode almost simul-

taneously, and with awful roaring and throbbing
a round, tapering flame shoots up two or three
hundred feet, and in a second or two is quenched,
leaving the green spire a black, dead mast, bris-
tled and roughened with down-curling boughs.
Nearly all the trees that have been burned
down are lying with their heads uphill, because
they are burned far more deeply on the upper
side, on account of broken limbs rolling down
against them to make hot fires, while only leaves
and twigs accumulate on the lower side and
are quickly consumed without injury to the tree.
But green, resinless Sequoia wood burns very
slowly, and many successive fires are required to
burn down a large tree. Fires can run only at
intervals of several years, and when the ordinary
amount of firewood that has rolled against the
gigantic trunk is consumed, only a shallow scar
is made, which is slowly deepened by recurring
fires until far beyond the centre of gravity, and
when at last the tree falls, it of course falls uphill.
The healing folds of wood layers on some of the
deeply burned trees show that centuries have
elapsed since the last wounds were made.

When a great Sequoia falls, its head is smashed
into fragments about as small as those made by
lightning, which are mostly devoured by the first
running, hunting fire that finds them, while the
trunk is slowly wasted away by centuries of fire
and weather. One of the most interesting fire

actions on the trunk is the boring of those great tunnel-like hollows through which horsemen may gallop. All of these famous hollows are burned out of the solid wood, for no Sequoia is ever hollowed by decay. When the tree falls the brash trunk is often broken straight across into sections as if sawed; into these joints the fire creeps, and, on account of the great size of the broken ends, burns for weeks or even months without being much influenced by the weather. After the great glowing ends fronting each other have burned so far apart that their rims cease to burn, the fire continues to work on in the centres, and the ends become deeply concave. Then heat being radiated from side to side, the burning goes on in each section of the trunk independent of the other, until the diameter of the bore is so great that the heat radiated across from side to side is not sufficient to keep them burning. It appears, therefore, that only very large trees can receive the fire-auger and have any shell rim left.

Fire attacks the large trees only at the ground, consuming the fallen leaves and humus at their feet, doing them but little harm unless considerable quantities of fallen limbs happen to be piled about them, their thick mail of spongy, unpitchy, almost unburnable bark affording strong protection. Therefore the oldest and most perfect unscarred trees are found on ground that is nearly level, while those growing on hillsides,

against which falling branches roll, are always
deeply scarred on the upper side, and as we have
seen are sometimes burned down. The saddest
thing of all was to see the hopeful seedlings,
many of them crinkled and bent with the pressure of winter snow, yet bravely aspiring at the
top, helplessly perishing, and young trees, perfect spires of verdure and naturally immortal,
suddenly changed to dead masts. Yet the sun
looked cheerily down the openings in the forest
roof, turning the black smoke to a beautiful
brown, as if all was for the best.

Beneath the smoke-clouds of the suffering
forest we again pushed southward, descending a
side-gorge of the East Fork cañon and climbing
another into new forests and groves not a whit
less noble. Brownie, the meanwhile, had been
resting, while I was weary and sleepy with almost
ceaseless wanderings, giving only an hour or two
each night or day to sleep in my log home.
Way-making here seemed to become more and
more difficult, "impossible," in common phrase,
for four-legged travelers. Two or three miles
was all the day's work as far as distance was concerned. Nevertheless, just before sundown we
found a charming camp ground with plenty of
grass, and a forest to study that had felt no fire
for many a year. The camp hollow was evidently a favorite home of bears. On many of
the trees, at a height of six or eight feet, their

autographs were inscribed in strong, free, flowing strokes on the soft bark where they had stood
up like cats to stretch their limbs. Using both
hands, every claw a pen, the handsome curved
lines of their writing take the form of remarkably regular interlacing pointed arches, producing a truly ornamental effect. I looked and
listened, half expecting to see some of the writers
alarmed and withdrawing from the unwonted
disturbance. Brownie also looked and listened,
for mules fear bears instinctively and have a very
keen nose for them. When I turned him loose,
instead of going to the best grass, he kept
cautiously near the camp-fire for protection, but
was careful not to step on me. The great starry
night passed away in deep peace and the rosy
morning sunbeams were searching the grove ere
I awoke from a long, blessed sleep.

The breadth of the Sequoia belt here is about
the same as on the north side of the river, extending, rather thin and scattered in some places,
among the noble pines from near the main forest
belt of the range well back towards the frosty
peaks, where most of the trees are growing on
moraines but little changed as yet.

Two days' scramble above Bear Hollow I enjoyed an interesting interview with deer. Soon
after sunrise a little company of four came to my
camp in a wild garden imbedded in chaparral,
and after much cautious observation quietly

began to eat breakfast with me. Keeping perfectly still I soon had their confidence, and they
came so near I found no difficulty, while admiring their graceful manners and gestures, in
determining what plants they were eating, thus
gaining a far finer knowledge and sympathy
than comes by killing and hunting.

Indian summer gold with scarce a whisper of
winter in it was painting the glad wilderness in
richer and yet richer colors as we scrambled
across the South cañon into the basin of the
Tule. Here the Big Tree forests are still more
extensive, and furnished abundance of work in
tracing boundaries and gloriously crowned ridges
up and down, back and forth, exploring, studying, admiring, while the great measureless days
passed on and away uncounted. But in the
calm of the camp-fire the end of the season
seemed near. Brownie too often brought snowstorms to mind. He became doubly jaded,
though I never rode him, and always left him in
camp to feed and rest while I explored. The invincible bread business also troubled me again;
the last mealy crumbs were consumed, and grass
was becoming scarce even in the roughest rock-
piles, naturally inaccessible to sheep. One afternoon, as I gazed over the rolling bossy Sequoia
billows stretching interminably southward, seeking a way and counting how far I might go
without food, a rifle shot rang out sharp and

clear. Marking the direction I pushed gladly on, hoping to find some hunter who could spare a little food. Within a few hundred rods I struck the track of a shod horse, which led to the camp of two Indian shepherds. One of them was cooking supper when I arrived. Glancing curiously at me he saw that I was hungry, and gave me some mutton and bread, and said encouragingly as he pointed to the west, "Putty soon Indian come, heap speak English." Toward sundown two thousand sheep beneath a cloud of dust came streaming through the grand Sequoias to a meadow below the camp, and presently the English-speaking shepherd came in, to whom I explained my wants and what I was doing. Like most white men, he could not conceive how anything other than gold could be the object of such rambles as mine, and asked repeatedly whether I had discovered any mines. I tried to make him talk about trees and the wild animals, but unfortunately he proved to be a tame Indian from the Tule Reservation, had been to school, claimed to be civilized, and spoke contemptuously of " wild Indians," and so of course his inherited instincts were blurred or lost. The Big Trees, he said, grew far south, for he had seen them in crossing the mountains from Porterville to Lone Pine. In the morning he kindly gave me a few pounds of flour, and assured me that I would get plenty more at a sawmill on the South Fork if I reached it before it was shut down for the season.

Of all the Tule basin forest the section on the North Fork seemed the finest, surpassing, I think, even the Giant Forest of the Kaweah. Southward from here, though the width and general continuity of the belt is well sustained, I thought I could detect a slight falling off in the height of the trees and in closeness of growth. All the basin was swept by swarms of hoofed locusts, the southern part over and over again, until not a leaf within reach was left on the wettest bogs, the outer edges of the thorniest chaparral beds, or even on the young conifers, which, unless under the stress of dire famine, sheep never touch. Of course Brownie suffered, though I made diligent search for grassy sheep-proof spots. Turning him loose one evening on the side of a carex bog, he dolefully prospected the desolate neighborhood without finding anything that even a starving mule could eat. Then, utterly discouraged, he stole up behind me while I was bent over on my knees making a fire for tea, and in a pitiful mixture of bray and neigh, begged for help. It was a mighty touching prayer, and I answered it as well as I could with half of what was left of a cake made from the last of the flour given me by the Indians, hastily passing it over my shoulder, and saying, " Yes, poor fellow, I know, but soon you 'll have plenty. To-morrow down we go to alfalfa and barley," speaking to him as if he were human, as through stress of trouble plainly he was. After eating his portion of bread he seemed content, for he said no more, but patiently turned away to gnaw leafless ceanothus stubs. Such clinging, confiding dependence after all our scrambles and adventures together was very touching, and I felt conscience-stricken for having led him so far in so rough and desolate a country. "Man," says Lord Bacon, "is the god of the dog." So, also, he is of the mule and many other dependent fellow mortals.

Next morning I turned westward, determined to force a way straight to pasture, letting Sequoia wait. Fortunately ere we had struggled down through half a mile of chaparral we heard a mill whistle, for which we gladly made a bee line. At the sawmill we both got a good meal, then taking the dusty lumber road pursued our way to the lowlands. The nearest good pasture I counted might be thirty or forty miles away. But scarcely had we gone ten when I noticed a little log cabin a hundred yards or so back from the road, and a tall man straight as a pine standing in front of it observing us as we came plodding down through the dust. Seeing no sign of grass or hay, I was going past without stopping, when he shouted, "Travelin'?" Then drawing nearer, "Where have you come from? I did n't

notice you go up." I replied I had come through
the woods from the north, looking at the trees.
" Oh, then, you must be John Muir. Halt,
you 're tired; come and rest and I 'll cook for
you." Then I explained that I was tracing the
Sequoia belt, that on account of sheep my mule
was starving, and therefore must push on to the
lowlands. " No, no," he said, " that corral over
there is full of hay and grain. Turn your mule
into it. I don't own it, but the fellow who does
is hauling lumber, and it will be all right. He 's
a white man. Come and rest. How tired you
must be! The Big Trees don't go much farther
south, nohow. I know the country up there, have
hunted all over it. Come and rest, and let your
little doggone rat of a mule rest. How in heavens
did you get him across the cañons — roll him? or
carry him? He 's poor, but he 'll get fat, and
I 'll give you a horse and go with you up the
mountains, and while you 're looking at the trees
I 'll go hunting. It will be a short job, for the
end of the Big Trees is not far." Of course I
stopped. No true invitation is ever declined.
He had been hungry and tired himself many a
time in the Rocky Mountains as well as in the
Sierra. Now he owned a band of cattle and
lived alone. His cabin was about eight by ten
feet, the door at one end, a fireplace at the other,
and a bed on one side fastened to the logs.
Leading me in without a word of mean apology,

he made me lie down on the bed, then reached under it, brought forth a sack of apples and advised me to keep "chawing" at them until he got supper ready. Finer, braver hospitality I never found in all this good world so often called selfish.

Next day with hearty, easy alacrity the mountaineer procured horses, prepared and packed provisions, and got everything ready for an early start the following morning. Well mounted, we pushed rapidly up the South Fork of the river and soon after noon were among the giants once more. On the divide between the Tule and Deer Creek a central camp was made, and the mountaineer spent his time in deer-hunting, while with provisions for two or three days I explored the woods, and in accordance with what I had been told soon reached the southern extremity of the belt on the South Fork of Deer Creek. To make sure, I searched the woods a considerable distance south of the last Deer Creek grove, passed over into the basin of the Kern, and climbed several high points commanding extensive views over the sugar-pine woods, without seeing a single Sequoia crown in all the wide expanse to the southward. On the way back to camp, however, I was greatly interested in a grove I discovered on the east side of the Kern River divide, opposite the North Fork of Deer Creek. The height of the pass where the species crossed over

is about 7000 feet, and I heard of still another
grove whose waters drain into the upper Kern
opposite the Middle Fork of the Tule.

It appears, therefore, that though the Sequoia
belt is two hundred and sixty miles long, most of
the trees are on a section to the south of Kings
River only about seventy miles in length.   But
though the area occupied by the species increases
so much to the southward, there is but little
difference in the size of the trees.   A diameter
of twenty feet and height of two hundred and
seventy-five is perhaps about the average for
anything like mature and favorably situated
trees.   Specimens twenty-five feet in diameter
are not rare, and a good many approach a height
of three hundred feet.   Occasionally one meets
a specimen thirty feet in diameter, and rarely one
that is larger.   The majestic stump on Kings
River is the largest I saw and measured on the
entire trip.   Careful search around the boundaries of the forests and groves and in the gaps
of the belt failed to discover any trace of the
former existence of the species beyond its present
limits.   On the contrary, it seems to be slightly
extending its boundaries; for the outstanding
stragglers, occasionally met a mile or two from
the main bodies, are young instead of old monumental trees.   Ancient ruins and the ditches
and root-bowls the big trunks make in falling
were found in all the groves, but none outside

of them. We may therefore conclude that the
area covered by the species has not been diminished during the last eight or ten thousand
years, and probably not at all in post-glacial
times. For admitting that upon those areas
supposed to have been once covered by Sequoia
every tree may have fallen, and that fire and the
weather had left not a vestige of them, many
of the ditches made by the fall of the ponderous trunks, weighing five hundred to nearly a
thousand tons, and the bowls made by their upturned roots would remain visible for thousands
of years after the last remnants of the trees had
vanished. Some of these records would doubt-
less be effaced in a comparatively short time by
the inwashing of sediments, but no inconsider-
able part of them would remain enduringly en-
graved on flat ridge tops, almost wholly free
from such action.

In the northern groves, the only ones that at
first came under the observation of students, there
are but few seedlings and young trees to take the
places of the old ones. Therefore the species
was regarded as doomed to speedy extinction, as
being only an expiring remnant vanquished in
the so-called struggle for life, and shoved into
its last strongholds in moist glens where conditions are exceptionally favorable. But the
majestic continuous forests of the south end of
the belt create a very different impression. Here,

as we have seen, no tree in the forest is more enduringly established. Nevertheless it is oftentimes vaguely said that the Sierra climate is drying out, and that this oncoming, constantly increasing drought will of itself surely extinguish King Sequoia, though sections of wood-rings show that there has been no appreciable change of climate during the last forty centuries. Furthermore, that Sequoia can grow and is growing on as dry ground as any of its neighbors or rivals, we have seen proved over and over again. " Why, then," it will be asked, " are the Big Tree groves always found on well-watered spots? " Simply because Big Trees give rise to streams. It is a mistake to suppose that the water is the cause of the groves being there. On the contrary, the groves are the cause of the water being there. The roots of this immense tree fill the ground, forming a sponge which hoards the bounty of the clouds and sends it forth in clear perennial streams instead of allowing it to rush headlong in short-lived destructive floods. Evaporation is also checked, and the air kept still in the shady Sequoia depths, while thirsty robber winds are shut out.

Since, then, it appears that Sequoia can and does grow on as dry ground as its neighbors and that the greater moisture found with it is an effect rather than a cause of its presence, the notions as to the former greater extension of

the species and its near approach to extinction,
based on its supposed dependence on greater
moisture, are seen to be erroneous. Indeed, all
my observations go to show that in case of pro-
longed drought the sugar pines and firs would
die before Sequoia. Again, if the restricted and
irregular distribution of the species be interpreted
as the result of the desiccation of the range,
then, instead of increasing in individuals toward
the south, where the rainfall is less, it should
diminish.

If, then, its peculiar distribution has not been
governed by superior conditions of soil and
moisture, by what has it been governed? Several years before I made this trip, I noticed that
the northern groves were located on those parts
of the Sierra soil-belt that were first laid bare
and opened to preëmption when the ice-sheet
began to break up into individual glaciers. And
when I was examining the basin of the San
Joaquin and trying to account for the absence of
Sequoia, when every condition seemed favorable
for its growth, it occurred to me that this remarkable gap in the belt is located in the channel of
the great ancient glacier of the San Joaquin and
Kings River basins, which poured its frozen
floods to the plain, fed by the snows that fell on
more than fifty miles of the Summit peaks of the
range. Constantly brooding on the question, I
next perceived that the great gap in the belt to

the northward, forty miles wide, between the
Stanislaus and Tuolumne groves, occurs in the
channel of the great Stanislaus and Tuolumne
glacier, and that the smaller gap between the
Merced and Mariposa groves occurs in the channel of the smaller Merced glacier. The wider
the ancient glacier, the wider the gap in the
Sequoia belt, while the groves and forests attain
their greatest development in the Kaweah and
Tule River basins, just where, owing to topographical conditions, the region was first cleared
and warmed, while protected from the main ice-
rivers, that flowed past to right and left down
the Kings and Kern valleys. In general, where
the ground on the belt was first cleared of ice,
there the Sequoia now is, and where at the same
elevation and time the ancient glaciers lingered,
there the Sequoia is not. What the other conditions may have been which enabled the Sequoia
to establish itself upon these oldest and warmest parts of the main soil-belt I cannot say. I
might venture to state, however, that since the
Sequoia forests present a more and more ancient
and long established aspect to the southward, the
species was probably distributed from the south
toward the close of the glacial period, before the
arrival of other trees. About this branch of the
question, however, there is at present much fog,
but the general relationship we have pointed out
between the distribution of the Big Tree and the

ancient glacial system is clear. And when we
bear in mind that all the existing forests of the
Sierra are growing on comparatively fresh moraine soil, and that the range itself has been
recently sculptured and brought to light from
beneath the ice-mantle of the glacial winter,
then many lawless mysteries vanish, and harmo-
nies take their places.

But notwithstanding all the observed phenomena bearing on the post-glacial history of
this colossal tree, point to the conclusion that it
never was more widely distributed on the Sierra
since the close of the glacial epoch ; that its
present forests are scarcely past prime ; if, indeed, they have reached prime ; that the post-
glacial day of the species is probably not half
done ; yet, when from a wider outlook the vast
antiquity of the genus is considered, and its
ancient richness in species and individuals, comparing our Sierra giant and Sequoia semperv-
rens of the coast, the only other living species,
with the many fossil species already discovered,
and described by Heer and Lesquereux, some of
which flourished over large areas around the
Arctic Circle, and in Europe and our own territories, during tertiary and cretaceous times, —
then, indeed, it becomes plain that our two sur-
viving species, restricted to narrow belts within
the limits of California, are mere remnants of
the genus both as to species and individuals, and

that they probably are verging to extinction.
But the verge of a period beginning in cretaceous
times may have a breadth of tens of thousands
of years, not to mention the possible existence of
conditions calculated to multiply and reëxtend
both species and individuals. No unfavorable
change of climate, so far as I can see, no disease,
but only fire and the axe and the ravages of
flocks and herds threaten the existence of these
noblest of God's trees. In Nature's keeping
they are safe, but through man's agency destruction is making rapid progress, while in the
work of protection only a beginning has been
made. The Mariposa Grove belongs to and is
guarded by the State; the General Grant and
Sequoia National Parks, established ten years
ago, are efficiently guarded by a troop of cavalry
under the direction of the Secretary of the Interior; so also are the small Tuolumne and Merced groves, which are included in the Yosemite
National Park, while a few scattered patches and
fringes, scarce at all protected, though belonging
to the national government, are in the Sierra
Forest Reservation.

Perhaps more than half of all the Big Trees
have been sold, and are now in the hands of
speculators and mill men. Even the beautiful
little Calaveras Grove of ninety trees, so histori-
cally interesting from its being the first discovered, is now owned, together with the much

larger South or Stanislaus Grove, by a lumber
company.

Far the largest and most important section
of protected Big Trees is in the grand Sequoia
National Park, now easily accessible by stage from
Visalia. It contains seven townships and extends across the whole breadth of the magnificent
Kaweah basin. But large as it is, it should be
made much larger. Its natural eastern boundary
is the high Sierra, and the northern and southern
boundaries, the Kings and Kern rivers, thus including the sublime scenery on the headwaters of
these rivers and perhaps nine tenths of all the
Big Trees in existence. Private claims cut and
blotch both of the Sequoia parks as well as all
the best of the forests, every one of which the
government should gradually extinguish by purchase, as it readily may, for none of these hold-
ings are of much value to their owners. Thus
as far as possible the grand blunder of selling
would be corrected. The value of these forests
in storing and dispensing the bounty of the
mountain clouds is infinitely greater than lumber
or sheep. To the dwellers of the plain, dependent on irrigation, the Big Tree, leaving all its
higher uses out of the count, is a tree of life, a
never-failing spring, sending living water to the
lowlands all through the hot, rainless summer.
For every grove cut down a stream is dried up.
Therefore, all California is crying, " Save the

trees of the fountains," nor, judging by the signs of the times, is it likely that the cry will cease until the salvation of all that is left of Sequoia gigantea is sure.

CHAPTER X

THE forests of America, however slighted by
man, must have been a great delight to God;
for they were the best he ever planted. The
whole continent was a garden, and from the beginning it seemed to be favored above all the
other wild parks and gardens of the globe. To
prepare the ground, it was rolled and sifted in
seas with infinite loving deliberation and fore-
thought, lifted into the light, submerged and
warmed over and over again, pressed and crumpled into folds and ridges, mountains, and hills,
subsoiled with heaving volcanic fires, ploughed
and ground and sculptured into scenery and
soil with glaciers and rivers, — every feature
growing and changing from beauty to beauty,
higher and higher. And in the fullness of time
it was planted in groves, and belts, and broad,
exuberant, mantling forests, with the largest,
most varied, most fruitful, and most beautiful
trees in the world. Bright seas made its border,
with wave embroidery and icebergs; gray deserts were outspread in the middle of it, mossy

tundras on the north, savannas on the south, and blooming prairies and plains; while lakes and rivers shone through all the vast forests and openings, and happy birds and beasts gave delightful animation. Everywhere, everywhere over all the blessed continent, there were beauty and melody and kindly, wholesome, foodful abundance.

These forests were composed of about five hundred species of trees, all of them in some way useful to man, ranging in size from twenty-five feet in height and less than one foot in diameter at the ground to four hundred feet in height and more than twenty feet in diameter, — lordly monarchs proclaiming the gospel of beauty like apostles.   For many a century after the ice-ploughs were melted, nature fed them and dressed them every day, — working like a man, a loving, devoted, painstaking gardener; fingering every leaf and flower and mossy furrowed bole; bending, trimming, modeling, balancing; painting them with the loveliest colors; bringing over them now clouds with cooling shadows and showers, now sunshine; fanning them with gentle winds and rustling their leaves; exercising them in every fibre with storms, and pruning them; loading them with flowers and fruit, loading them with snow, and ever making them more beautiful as the years rolled by.   Wide-branching oak and elm in endless variety, walnut and maple, chestnut and beech, ilex and locust, touching limb to limb, spread a leafy translucent canopy along the coast of the Atlantic over the wrinkled folds and ridges of the Alleghanies, — a green billowy sea in summer, golden and purple in autumn, pearly gray like a steadfast frozen mist of interlacing branches and sprays in leafless, restful winter.

To the southward stretched dark, level-topped cypresses in knobby, tangled swamps, grassy savannas in the midst of them like lakes of light, groves of gay, sparkling spice-trees, magnolias and palms, glossy-leaved and blooming and shining continually. To the northward, over Maine and Ottawa, rose hosts of spiry, rosiny evergreens, — white pine and spruce, hemlock and cedar, shoulder to shoulder, laden with purple cones, their myriad needles sparkling and shimmering, covering hills and swamps, rocky headlands and domes, ever bravely aspiring and seeking the sky; the ground in their shade now snow-clad and frozen, now mossy and flowery; beaver meadows here and there, full of lilies and grass; lakes gleaming like eyes, and a silvery embroidery of rivers and creeks watering and brightening all the vast glad wilderness.

Thence westward were oak and elm, hickory and tupelo, gum and liriodendron, sassafras and ash, linden and laurel, spreading on ever wider in glorious exuberance over the great fer-

tile basin of the Mississippi, over damp level
bottoms, low dimpling hollows, and round dotting hills, embosoming sunny prairies and cheery
park openings, half sunshine, half shade; while
a dark wilderness of pines covered the region
around the Great Lakes. Thence still westward swept the forests to right and left around
grassy plains and deserts a thousand miles wide:
irrepressible hosts of spruce and pine, aspen and
willow, nut-pine and juniper, cactus and yucca,
caring nothing for drought, extending undaunted
from mountain to mountain, over mesa and
desert, to join the darkening multitudes of
pines that covered the high Rocky ranges and the
glorious forests along the coast of the moist and
balmy Pacific, where new species of pine, giant
cedars and spruces, silver firs and Sequoias, kings
of their race, growing close together like grass
in a meadow, poised their brave domes and
spires in the sky, three hundred feet above the
ferns and the lilies that enameled the ground;
towering serene through the long centuries,
preaching God's forestry fresh from heaven.

Here the forests reached their highest development. Hence they went wavering northward
over icy Alaska, brave spruce and fir, poplar and
birch, by the coasts and the rivers, to within
sight of the Arctic Ocean. American forests!
the glory of the world! Surveyed thus from
the east to the west, from the north to the south,

they are rich beyond thought, immortal, immeasurable, enough and to spare for every feeding, sheltering beast and bird, insect and son of Adam; and nobody need have cared had there been no pines in Norway, no cedars and deodars on Lebanon and the Himalayas, no vine-clad selvas in the basin of the Amazon. With such variety, harmony, and triumphant exuberance, even nature, it would seem, might have rested content with the forests of North America, and planted no more.

So they appeared a few centuries ago when they were rejoicing in wildness. The Indians with stone axes could do them no more harm than could gnawing beavers and browsing moose. Even the fires of the Indians and the fierce shattering lightning seemed to work together only for good in clearing spots here and there for smooth garden prairies, and openings for sunflowers seeking the light. But when the steel axe of the white man rang out on the startled air their doom was sealed. Every tree heard the bodeful sound, and pillars of smoke gave the sign in the sky.

I suppose we need not go mourning the buffaloes. In the nature of things they had to give place to better cattle, though the change might have been made without barbarous wickedness. Likewise many of nature's five hundred kinds of wild trees had to make way for orchards

and cornfields. In the settlement and civilization of the country, bread more than timber or
beauty was wanted; and in the blindness of
hunger, the early settlers, claiming Heaven as
their guide, regarded God's trees as only a larger
kind of pernicious weeds, extremely hard to get
rid of. Accordingly, with no eye to the future,
these pious destroyers waged interminable forest
wars; chips flew thick and fast; trees in their
beauty fell crashing by millions, smashed to confusion, and the smoke of their burning has been rising to heaven more than two hundred years. After
the Atlantic coast from Maine to Georgia had
been mostly cleared and scorched into melancholy ruins, the overflowing multitude of bread
and money seekers poured over the Alleghanies
into the fertile middle West, spreading ruthless
devastation ever wider and farther over the rich
valley of the Mississippi and the vast shadowy
pine region about the Great Lakes. Thence still
westward, the invading horde of destroyers called
settlers made its fiery way over the broad Rocky
Mountains, felling and burning more fiercely
than ever, until at last it has reached the wild
side of the continent, and entered the last of
the great aboriginal forests on the shores of the
Pacific.

Surely, then, it should not be wondered at
that lovers of their country, bewailing its bald-
ness, are now crying aloud, " Save what is left of

the forests!" Clearing has surely now gone far enough; soon timber will be scarce, and not a grove will be left to rest in or pray in. The remnant protected will yield plenty of timber, a perennial harvest for every right use, without further diminution of its area, and will continue to cover the springs of the rivers that rise in the mountains and give irrigating waters to the dry valleys at their feet, prevent wasting floods and be a blessing to everybody forever.

Every other civilized nation in the world has been compelled to care for its forests, and so must we if waste and destruction are not to go on to the bitter end, leaving America as barren as Palestine or Spain. In its calmer moments, in the midst of bewildering hunger and war and restless over-industry, Prussia has learned that the forest plays an important part in human progress, and that the advance in civilization only makes it more indispensable. It has, therefore, as shown by Mr. Pinchot, refused to deliver its forests to more or less speedy destruction by permitting them to pass into private ownership. But the state woodlands are not allowed to lie idle. On the contrary, they are made to produce as much timber as is possible without spoiling them. In the administration of its forests, the state righteously considers itself bound to treat them as a trust for the nation as a whole, and to keep in view the common good of the people for all time.

In France no government forests have been
sold since 1870. On the other hand, about one
half of the fifty million francs spent on forestry
has been given to engineering works, to make
the replanting of denuded areas possible. The
disappearance of the forests in the first place, it
is claimed, may be traced in most cases directly
to mountain pasturage. The provisions of the
Code concerning private woodlands are substan-
tially these : no private owner may clear his
woodlands without giving notice to the government at least four months in advance, and the
forest service may forbid the clearing on the
following grounds, — to maintain the soil on
mountains, to defend the soil against erosion and
flooding by rivers or torrents, to insure the existence of springs or watercourses, to protect the
dunes and seashore, etc. A proprietor who has
cleared his forest without permission is subject to
heavy fine, and in addition may be made to re-
plant the cleared area.

In Switzerland, after many laws like our own
had been found wanting, the Swiss forest school
was established in 1865, and soon after the federal forest law was enacted, which is binding
over nearly two thirds of the country. Under
its provisions, the cantons must appoint and pay
the number of suitably educated foresters required for the fulfillment of the forest law ; and
in the organization of a normally stocked forest,

the object of first importance must be the cutting each year of an amount of timber equal to the total annual increase, and no more.

The Russian government passed a law in 1888, declaring that clearing is forbidden in protected forests, and is allowed in others " only when its effects will not be to disturb the suitable relations which should exist between forest and agricultural lands."

Even Japan is ahead of us in the management of her forests. They cover an area of about twenty-nine million acres. The feudal lords valued the woodlands, and enacted vigorous protective laws; and when, in the latest civil war, the Mikado government destroyed the feudal system, it declared the forests that had belonged to the feudal lords to be the property of the state, promulgated a forest law binding on the whole kingdom, and founded a school of forestry in Tokio. The forest service does not rest satisfied with the present proportion of woodland, but looks to planting the best forest trees it can find in any country, if likely to be useful and to thrive in Japan.

In India systematic forest management was begun about forty years ago, under difficulties — presented by the character of the country, the prevalence of running fires, opposition from lumbermen, settlers, etc. — not unlike those which confront us now. Of the total area of government forests, perhaps seventy million acres, fifty-five

million acres have been brought under the control of the forestry department, — a larger area
than that of all our national parks and reservations. The chief aims of the administration are
effective protection of the forests from fire, an
efficient system of regeneration, and cheap transportation of the forest products; the results so
far have been most beneficial and encouraging.

It seems, therefore, that almost every civilized
nation can give us a lesson on the management
and care of forests. So far our government has
done nothing effective with its forests, though
the best in the world, but is like a rich and
foolish spendthrift who has inherited a magnificent estate in perfect order, and then has left his
fields and meadows, forests and parks, to be sold
and plundered and wasted at will, depending on
their inexhaustible abundance. Now it is plain
that the forests are not inexhaustible, and that
quick measures must be taken if ruin is to be
avoided. Year by year the remnant is growing
smaller before the axe and fire, while the laws
in existence provide neither for the protection
of the timber from destruction nor for its use
where it is most needed.

As is shown by Mr. E. A. Bowers, formerly
Inspector of the Public Land Service, the foundation of our protective policy, which has never
protected, is an act passed March 1, 1817, which
authorized the Secretary of the Navy to reserve

lands producing live-oak and cedar, for the sole purpose of supplying timber for the navy of the United States. An extension of this law by the passage of the act of March 2, 1831, provided that if any person should cut live-oak or red cedar trees or *other timber* from the lands of the United States for any other purpose than the construction of the navy, such person should pay a fine not less than triple the value of the timber cut, and be imprisoned for a period not exceeding twelve months. Upon this old law, as Mr. Bowers points out, having the construction of a wooden navy in view, the United States government has to-day chiefly to rely in protecting its timber throughout the arid regions of the West, where none of the naval timber which the law had in mind is to be found.

By the act of June 3, 1878, timber can be taken from public lands not subject to entry under any existing laws except for minerals, by *bona fide* residents of the Rocky Mountain states and territories and the Dakotas. Under the timber and stone act, of the same date, land in the Pacific States and Nevada, valuable mainly for timber, and unfit for cultivation if the timber is removed, can be purchased for two dollars and a half an acre, under certain restrictions. By the act of March 3, 1875, all land-grant and right-of-way railroads are authorized to take timber from the public lands adjacent to their lines for construction purposes; and they have taken it with a vengeance, destroying a hundred times more than they have used, mostly by allowing fires to run in the woods. The settlement laws, under which a settler may enter lands valuable for timber as well as for agriculture, furnish another means of obtaining title to public timber.

With the exception of the timber culture act, under which, in consideration of planting a few acres of seedlings, settlers on the treeless plains got 160 acres each, the above is the only legislation aiming to protect and promote the planting of forests. In no other way than under some one of these laws can a citizen of the United States make any use of the public forests. To show the results of the timber-planting act, it need only be stated that of the thirty-eight million acres entered under it, less than one million acres have been patented. This means that less than fifty thousand acres have been planted with stunted, woebegone, almost hopeless sprouts of trees, while at the same time the government has allowed millions of acres of the grandest forest trees to be stolen or destroyed, or sold for nothing. Under the act of June 3, 1878, settlers in Colorado and the Territories were allowed to cut timber for mining and educational purposes from mineral land, which in the practical West means both cutting and burning anywhere and everywhere, for any purpose, on any sort of public land.

Thus, the prospector, the miner, and mining and railroad companies are allowed by law to take all the timber they like for their mines and roads, and the forbidden settler, if there are no mineral lands near his farm or stock-ranch, or none that he knows of, can hardly be expected to forbear taking what he needs wherever he can find it. Timber is as necessary as bread, and no scheme of management failing to recognize and properly provide for this want can possibly be maintained. In any case, it will be hard to teach the pioneers that it is wrong to steal government timber. Taking from the government is with them the same as taking from nature, and their consciences flinch no more in cutting timber from the wild forests than in drawing water from a lake or river. As for reservation and protection of forests, it seems as silly and needless to them as protection and reservation of the ocean would be, both appearing to be boundless and inexhaustible.

The special land agents employed by the General Land Office to protect the public domain from timber depredations are supposed to collect testimony to sustain prosecution and to superintend such prosecution on behalf of the government, which is represented by the district attorneys. But timber thieves of the Western class are seldom convicted, for the good reason that most of the jurors who try such cases are

themselves as guilty as those on trial.   The effect
of the present confused, discriminating, and un-
just system has been to place almost the whole
population in opposition to the government; and
as conclusive of its futility, as shown by Mr.
Bowers, we need only state that during the seven
years from 1881 to 1887 inclusive, the value of
the timber reported stolen from the government
lands was $36,719,935, and the amount recov-
ered was $478,073, while the cost of the ser-
vices of special agents alone was $455,000, to
which must be added the expense of the trials.
Thus for nearly thirty-seven million dollars' worth
of timber the government got less than nothing;
and the value of that consumed by running fires
during the same period, without benefit even to
thieves, was probably over two hundred millions
of dollars.   Land commissioners and Secretaries
of the Interior have repeatedly called attention
to this ruinous state of affairs, and asked Congress to enact the requisite legislation for reasonable reform.   But, busied with tariffs, etc.,
Congress has given no heed to these or other
appeals, and our forests, the most valuable and
the most destructible of all the natural resources
of the country, are being robbed and burned
more rapidly than ever.   The annual appropria-
tion for so-called " protection service " is hardly
sufficient to keep twenty-five timber agents in
the field, and as far as any efficient protection

of timber is concerned these agents themselves might as well be timber.[1]

That a change from robbery and ruin to a permanent rational policy is urgently needed nobody with the slightest knowledge of American forests will deny. In the East and along the northern Pacific coast, where the rainfall is abundant, comparatively few care keenly what becomes of the trees so long as fuel and lumber are not noticeably dear. But in the Rocky Mountains and California and Arizona, where the forests are inflammable, and where the fertility of the lowlands depends upon irrigation, public opinion is growing stronger every year in favor of permanent protecton by the federal government of all the forests that cover the sources of the streams. Even lumbermen in these regions, long accustomed to steal, are now willing and anxious to buy lumber for their mills under cover of law: some possibly from a late second growth of honesty, but most, especially the small mill-owners, simply because it no longer pays to steal where all may not only steal, but also destroy, and in particular because it costs about as much to steal timber for one mill as for ten, and, therefore, the ordinary lumberman can no longer compete with the large corporations. Many of the miners find that timber is already becoming scarce and dear on

[1] A change for the better, compelled by public opinion, is now going on, — 1901.

the denuded hills around their mills, and they, too, are asking for protection of forests, at least against fire. The slow-going, unthrifty farmers, also, are beginning to realize that when the timber is stripped from the mountains the irrigating streams dry up in summer, and are destructive in winter; that soil, scenery, and everything slips off with the trees: so of course they are coming into the ranks of tree-friends.

Of all the magnificent coniferous forests around the Great Lakes, once the property of the United States, scarcely any belong to it now. They have disappeared in lumber and smoke, mostly smoke, and the government got not one cent for them; only the land they were growing on was considered valuable, and two and a half dollars an acre was charged for it. Here and there in the Southern States there are still considerable areas of timbered government land, but these are comparatively unimportant. Only the forests of the West are significant in size and value, and these, although still great, are rapidly vanishing. Last summer, of the unrivaled redwood forests of the Pacific Coast Range, the United States Forestry Commission could not find a single quarter-section that remained in the hands of the government.[1]

---

[1] The State of California recently appropriated two hundred and fifty thousand dollars to buy a block of redwood land near Santa Cruz for a state park. A much larger national park should be made in Humboldt or Mendocino county.

Under the timber and stone act of 1878,
which might well have been called the "dust
and ashes act," any citizen of the United States
could take up one hundred and sixty acres of
timber land, and by paying two dollars and a
half an acre for it obtain title.   There was some
virtuous effort made with a view to limit the operations of the act by requiring that the pur-
chaser should make affidavit that he was entering
the land exclusively for his own use, and by not
allowing any association to enter more than one
hundred and sixty acres.   Nevertheless, under
this act wealthy corporations have fraudulently
obtained title to from ten thousand to twenty
thousand acres or more.   The plan was usually
as follows : A mill company, desirous of getting
title to a large body of redwood or sugar-pine
land, first blurred the eyes and ears of the land
agents, and then hired men to enter the land
they wanted, and immediately deed it to the
company after a nominal compliance with the
law ; false swearing in the wilderness against the
government being held of no account.   In one
case which came under the observation of Mr.
Bowers, it was the practice of a lumber company
to hire the entire crew of every vessel which
might happen to touch at any port in the redwood belt, to enter one hundred and sixty acres
each and immediately deed the land to the company, in consideration of the company's paying

all expenses and giving the jolly sailors fifty dollars apiece for their trouble.

By such methods have our magnificent redwoods and much of the sugar-pine forests of the Sierra Nevada been absorbed by foreign and resident capitalists. Uncle Sam is not often called a fool in business matters, yet he has sold millions of acres of timber land at two dollars and a half an acre on which a single tree was worth more than a hundred dollars. But this priceless land has been patented, and nothing can be done now about the crazy bargain. According to the everlasting law of righteousness, even the fraudulent buyers at less than one per cent of its value are making little or nothing, on account of fierce competition. The trees are felled, and about half of each giant is left on the ground to be converted into smoke and ashes; the better half is sawed into choice lumber and sold to citizens of the United States or to foreigners: thus robbing the country of its glory and impoverishing it without right benefit to anybody, — a bad, black business from beginning to end.

The redwood is one of the few conifers that sprout from the stump and roots, and it declares itself willing to begin immediately to repair the damage of the lumberman and also that of the forest-burner. As soon as a redwood is cut down or burned it sends up a crowd of eager, hopeful shoots, which, if allowed to grow, would in a few decades attain a height of a hundred feet, and the strongest of them would finally become giants as great as the original tree. Gigantic second and third growth trees are found in the redwoods, forming magnificent temple-like circles around charred ruins more than a thousand years old. But not one denuded acre in a hundred is allowed to raise a new forest growth. On the contrary, all the brains, religion, and superstition of the neighborhood are brought into play to prevent a new growth. The sprouts from the roots and stumps are cut off again and again, with zealous concern as to the best time and method of making death sure. In the clearings of one of the largest mills on the coast we found thirty men at work, last summer, cutting off redwood shoots " in the dark of the moon," claiming that all the stumps and roots cleared at this auspicious time would send up no more shoots. Anyhow, these vigorous, almost immortal trees are killed at last, and black stumps are now their only monuments over most of the chopped and burned areas.

The redwood is the glory of the Coast Range. It extends along the western slope, in a nearly continuous belt about ten miles wide, from beyond the Oregon boundary to the south of Santa Cruz, a distance of nearly four hundred miles, and in massive, sustained grandeur and closeness of growth surpasses all the other timber woods of the world. Trees from ten to fifteen feet in diameter and three hundred feet high are not uncommon, and a few attain a height of three hundred and fifty feet or even four hundred, with a diameter at the base of fifteen to twenty feet or more, while the ground beneath them is a garden of fresh, exuberant ferns, lilies, gaultheria, and rhododendron. This grand tree, Sequoia sempervirens, is surpassed in size only by its near relative, Sequoia gigantea, or Big Tree, of the Sierra Nevada, if, indeed, it is surpassed. The sempervirens is certainly the taller of the two. The gigantea attains a greater girth, and is heavier, more noble in port, and more sublimely beautiful. These two Sequoias are all that are known to exist in the world, though in former geological times the genus was common and had many species. The redwood is restricted to the Coast Range, and the Big Tree to the Sierra.

As timber the redwood is too good to live. The largest sawmills ever built are busy along its seaward border, " with all the modern improvements," but so immense is the yield per acre it will be long ere the supply is exhausted. The Big Tree is also, to some extent, being made into lumber. It is far less abundant than the redwood, and is, fortunately, less accessible, extending along the western flank of the Sierra in a partially interrupted belt, about two hundred and fifty miles long, at a height of from four to eight

ROAD THROUGH THE SEQUOIAS, MARIPOSA GROVE

thousand feet above the sea.   The enormous logs,
too heavy to handle, are blasted into manageable
dimensions with gunpowder.   A large portion of
the best timber is thus shattered and destroyed,
and, with the huge, knotty tops, is left in ruins
for tremendous fires that kill every tree within
their range, great and small.   Still, the species is
not in danger of extinction.   It has been planted
and is flourishing over a great part of Europe,
and magnificent sections of the aboriginal forests
have been reserved as national and State parks,
— the Mariposa Sequoia Grove, near Yosemite,
managed by the State of California, and the
General Grant and Sequoia national parks on the
Kings, Kaweah, and Tule rivers, efficiently
guarded by a small troop of United States cavalry under the direction of the Secretary of the
Interior.   But there is not a single specimen of
the redwood in any national park.   Only by gift
or purchase, so far as I know, can the government get back into its possession a single acre of
this wonderful forest.

The legitimate demands on the forests that
have passed into private ownership, as well as
those in the hands of the government, are increasing every year with the rapid settlement and up-
building of the country, but the methods of lumbering are as yet grossly wasteful.   In most mills
only the best portions of the best trees are used,
while the ruins are left on the ground to feed

great fires, which kill much of what is left of the
less desirable timber, together with the seedlings,
on which the permanence of the forest depends.
Thus every mill is a centre of destruction far
more severe from waste and fire than from use.
The same thing is true of the mines, which consume and destroy indirectly immense quantities
of timber with their innumerable fires, accidental or set to make open ways, and often without
regard to how far they run. The prospector
deliberately sets fires to clear off the woods just
where they are densest, to lay the rocks bare and
make the discovery of mines easier. Sheep-
owners and their shepherds also set fires everywhere through the woods in the fall to facilitate
the march of their countless flocks the next summer, and perhaps in some places to improve the
pasturage. The axe is not yet at the root of
every tree, but the sheep is, or was before the
national parks were established and guarded by
the military, the only effective and reliable arm of
the government free from the blight of politics.
Not only do the shepherds, at the driest time of
the year, set fire to everything that will burn,
but the sheep consume every green leaf, not
sparing even the young conifers, when they are
in a starving condition from crowding, and they
rake and dibble the loose soil of the mountain
sides for the spring floods to wash away, and
thus at last leave the ground barren.

Of all the destroyers that infest the woods, the shake-maker seems the happiest. Twenty or thirty years ago, shakes, a kind of long, board-like shingles split with a mallet and a frow, were in great demand for covering barns and sheds, and many are used still in preference to common shingles, especially those made from the sugar-pine, which do not warp or crack in the hottest sunshine. Drifting adventurers in California, after harvest and threshing are over, oftentimes meet to discuss their plans for the winter, and their talk is interesting. Once, in a company of this kind, I heard a man say, as he peacefully smoked his pipe: "Boys, as soon as this job's done I'm goin' into the duck business. There's big money in it, and your grub costs nothing. Tule Joe made five hundred dollars last winter on mallard and teal. Shot 'em on the Joaquin, tied 'em in dozens by the neck, and shipped 'em to San Francisco. And when he was tired wading in the sloughs and touched with rheumatiz, he just knocked off on ducks, and went to the Contra Costa hills for dove and quail. It's a mighty good business, and you're your own boss, and the whole thing's fun."

Another of the company, a bushy-bearded fellow, with a trace of brag in his voice, drawled out: "Bird business is well enough for some, but bear is my game, with a deer and a California lion thrown in now and then for change. There's

always market for bear grease, and sometimes
you can sell the hams. They're good as hog
hams any day. And you are your own boss in
my business, too, if the bears ain't too big and
too many for you. Old grizzlies I despise, —
they want cannon to kill 'em; but the blacks
and browns are beauties for grease, and when
once I get 'em just right, and draw a bead on
'em, I fetch 'em every time." Another said he
was going to catch up a lot of mustangs as
soon as the rains set in, hitch them to a gang-
plough, and go to farming on the San Joaquin
plains for wheat. But most preferred the shake
business, until something more profitable and as
sure could be found, with equal comfort and
independence.

With a cheap mustang or mule to carry a pair
of blankets, a sack of flour, a few pounds of
coffee, and an axe, a frow, and a cross-cut saw,
the shake-maker ascends the mountains to the
pine belt where it is most accessible, usually
by some mine or mill road. Then he strikes off
into the virgin woods, where the sugar pine, king
of all the hundred species of pines in the world
in size and beauty, towers on the open sunny
slopes of the Sierra in the fullness of its glory.
Selecting a favorable spot for a cabin near a
meadow with a stream, he unpacks his animal
and stakes it out on the meadow. Then he
chops into one after another of the pines, until

he finds one that he feels sure will split freely, cuts
this down, saws off a section four feet long, splits
it, and from this first cut, perhaps seven feet in
diameter, he gets shakes enough for a cabin and
its furniture, — walls, roof, door, bedstead, table,
and stool.   Besides his labor, only a few pounds
of nails are required.   Sapling poles form the
frame of the airy building, usually about six feet
by eight in size, on which the shakes are nailed,
with the edges overlapping.   A few bolts from the
same section that the shakes were made from are
split into square sticks and built up to form a
chimney, the inside and interspaces being plas-
tered and filled in with mud.   Thus, with abundance of fuel, shelter and comfort by his own
fireside are secured.   Then he goes to work saw-
ing and splitting for the market, tying the shakes
in bundles of fifty or a hundred.   They are four
feet long, four inches wide, and about one fourth
of an inch thick.   The first few thousands he
sells or trades at the nearest mill or store, getting
provisions in exchange.   Then he advertises, in
whatever way he can, that he has excellent sugar-
pine shakes for sale, easy of access and cheap.

Only the lower, perfectly clear, free-splitting
portions of the giant pines are used, — perhaps
ten to twenty feet from a tree two hundred and
fifty in height; all the rest is left a mass of
ruins, to rot or to feed the forest fires, while thousands are hacked deeply and rejected in proving

the grain.   Over nearly all of the more accessible slopes of the Sierra and Cascade mountains in southern Oregon, at a height of from
three to six thousand feet above the sea, and for
a distance of about six hundred miles, this waste
and confusion extends.   Happy robbers! dwell-
ing in the most beautiful woods, in the most
salubrious climate, breathing delightful odors
both day and night, drinking cool living water,
— roses and lilies at their feet in the spring,
shedding fragrance and ringing bells as if cheering them on in their desolating work.   There is
none to say them nay.   They buy no land, pay
no taxes, dwell in a paradise with no forbidding
angel either from Washington or from heaven.
Every one of the frail shake shanties is a centre
of destruction, and the extent of the ravages
wrought in this quiet way is in the aggregate
enormous.

It is not generally known that, notwithstanding the immense quantities of timber cut every
year for foreign and home markets and mines,
from five to ten times as much is destroyed as is
used, chiefly by running forest fires that only the
federal government can stop.   Travelers through
the West in summer are not likely to forget the fire-
work displayed along the various railway tracks.
Thoreau, when contemplating the destruction of
the forests on the east side of the continent, said
that soon the country would be so bald that every

man would have to grow whiskers to hide its
nakedness, but he thanked God that at least the
sky was safe. Had he gone West he would
have found out that the sky was not safe ; for all
through the summer months, over most of the
mountain regions, the smoke of mill and forest
fires is so thick and black that no sunbeam can
pierce it. The whole sky, with clouds, sun,
moon, and stars, is simply blotted out. There is
no real sky and no scenery. Not a mountain is
left in the landscape. At least none is in sight
from the lowlands, and they all might as well be
on the moon, as far as scenery is concerned.

The half-dozen transcontinental railroad companies advertise the beauties of their lines in gorgeous many-colored folders, each claiming its as
the "scenic route." "The route of superior
desolation " — the smoke, dust, and ashes route
— would be a more truthful description. Every
train rolls on through dismal smoke and barbarous, melancholy ruins; and the companies
might well cry in their advertisements: " Come !
travel our way. Ours is the blackest. It is the
only genuine Erebus route. The sky is black
and the ground is black, and on either side there
is a continuous border of black stumps and logs
and blasted trees appealing to heaven for help as
if still half alive, and their mute eloquence is most
interestingly touching. The blackness is perfect.
On account of the superior skill of our workmen,

advantages of climate, and the kind of trees, the charring is generally deeper along our line, and the ashes are deeper, and the confusion and desolation displayed can never be rivaled. No other route on this continent so fully illustrates the abomination of desolation." Such a claim would be reasonable, as each seems the worst, whatever route you chance to take.

Of course a way had to be cleared through the woods. But the felled timber is not worked up into firewood for the engines and into lumber for the company's use; it is left lying in vulgar confusion, and is fired from time to time by sparks from locomotives or by the workmen camping along the line. The fires, whether accidental or set, are allowed to run into the woods as far as they may, thus assuring comprehensive destruction. The directors of a line that guarded against fires, and cleared a clean gap edged with living trees, and fringed and mantled with the grass and flowers and beautiful seedlings that are ever ready and willing to spring up, might justly boast of the beauty of their road; for nature is always ready to heal every scar. But there is no such road on the western side of the continent. Last summer, in the Rocky Mountains, I saw six fires started by sparks from a locomotive within a distance of three miles, and nobody was in sight to prevent them from spreading. They might run into the adjacent forests and burn the timber from hundreds of square miles; not a man in the State would care to spend an hour in fighting them, as long as his own fences and buildings were not threatened.

Notwithstanding all the waste and use which have been going on unchecked like a storm for more than two centuries, it is not yet too late — though it is high time — for the government to begin a rational administration of its forests. About seventy million acres it still owns, — enough for all the country, if wisely used. These residual forests are generally on mountain slopes, just where they are doing the most good, and where their removal would be followed by the greatest number of evils; the lands they cover are too rocky and high for agriculture, and can never be made as valuable for any other crop as for the present crop of trees. It has been shown over and over again that if these mountains were to be stripped of their trees and underbrush, and kept bare and sodless by hordes of sheep and the innumerable fires the shepherds set, besides those of the millmen, prospectors, shake-makers, and all sorts of adventurers, both lowlands and mountains would speedily become little better than deserts, compared with their present beneficent fertility. During heavy rainfalls and while the winter accumulations of snow were melting, the larger streams would swell into destructive torrents, cutting deep, rugged-edged

gullies, carrying away the fertile humus and soil
as well as sand and rocks, filling up and overflowing their lower channels, and covering the
lowland fields with raw detritus.   Drought and
barrenness would follow.

In their natural condition, or under wise management, keeping out destructive sheep, preventing fires, selecting the trees that should be cut for
lumber, and preserving the young ones and the
shrubs and sod of herbaceous vegetation, these forests would be a never failing fountain of wealth
and beauty.   The cool shades of the forest give
rise to moist beds and currents of air, and the sod
of grasses and the various flowering plants and
shrubs thus fostered, together with the network
and sponge of tree roots, absorb and hold back
the rain and the waters from melting snow,
compelling them to ooze and percolate and flow
gently through the soil in streams that never
dry.   All the pine needles and rootlets and
blades of grass, and the fallen, decaying trunks
of trees, are dams, storing the bounty of the
clouds and dispensing it in perennial life-giving
streams, instead of allowing it to gather suddenly
and rush headlong in short-lived devastating
floods.   Everybody on the dry side of the continent is beginning to find this out, and, in view
of the waste going on, is growing more and
more anxious for government protection.   The
outcries we hear against forest reservations come

mostly from thieves who are wealthy and steal timber by wholesale. They have so long been allowed to steal and destroy in peace that any impediment to forest robbery is denounced as a cruel and irreligious interference with " vested rights," likely to endanger the repose of all ungodly welfare.

Gold, gold, gold ! How strong a voice that metal has !

" O wae for the siller, it is sae preva'lin' ! "

Even in Congress a sizable chunk of gold, carefully concealed, will outtalk and outfight all the nation on a subject like forestry, well smothered in ignorance, and in which the money interests of only a few are conspicuously involved. Under these circumstances, the bawling, blethering oratorical stuff drowns the voice of God himself. Yet the dawn of a new day in forestry is breaking. Honest citizens see that only the rights of the government are being trampled, not those of the settlers. Only what belongs to all alike is reserved, and every acre that is left should be held together under the federal government as a basis for a general policy of administration for the public good. The people will not always be deceived by selfish opposition, whether from lumber and mining corporations or from sheepmen and prospectors, however cunningly brought forward underneath fables and gold.

Emerson says that things refuse to be mismanaged long. An exception would seem to be found in the case of our forests, which have been mismanaged rather long, and now come desperately near being like smashed eggs and spilt milk. Still, in the long run the world does not move backward. The wonderful advance made in the last few years, in creating four national parks in the West, and thirty forest reservations, embracing nearly forty million acres; and in the planting of the borders of streets and highways and spacious parks in all the great cities, to satisfy the natural taste and hunger for landscape beauty and righteousness that God has put, in some measure, into every human being and animal, shows the trend of awakening public opinion. The making of the far-famed New York Central Park was opposed by even good men, with misguided pluck, perseverance, and ingenuity; but straight right won its way, and now that park is appreciated. So we confidently believe it will be with our great national parks and forest reservations. There will be a period of indifference on the part of the rich, sleepy with wealth, and of the toiling millions, sleepy with poverty, most of whom never saw a forest; a period of screaming protest and objection from the plunderers, who are as unconscionable and enterprising as Satan. But light is surely coming, and the friends of destruction will preach and bewail in vain.

The United States government has always been proud of the welcome it has extended to good men of every nation, seeking freedom and homes and bread. Let them be welcomed still as nature welcomes them, to the woods as well as to the prairies and plains. No place is too good for good men, and still there is room. They are invited to heaven, and may well be allowed in America. Every place is made better by them. Let them be as free to pick gold and gems from the hills, to cut and hew, dig and plant, for homes and bread, as the birds are to pick berries from the wild bushes, and moss and leaves for nests. The ground will be glad to feed them, and the pines will come down from the mountains for their homes as willingly as the cedars came from Lebanon for Solomon's temple. Nor will the woods be the worse for this use, or their benign influences be diminished any more than the sun is diminished by shining. Mere destroyers, however, tree-killers, wool and mutton men, spreading death and confusion in the fairest groves and gardens ever planted, — let the government hasten to cast them out and make an end of them. For it must be told again and again, and be burningly borne in mind, that just now, while protective measures are being deliberated languidly, destruction and use are speeding on faster and farther every day. The axe and saw are insanely busy, chips are flying thick as snowflakes, and every summer thousands of acres of priceless forests, with their underbrush, soil, springs, climate, scenery, and religion, are vanishing away in clouds of smoke, while, except in the national parks, not one forest guard is employed.

All sorts of local laws and regulations have been tried and found wanting, and the costly lessons of our own experience, as well as that of every civilized nation, show conclusively that the fate of the remnant of our forests is in the hands of the federal government, and that if the remnant is to be saved at all, it must be saved quickly.

Any fool can destroy trees. They cannot run away ; and if they could, they would still be destroyed, — chased and hunted down as long as fun or a dollar could be got out of their bark hides, branching horns, or magnificent bole backbones. Few that fell trees plant them ; nor would planting avail much towards getting back anything like the noble primeval forests. During a man's life only saplings can be grown, in the place of the old trees — tens of centuries old — that have been destroyed. It took more than three thousand years to make some of the trees in these Western woods, — trees that are still standing in perfect strength and beauty, waving and singing in the mighty forests of the Sierra. Through all the wonderful, eventful centuries since Christ's time — and long before that —

God has cared for these trees, saved them from drought, disease, avalanches, and a thousand straining, leveling tempests and floods; but he cannot save them from fools, — only Uncle Sam can do that.

INDEX